A John Hick Reader

Edited by

PAUL BADHAM

TRINITY PRESS INTERNATIONAL
Philadelphia

First U.S. edition 1990

Trinity Press International
3725 Chestnut Street
Philadelphia, Pa. 19104

Printed in Hong Kong

Library of Congress Cataloging-in-Publication Data
Hick, John.
  [Selections.   1990]
  A John Hick reader / edited by Paul Badham.
      p.   cm.
  Includes bibliographical references.
  ISBN 0–334–00599–X
  1. Philosophical theology.   2. Religion—Philosophy.   I. Badham, Paul.
  II. Title.
BT40.H53   1990
200—dc20   89–38417
                                              CIP

Contents

Acknowledgements

The individual chapters of this reader are drawn from a variety of sources. Each chapter represents one of the major aspects of John Hick's thought. Grateful thanks are due to the various editors and publishers of the journals and books where these pieces first saw the light of day.

Chapter 2, 'Religion as Fact-asserting', was derived from two articles which appeared in the journals *Theology Today* (April 1961) and *Theology* (March 1968). The complete article was first published in *God and the Universe of Faiths* (London: Macmillan; New York: St Martin's Press, 1973; reissued with a new preface, 1988).

Chapter 3, 'Religious Faith as Experiencing-as', was first published in *Talk of God*, ed. G. N. A. Vesey for the Royal Institute of Philosophy (London: Macmillan; New York: St Martin's Press, 1969).

Chapter 4, 'Rational Theistic Belief without Proofs', first appeared in John Hick, *Arguments for the Existence of God* (London: Macmillan; New York: Herder and Herder, 1971).

Chapter 5, 'Theology and Verification', first appeared in *Theology Today* (April 1960), and was republished in John Hick, *The Existence of God* (New York: Macmillan, 1964), and in John Hick, *Faith and Knowledge*, 2nd edn (Ithaca, NY: Cornell University Press, 1966; London: Macmillan, 1967; reissued with a new preface, 1988).

Chapter 6, 'An Irenaean Theodicy', was published in Stephen T. Davis (ed.), *Encountering Evil* (Edinburgh: T. & T. Clark; Atlanta: John Knox Press, 1981).

Chapter 7, 'Jesus and the World Religions', was initially published in John Hick (ed.), *The Myth of God Incarnate* (London: SCM Press; Philadelphia: Westminster Press, 1977), and republished in his *God Has Many Names* (London: Macmillan, 1980).

Chapter 8, 'Eschatological Verification Reconsidered', first appeared in *Religious Studies*, xiii (1977), and was republished in John Hick, *Problems of Religious Pluralism* (London: Macmillan; New York: St Martin's Press, 1985).

Chapter 9, 'Present and Future Life', was the 1977 Ingersoll Lecture on Immortality, delivered at Harvard University and first printed in the *Harvard Theological Review*, lxxi, nos 1–2 (Jan–Apr 1978). It was republished in *Problems of Religious Pluralism*.

Chapter 10, 'A Philosophy of Religious Pluralism', was first published in *The World's Religious Traditions: Essays in Honour of Wilfrid Cantwell Smith*, ed. Frank Whaling (Edinburgh: T. & T. Clark, 1984), and was reprinted in *Problems of Religious Pluralism*.

Chapter 11, 'On Grading Religions', was first published in *Religious Studies*, xvii (1982), and was reprinted in *Problems of Religious Pluralism*.

A Note on Inclusive Language

During the last decade – whilst teaching in the United States – John Hick has changed from traditional 'patriarchal' language in which, for example, the human race is referred to as 'man', to the more inclusive language which is gradually becoming standard. This change is reflected in the more recent essays in this Reader and in my Introduction, but we have not altered the format of those pieces which come from an earlier period of Hick's life and thought.

1

The Philosophical Theology of John Hick

PAUL BADHAM

I CHRISTIAN THEOLOGY IN DIALOGUE WITH WESTERN PHILOSOPHY

John Hick is one of the most widely read and discussed philosophers of religion in the contemporary world. Scholars who take up topics on which Hick has written normally find it essential to engage themselves in dialogue with or criticism of what he has said. And what is striking is the range of topics in which this is true. Many world-renowned scholars build their reputations in one area of thought and devote their lives to the clarification and defence of their work in this field. This option was open to John Hick, for the success of his early works *Faith and Knowledge* and *Evil and the God of Love* established his name as a Christian philosopher of originality, clarity and power. But, instead of resting on his laurels, he has gone on to apply the same searching and questing spirit to other central issues of the contemporary debate, such as the meaning and coherence of claims concerning the divinity of Christ, the hope of a future life, and the place of Christianity among the religions of the world.

John Hick started his academic life as a student of law. He then went on to philosophy, and finally to theology. Each of these disciplines has affected his approach: from his legal training he learnt the need to weigh and evaluate evidence; from philosophy he learnt the importance of clarity and coherence in argument; and from his theological and ministerial training he obtained a wide knowledge of the history of Christian thought and the complexity of Christian belief. But to tell Hick's academic history is to tell only one side of his character; for the foundation of his work, like that of

1

all the major figures of Christian theology, is a deep, experientially based awareness of faith. For him, this came initially through a spiritual conversion of a strongly evangelical kind, and his approach to theology was from the beginning that of faith seeking understanding. And, although over the years he has moved increasingly away from a conservative evangelical framework of thought, he remains devoted to that encounter with a higher reality which lies at its heart.[1] This has been of the utmost benefit to his work. Many philosophers of religion discuss their subject without themselves understanding the workings of the religious mind or the things that matter to religious faith. This has never been true of John Hick, which is why his work has always been focused on the central issues confronting faith in the world of today.

But this awareness of what confronts faith is also crucial to understanding Hick. He has found it impossible to confine his theological thinking within a self-authenticating circle of faith. Rather he has sought to take up the challenge of making sense of faith to the thoughtful inquirer, and of responding to the challenge of the sceptic. And he has done this not in the spirit of a debater wishing to out-argue an adversary, but as a sensitive and perceptive thinker who has himself experienced the force of the intellectual challenge that faith encounters today.

John Hick began his academic career in the 1950s, when Christian theology in Britain was under the sharpest philosophical attack from the then dominant logical positivist position. This put the challenge of whether there was any way in which the understanding and expectations of a well-educated and informed believer essentially differed from the understanding and beliefs of an atheist. For, if belief in God makes no difference, the alleged belief would appear to be wholly vacuous. One characteristic response of Christian intellectuals was to accept the thrust of the positivist critique and deny that Christianity made any factual claims at all. Some suggested that religion be defended on grounds of its utility rather than its truth-claims. Others contended that religious language should be seen as expressing emotion, attitude or intention rather than as consisting of propositional statements.

For Hick, none of these 'defences' will do. He argues that no religious claim can be defended on grounds of utility unless it actually corresponds to reality. Moreover, if one attends to the actual usage of religious language by Christian believers from biblical times to the present day, it becomes apparent that their language is inextricably associated with substantive beliefs about the real existence of God and living hope in a genuinely personal life after death. This does not mean that Hick assumes that *all* religious language must be propositional, for he fully recognises the place of metaphor and poetry in religious language, and is indeed well-known for his advocacy of a non-literal understanding of the divinity of Christ. Nevertheless, he insists that a basic structure of factual belief is essential for any religious world-view. Hence John Hick wholly repudiates a non-cognitive account of Christian belief, and seeks to defend a fact-asserting, experientially grounded and ultimately verifiable faith in a living, personal God.

Hick does not believe that a religious interpretation of reality could be unequivocally established to be true. He thinks that it is religiously important that we live at an 'epistemic' distance from God so that faith is always a free personal response rather than something imposed upon us by coercive proof of divine reality. On the other hand, it is important that the religious vision should be capable of defence as one possible way of rationally interpreting the world. Hence Hick seeks to defend faith as a valid way of experiencing life. He points out that much that we perceive is ambiguous, and can legitimately be interpreted in various ways. A painting, particularly of an abstract kind, can be thought of simply as paint randomly applied to canvas, or experienced-as a great work of art full of sensitivity and expression. A drowning man can be viewed simply as a form disappearing below the waves, or can be experienced-as a moral challenge to us to rush to the rescue. Likewise, the chronicles of ancient Israel, or the life of Jesus of Nazareth, can be studied as history and biography, or experienced-as having distinctively religious significance in revealing God's presence and activity in the world. The same is true of our own experience of life here and now. It can be understood in completely natural terms, or it can be experienced-as the place of our encounter with God.

But is it reasonable to believe that there is a God who can be thus encountered? Hick suggests that in discussing this issue we should not focus on the abstract question of whether or not it is possible to prove, starting from zero, that God exists. Instead we should focus on the question of whether or not persons who believe themselves to be in living contact with God are acting rationally in trusting in the reality of their own experience. He believes that they are. He points out that it is notoriously difficult to establish philosophically the reality of the external world, but that every sane person does accept it as a natural belief, embodied in our language, and essential for coping successfully with the demands of human existence. We accept the reality of the world we perceive because our perceptual experience has a givenness or involuntary character about it and accepting its reality enables us to function efficiently. But, for the primary religious figures of the theistic traditions, religious experience of God seems to have felt just as real as their perceptual experience of the external world. It possessed the same involuntary and compelling quality, and, as they lived with it, they found that their experience confirmed the reality of that which they believed themselves to be encountering. Hick concludes that, for all such persons, belief in God is as rational as belief in the external world is for the vast mass of humanity.

Hick is of course aware of the problem facing this analogy: namely, that those whose experience of God is of this overwhelming quality are relatively rare. So perhaps their claims to such a divine relationship should be dismissed in the same way as we habitually dismiss the experiential claims of paranoiacs or alcoholics. But the problem with doing this is that the reason why we reject the claims of paranoiacs or alcoholics is that we have other grounds for thinking them out of touch with reality. By contrast, primary religious figures have been considered to be among the most perceptive people in the history of the human race. Jesus of Nazareth has been thought by hundreds of millions to embody the ideal fulfilment of human nature. Likewise Muhammad, another wholly God-centred person, was also on any reckoning a brilliant general, statesman and lawgiver, and even today is thought by countless other millions to be the supreme example of how to live. And consider the prophets of Israel. What was notable about them was not just that God was so overwhelmingly real to them, but that their social and political judgement was so much more penetrating than that of their contemporaries. Hence, Hick argues, it would seem wholly unjustified to dismiss the primary religious figures as psychologically deluded if they so triumphantly pass our normal tests of mental equilibrium. Therefore, even the non-believer would have to acknowledge that such religious leaders, on the basis of their own experiences, were justified in believing as they did. This does not of course mean that those who have not in any way shared their experiences are compelled to accept the reality of that to which they testify. Hick does not accept the validity of arguing from other people's experience. On the other hand, those of us who have had at least a sufficient acquaintance with what they are talking about to understand them may feel that their larger experience gives us the right to trust our own tentative and partial awarenesses.

Thus far in our exploration of Hick's theology, we have looked at his reasons for seeing faith in God as fact-asserting, as a possible way of interpreting the world, and as authenticated for the believer by the data of personal religious experience. The next problem to be tackled is whether such belief makes any real difference to our expectations. For, as Antony Flew pointed out so vigorously in the *Theology and Falsification* debate of the 1950s, a belief can only have content if it does make a difference.[2] What became apparent from that debate was that, within this life, the substantive beliefs and expectations of well-educated and informed believers and non-believers in God are virtually identical. Hence, for many intellectuals, belief in God dies the death of a thousand qualifications when it is really probed.

John Hick does not think that God intervenes in the world. Particular providence, answered prayer and miracle play no part in his philosophical theology. This is not because he has a closed mind, for Hick is actually quite open to the possibility of strange phenomena. However, with the advance of parapsychology, non-theistic accounts of supposed 'miraculous happenings' have become available. For example, an 'answered prayer' might well be explained by telepathy in a more open, but still thoroughly naturalistic, world-view. More importantly, Hick rejects particular providence on theological grounds. His answer to the problem of evil is contingent on the notion that God has created an autonomous universe in whose workings he does not intervene. But, if God does not intervene in our world, what difference does belief in him make to any of our expectations?

Hick's answer is 'eschatological verification'. This view gives supreme importance to the Christian hope of a life after death in which God's purposes will ultimately triumph. Our present life is, for the Christian, like a journey to a heavenly city. Atheists walk the same path, and both the Christian and the atheist experience similar trials, tribulations and joys, along the way. But the one looks forward to a glorious destiny, while the other takes for granted that the road leads nowhere. This difference in expectations colours the way they experience the journey. There is thus a real difference between the Christian and the atheist visions of life, and the difference is a factual one in that it will be verified if it turns out that there is indeed a life after death, and if that life is such as to accord with Christian expectations concerning the ultimate triumph of God's will.

This theory depends on supposing that life after death is a thinkable possibility. This raises many problems. Most contemporary philosophers believe that life after death is literally non-sense. Persons are essentially the embodied creatures we know ourselves to be in our present existence, and hence it can make no sense at all to suppose that we can survive our own dissolution. To meet this problem Hick has put forward a reinterpretation of the doctrine of the resurrection of the body. This is known as the 'replica' theory. It suggests that, if God were to create exact replicas of us in another space, replicas possessing complete similarity of all bodily features and full continuity of memory and mental dispositions, then the basic criteria of personal identity would be met; that is, such a person replicated after death could be said to have survived death. This thesis has been one of the most intensely discussed theories of life after death put forward in our time. Much of this discussion has focused on the sense in which the term 'exact' can be ascribed to a replica which by definition is living under very different conditions of life in the postulated 'other space'. However, this difficulty is by no means insuperable, and in his summing-up of the hypothesis Hick modifies his talk of an 'exact' replica and speaks instead of 'sufficient correspondence of characteristics with our present bodies, and sufficient continuity of memory with our present consciousness, for us to speak of the same person being raised again to life in a new environment'.[3] With this modification, it does seem that a concept of bodily resurrection is at least conceivable, and thus Hick's 'replica' theory makes a very valuable contribution to contemporary debate on death and immortality.

Life after death is absolutely central to Hick's philosophical theology. This comes out not only in his work on eschatological verification, but also, and even more strikingly, in the book for which he is probably best known, *Evil and the God of Love*, the argument of which is summarised in this volume in his essay 'An Irenaean Theodicy' (Ch. 6). The essential feature of this approach to the problem of evil is that the changes and chances of this world, with all its potential for joy and sorrow, for good and evil, may make sense as an inevitable part of an environment in which persons can develop as free responsible agents. As a 'vale of soul-making' the hardships and challenges of life may serve a larger purpose; but, if there is no soul to make, no larger purpose to serve, then the fact of suffering in general, and its random character in particular, simply makes nonsense of Christian claims about God's character and power. It should be stressed that Hick's theodicy does not in any way imply that suffering is in itself ennobling or redemptive, for there would be very strong evidence against so simplistic a view. But what his theodicy does say is that a real objective physical world, governed by regular physical law, provides an environment more suited to the development of responsible agents than would an environment in which divine intervention consistently saved humanity from the consequences of its folly, or from the heartache and challenge implicit in any finite and physical existence. Hick's arguments do not 'solve' the problem of evil, the extent and nature of which remains a persistent challenge to the integrity of Christian believing, but what Hick's work does make clear is that, without a belief in a future life, no approach to the problem of evil can get off the ground. If death means extinction, then old age, suffering, disease and death gain the ultimate victory over each of us, and thereby bring to nothing any belief that each human person is eternally precious to an all-sovereign God.

II CHRISTIAN THEOLOGY IN DIALOGUE WITH WORLD RELIGION

For the first half of John Hick's academic life his central concern was to explore the intelligibility of Christian belief in the light of the questions raised by contemporary Western philosophy. But in 1967 he moved from the quintessentially English environment of Cambridge to a Chair in Theology at the University of Birmingham in one of the most multiracial areas of Britain. Hick has always been concerned with the pastoral implications of the Gospel, and he rapidly involved himself with the life of the city. In particular he became Chairman of a group called 'All Faiths for One Race', which sought to combat the endemic racism of Britain in the 1970s. At that time British society was slowly coming to terms with the ending of the Empire, and imperially engendered attitudes of mind still encouraged both conscious and unconscious prejudice against immigrants from former Colonies who sought to make a new life for themselves in vibrant cities such as Birmingham. Hick's concern for racial equality rapidly brought him into close acquaintanceship with the leaders of the Hindu, Sikh, Muslim and Jewish communities in the city. These relationships naturally deepened when Hick became Chairman both of the Religious and Cultural Panel of the Birmingham Community Relations Committee, and of the group set up to develop a new multi-religious syllabus for Religious Education in Birmingham's schools. Invitations to attend worship in mosque, gurdwara, temple and synagogue naturally followed, and an Inter-Faiths Council was set up to stimulate dialogue, co-operation and understanding. Attending non-Christian worship convinced Hick that phenomenologically the same kind of thing was going on in such worship as in worship in Christian churches. In each place of worship human beings were offering up themselves in dedication and praise to a personal God, addressed and reverenced as creator and Lord. Citing hymns from such worship in his book *God Has Many Names*, Hick sought to illustrate the common themes which occur in the theistic worship of the religions he had encountered. Clearly such experiences had a profound effect upon Hick's theological awareness and sensitivity, which were reinforced by intense study of Hinduism and Buddhism during a year of study and lecturing in India and Sri Lanka. As a result of such contacts, many assumptions Hick had previously accepted, such as the uniqueness of Christ and the impossibility of salvation except in his name, no longer seemed to be plausible, and the direction of his theological research and thinking began to change.

The most evident change was in Hick's Christology. One of his earliest ventures into print as a young scholar had been a review criticising D. M. Baillie's classic expression of liberal Christology, *God was in Christ*, as not orthodox enough![4] Later Hick came to a comparable liberal position himself, and sought to articulate Chalcedonian orthodoxy in terms of Christ expressing in history the divine love of God.[5] But gradually Hick became aware of three problems facing all attempts to make classical Christian doctrine intelligible. First, it seems impossible to present the incarnation of God in Christ as a wholly unique and utterly unprecedented phenomenon, without implicitly denying the significance of the extra-Christian religious experience of humanity. Second, all attempts to *explain* rather than simply *assert* the doctrine of the incarnation have been deemed to fail. Every explanation put forward in the ancient world was classified as a heresy, and no modern explanation, whether from liberal or traditional sources, has been felt to do justice simultaneously to Christ's true divinity and his full humanity. Third, New Testament scholarship seems to have reached a fairly substantial consensus that no first-century Jew could have made sense of the Christological formulations accepted by the Church in the Hellenistic world of the fourth and fifth centuries. For these reasons John Hick has come to believe that the doctrine of the incarnation cannot be understood as a factual hypothesis, and that the centre of Christianity should be focused on God rather than Christ. The language of incarnation should be understood as poetic, metaphorical or 'mythological'; expressive of the commitment felt by Christians to Jesus as the one through whom they have found themselves in God's presence, and discovered God's purpose for their lives.

Hick believes that to see the work of Jesus in this way is not a denial, but an affirmation, of the real significance of the historical figure. For, without the barriers set up by Christian doctrine round his person, people of other faiths can more easily draw inspiration from his life and teaching in the way that Gandhi did. The real historical Jesus may be released from the stained-glass windows of Christian piety and may once more become a source of inspiration and example to the world.

Hick believes that, from now on, all theology should be conducted in a global context, focusing on God (perhaps better described as 'the Real') and drawing on the religious experience and insights of all the traditions of humanity. Accordingly he has 'reconsidered' his theory of eschatological verification, originally developed within a Christian framework, so as to make it applicable to all the major religious traditions. In fact, nearly everything that Hick initially said from within the Christian tradition on this topic can be applied straightforwardly to Jewish, Muslim and theistic Hindu expectations also. And, although the details of the thesis need some modification to apply to advaitic Hinduism or Buddhist thought, this also can be done. For the basic question facing the human race is not 'whether the truth of a Christian, or a Muslim, or a Hindu, or a Buddhist interpretation is ultimately verifiable within human experience but whether the truth of a religious as opposed to a naturalistic interpretation of the Universe

is ultimately capable of being verified'.[6] The major divide between
a naturalistic and a religious world-view is that the former limits all
possible experience to this life only, while the latter looks to a
destiny which transcends the limits of this world.

That the major religions of the world have all traditionally given
considerable emphasis to belief in a life beyond death makes *Death
and Eternal Life* an appropriate subject for a global theology. John
Hick's encyclopaedic work on this theme illustrates the benefits of
approaching a major religious doctrine from the perspective of the
religious experience of the whole of humanity, rather than from
any one single tradition. For, as Hick pondered the difficulty of
seeking to articulate a possible vision of what life after death might
be like, he came to the conclusion that it was 'likely that the
different expectations cherished within the different traditions will
ultimately turn out to be partly correct and partly incorrect'.[7]
Hence a global theology uniting elements from various traditions
seems to present the most plausible schema.

Hick suggests that at death we temporarily enter a mind-
dependent world, somewhat as described in the *Tibetan Book of the
Dead*, or in the writings of the Oxford philosopher H. H. Price.[8]
This world would be a kind of dream environment built out of the
materials of our memories and desires and therefore providing an
opportunity for self-revelation and self-judgement. After a period
in this *bardo* world, the person would be reborn into another
embodied existence.

The idea of rebirth or reincarnation is open to serious objection
when thought of as taking place on this planet, but many references in Buddhist and Hindu scriptures suggest that rebirth
normally takes place in other worlds.[9] With this modification the
theory would correspond to the way many modern Christians
interpret the doctrine of resurrection (as something occurring in
another space), and Hick uses his re-created replica theory to
illustrate the possibility of this.[10] He believes that a succession of
such lives with intervals for reflection in between would provide
the most suitable means for the human pilgrimage towards the
divine Reality. The alternative would be to enter immediately into
unlimited and immortal life, but, according to Hick, 'if we were
faced with a limitlessly open future ... what we now know as
human nature would be transformed out of existence'.[11]

A succession of lives would enable the person gradually to adapt
and advance in moral and religious insight until the attainment of

ultimate union with God. Hick notes that in Hinduism and Buddhism the ultimate goal is absorption into the divine or into *nirvāṇa*, and suggests that such absorption corresponds with what Western mystics have written about the unitive state when the perfected soul comes to be truly one with God.[12]

Hick is vividly aware that, for many who presuppose a wholly naturalistic world-view, such speculation must seem bizarre, as indeed it may for some who take a very dogmatic stance concerning the teaching of their own particular religious tradition. What is interesting, however, is that within each of the great world religions there are to be found elements congruent with the schema which Hick outlines, and he could strengthen his case here by looking to the Islamic tradition and incorporating al-Ghazali's description of the mind-dependent state of *barzakh* and the subsequent resurrection world.[13]

Religious pluralism is a controversial theme in Christianity. But Hick believes that it has a sounder theoretical basis than its alternatives. He suggests that there are three possible answers to the question posed by the existence of a plurality of religions: exclusivism, inclusivism and pluralism. The first has been the traditional response of Christianity: namely, a confident, brash certainty that it alone has the truth, and that all other religions are destined to perish before the ever-widening influence of the Gospel. The ebbing of the missionary tide, the resurgence of confidence in the other great religions, and the increasing secularisation of the traditional European heartlands of the Christian tradition have meant that such attitudes have faded in the mainstream Christian churches even though they remain strong among fundamentalists. The second attitude, inclusivism, has taken its place as the standard Christian response.

Inclusivism does not limit the salvific purposes of God to those who make a conscious decision for Christ, but it continues to claim that Christ is the one source of salvation. This salvation can be understood to mean that the sacrifice of Christ on Calvary achieved a change in the permanent relationship between God and the whole of humanity, irrespective of whether or not anyone is aware of this alleged fact. Alternatively it can claim that Christ, the divine Logos, is at work in all the religions of the world. Christians are simply uniquely privileged in being able to identify correctly the source of this saving knowledge.

The problem with this kind of inclusivism is to know what real content it has. Hick suggests that it keeps the outward form of the older beliefs while emptying them of any real substance. To attach a Christian label to people of other religions fails to take seriously their very real sense of not being Christians and their conscious commitment to their own faith and community. However, Hick recognises that many Christians feel a need to cling to this unstable position, and suggests that it stems from their sense of obligation to a quasi-literal understanding of the doctrine of the incarnation. On this view Christianity is the only source of salvation, because God has revealed himself in Christ in a wholly unique manner, without which we would be in a state of complete ignorance.

Hick suggests that a way out of this dilemma is available in the standard liberal interpretations of the doctrine of the incarnation which have been a commonplace of English theology for the past seventy years. This 'liberal' view fully accepts that Christ truly revealed God. But it argues that this revelation came through Jesus' human awareness of God, and of God's grace at work in him. Hence the self-disclosing activity of God in Christ differs in degree rather than in kind from the manner in which God is revealed in any holy and godly person who seeks to live in communion with God, and in harmony with God's will. One who holds to a degree Christology can completely accept that God has nowhere left himself without witness, and that he reveals himself to all who open their lives to him whatever religion they may belong to. And this view can be held while remaining wholly convinced that one's own faith came through the work of Christ in the Christian community.

Pluralism does not mean that there are no differences between religions. John Hick is fully aware that there are significant differences in the way in which the divine Reality is perceived in the various religious traditions of humanity. Each 'name' of God represents a different *persona* of the divine Reality as responded to in human history. Shiva and Yahweh, for example, have significantly different characteristics. These derive from the distinctive interpretations of the encounter between God and humanity in differing faith communities. It is not intelligible to suppose that these *personae* are rival gods in some kind of polytheistic pantheon. Rather the one God is differently described because experience of God, like all other human experience, is necessarily coloured by the differing cultural traditions and historical experiences of particular human groups. Hick believes that this perspective also applies to those religious traditions which reject the notion of a personal deity and think of the Real in impersonal terms as the Absolute. This Absolute is also differently signified in different cultures as Brahman, or the Tao, or the Dharma, *nirvāṇa*, or *śūnyāta*. These differences in terminology reflect different apprehensions of the Real as it is mediated through, and affected by, the conceptual framework and spiritual training of people of different human traditions. Nevertheless Hick believes that there is a common underlying experience, and a common soteriological efficacy, in each of the world's great religions. We might note too that the differences do not lie solely between the differing historic religions but also within them, in that both personal and impersonal concepts of the divine Reality are to be found in each of the world's major faiths.

Does this mean that all religions are equally 'good'? It would be hard to maintain this, for, as Hick points out, one characteristic of most of the primary religious figures is that they distanced themselves from the religion out of which their own movement sprang. And almost all believers do tend to grade religions in a variety of ways. But on any objective criteria this is an exceedingly difficult thing to do in relation to the major world faiths. If all Christians, Muslims, Hindus and Buddhists lived up to the highest ideals of their respective religions, we would realise the goal of human brotherhood on earth. Yet each tradition is marred in different ways by human failings. The only conclusion one can come to is that each of the great traditions is equally capable of leading to human fulfilment, and of producing a sanctity in which selfishness is overcome and ultimate reality encountered and experienced.

NOTES

1. For details of John Hick's spiritual pilgrimage and the controversies of his life, see the opening chapters of his books *God Has Many Names* (London: Macmillan, 1980) and *Problems of Religious Pluralism* (London: Macmillan, 1985).

2. Antony Flew and Alasdair MacIntyre, *New Essays in Philosophical Theology* (London: SCM Press; New York: Macmillan, 1955) ch. 6.

3. See below, Ch. 5, section v.

4. John Hick, 'The Christology of D. M. Baillie', *Scottish Journal of Theology*, 11, no. 1 (Mar) 1–12.

5. John Hick, 'Christ and Incarnation', *God and the Universe of Faiths*

14 *A John Hick Reader*

(London: Macmillan, 1973) ch. 11.
6. Hick, *Problems of Religious Pluralism*, p. 125.
7. Ibid., p. 124.
8. H. H. Price, 'Survival and the Idea of "Another World"', in J. R. Smythies (ed.), *Brain and Mind* (London: Routledge and Kegan Paul, 1965) pp. 1–24.
9. John Hick, *Death and Eternal Life* (London: Macmillan, 1976) p. 36.
10. Ibid., pp. 279–85; and compare the discussion in Chapter 5 below.
11. Ibid., p. 413; and see Chapter 9 below.
12. Ibid., pp. 442–6; and see Chapter 9 below.
13. Salih Tug, 'Death and Immortality in Islamic Thought', in Paul and Linda Badham (eds), *Death and Immortality in the Religions of the World* (New York: Paragon, 1987).

2
Religion as Fact-asserting

In [chapter 1 of *God and the Universe of Faiths*] I claimed that religion is concerned with reality and that its central affirmations are, ultimately, true or false factual assertions. In this chapter I want to criticise the opposite view, both in the crude assumption that the important question is not whether religious affirmations are true but whether they are useful; and in the highly sophisticated form of the current neo-Wittgensteinian treatment of religious discourse as an autonomous language-game.

I

As regards the crude pragmatic approach to religion, I can indicate the tendency which I have in mind by recalling an impression received on going to teach in the United States in the midst of the religious boom of the 1950s. Observing America through the ears of a philosopher interested in the problems of language, I was struck by the frequent use of the word 'religion' (or 'faith', used virtually as a synonym) and, within the same realm of discourse, the relatively infrequent occurrence of the word 'God'. In contexts in which a generation or so ago questions used to be raised and debated concerning God, his existence, attributes, purpose and deeds, the corresponding questions from at least the 1950s onwards have focused upon religion, its nature, function, forms and pragmatic value. A shift has apparently taken place from the term 'God' as the head of a certain family of words and locutions, to the term 'religion' as the new head of the same linguistic family.

One accordingly hears much talk of religion considered as an aspect of human culture. In many American universities and colleges there are departments devoted to studying the history and varieties of this phenomenon, and the contribution which it has brought to man's culture in general. And among the ideas treated in this connection, along with cult, priesthood, taboo, and many others, is the concept of God. For academic study God is thus a sub-topic within the larger subject of religion.

At a more popular level religion is widely conceived – sometimes articulately, often inarticulately – as a human activity whose general function is to enable the individual to achieve harmony within himself and with his environment. One of the distinctive ways in which religion fulfils this function is by preserving and promoting certain great ideas or symbols which have a power to invigorate men's finer aspirations; and the most important and enduring of these symbols is God. Both at the academic and at the popular levels, then, God is in effect defined in terms of religion, as one of the concepts with which religion works; rather than religion being defined in terms of God, as the realm of men's varying responses to a real supernatural Being.

This displacement of 'God' by 'religion' as the focus of a wide realm of discourse has brought with it a change in the character of the questions that are most persistently asked in this area. Concerning God the traditional question has naturally been whether he exists or is real. But this is not a question that arises with regard to religion. It is obvious that religion exists; the important queries concern the purposes which it serves in human life, whether it ought to be cultivated and, if so, in what directions it may most profitably be developed. Under the pressure of these concerns the question of the truth of religious beliefs has fallen into the background and the issue of their practical usefulness has come forward to occupy the centre of attention.

This situation was first impressed upon my own mind by reading hundreds of students' essays in a Philosophy of Religion course in a secular American university. It was evident from this sample that large numbers – indeed the majority – of the writers had only a very dim conception of religious beliefs as being true or false, but a much keener sense of their being (or failing to be) psychologically and socially valuable. The question of truth had not been explicitly repudiated; but the alternative question of practical usefulness was far more effectively to the fore.

The same basic standpoint lies behind sermons heard from many pulpits, in which the true relevance of the biblical teachings and narratives is seen to lie in their illustration of current principles of psychotherapy and mental hygiene. This tendency reaches its well-known peak in the virtual equation of the Christian gospel with the proclamation of the power of positive thinking; but to this extreme there are many approximations. The resulting favourable public image of the Protestant minister – conformity to which earns community approval – is that of a man who performs services of social welfare (validated by statistically certifiable results), primarily in such areas as moral education, mental health, national morale and family life.

I am very far from wishing to question the real importance of such services, or their character as authentic expressions of Christian love. I am rather seeking to focus attention upon the way in which arguments centring upon pragmatic value have replaced the traditional conception that there are great and saving truths to be proclaimed and all-important transcendent realities to be witnessed to.

Is the new pragmatic emphasis a surrogate for the older religious conviction, a substitute natural to an age of waning faith? Such a diagnosis is suggested by the observations of the agnostic John Stuart Mill at the opening of his famous essay on *The Utility of Religion*:

> If religion, or any particular form of it, is true, its usefulness follows without other proof. If to know authentically in what order of things, under what government of the universe it is our destiny to live, were not useful, it is difficult to imagine what could be considered so. Whether a person is in a pleasant or in an unpleasant place, a palace or a prison, it cannot be otherwise than useful to him to know where he is. So long, therefore, as men accepted the teachings of their religion as positive facts, no more a matter of doubt than their own existence or the existence of the objects around them, to ask the use of believing it could not possibly occur to them. The utility of religion did not need to be asserted until the arguments for its truth had in a great measure ceased to convince. People must either have ceased to believe, or have ceased to rely on the belief of others, before they could take that inferior ground of defence without a consciousness of lowering what they were endeavouring to raise. An argument for the utility of religion is an appeal to unbelievers, to induce them to practise a well meant hypocrisy, or to semi-believers to make them avert their eyes from what might possibly shake their unstable belief, or finally to persons in general to abstain from expressing any doubts they may feel, since a fabric of immense importance to mankind is so insecure

at its foundations, that men must hold their breath in its neighbourhood for fear of blowing it down.

Mill's words refer to mid-nineteenth-century England, which had much in common religiously with recent American society. One also recalls the caustic remark of Bertrand Russell (likewise a nineteenth-century rationalist, although happily he lived on into the second half of the twentieth century): 'I can respect the men who argue that religion is true and therefore ought to be believed, but I can feel only profound moral reprobation for those who say that religion ought to be believed because it is useful, and that to ask whether it is true is a waste of time.'[1]

Comparing our current emphasis upon utility rather than truth with the thought of the great biblical exemplars of faith, we are at once struck by a startling reversal. There is a profound and momentous difference between serving and worshipping God, and being 'interested in religion'. God, if he is real, is our Creator. We stand before him as One who is infinitely superior to ourselves, in worth as well as in power, and 'to whom all hearts are open, all desires known, and from whom no secrets are hid'. But on the other hand religion stands before us as one of the various concerns which we may, at our own option, choose to cultivate. In dealing with religion and the religions we occupy the appraiser's role. And God is subsumed within that which we appraise. There need be no bearing of our lives and souls before the divine judgement and mercy. We can deal instead with religion, within which God is only an idea, a concept whose history we can trace, and which we can analyse, define, and even revise – instead of the living Lord of heaven and earth before whom we bow down in awe to worship and rise up with joy to serve.

There is, I think, no great mystery as to the historical sources of this prevalent view of religion as essentially an aspect of human culture, and of the consequent transformation of God into one of the terms of religious thought. It represents a logical development within an increasingly technological society of what has been variously called scientism, positivism and naturalism – the assumption engendered by the tremendous, dramatic and still accelerating growth of scientific knowledge and achievement, that the truth concerning any aspect or alleged aspect of reality consists in the results of the application to the relevant phenomena of the methods of scientific investigation. God is not a phenomenon available for scientific study; but religion is. There can be a history, a psychology, a sociology, and a comparative study of religion. Hence religion has become an object of intensive investigation, and God has perforce become identified as an idea which occurs within this complex phenomenon of religion.

Stated explicitly, the philosophical presupposition of the current mood is that the categories of truth and falsity do not apply to religious beliefs. Hence as a problem in contemporary theology and philosophy the issue centres upon the debate between the cognitive and non-cognitive, or the factual and mythological, understandings of religious language. Do such sentences as 'God loves mankind' or 'Men live after death' profess to describe objective realities; or do they perform a different function altogether? For language in its rich versatility can accomplish many other tasks than simply the making of assertions about what is alleged to be the case. We do not ask of a sonnet, for instance, whether it is literally true; poetry serves a quite different purpose from that of formulating factual assertions. And so the question naturally arises, Is the veracity properly claimed for religious statements more akin to 'poetic truth' than to ordinary factual truth? Are religious statements perhaps to be regarded as mythological and as having their own special kind of quasi-poetic truthfulness?

The problem is many-sided, and different aspects of it are at present engaging the attention of biblical scholars, theologians and philosophers of religion. A convenient way to raise some of the issues in short compass is by presenting a specific thesis. I shall therefore argue that: (a) it is vitally important to maintain the genuinely factual character of the central affirmations of the Christian faith; and (b) given a basic structure of factual belief, there is ample scope for the non-factual language of myth, symbol and poetry to express the believer's awareness of the illimitable mysteries which surround that core of religious fact. We may begin with this latter contention.

That there is a large admixture of mythological material (in the sense of statements which are non-factual but nevertheless religiously significant) in our scriptures, creeds, and other religious writings has long been recognised. It was as evident to Origen in the third century as it is to Bultmann in the twentieth. There will doubtless always be keen and even heated discussions about whether this or that specific item is to be regarded as factual or as mythological; but few thoughtful Christians today are disposed to deny that their religious discourse does include considerable mythological elements. Bishop James A. Pike, for instance, wrote:

> There are several phrases in the creed that I cannot affirm as literal prose sentences, but I can certainly sing them – as a kind of war song picturing major convictions in poetic terms. . . . Stated in plain prose, I certainly do not believe that Christ 'sitteth on the right hand of the Father'. . . . But I can sing this phrase with a real affirmation as to the place of Christ in the whole situation. I feel the same about 'ascended into Heaven'. And the same about 'conceived by the Holy Ghost, and born of the Virgin Mary'.[2]

Some would no doubt categorise differently one or other of the credal phrases cited. But it is impossible to repudiate the category itself which Bishop Pike used, or to deny that at least some religious utterances properly belong in it. Nor is there anything revolutionary in holding that the structure of fact-type Christian beliefs contains gaps which have to be filled, if at all, by myth. Such myths are distinguished from whimsical or arbitrary exercises of the poetic imagination by their relation to a framework of factual belief which they supplement and adorn. For myths of this kind are always products of a serious theological intention. For example, the myth of the ascended Christ's session at the right hand of the Father expresses the conviction that in some way which cannot be literally visualised our Lord is enthroned over the world. The myth derives its appropriateness and its point from the environment of non-mythological beliefs within which it lives – beliefs in the literal reality of God and of his action in Christ. It is thus possible to see large tracts of Christian discourse as significant although non-factual if one holds them within a context of genuinely factual beliefs.

If, however, the entire range of religious beliefs were regarded as non-factual, none of them could possess the kind of significance which depends upon a connection with objective reality. Myths that are embedded within a body of facts bear this kind of significance secondarily and derivatively, but myths which live in a system which is mythological throughout merely define an im-agined realm of their own. I suggest, then, that what might be called valuable or significant myth is necessarily parasitic upon non-mythological beliefs, and that if a set of myths becomes complete and autonomous it thereby forfeits its cognitive value.

This conclusion points to my other thesis, namely that Christianity, if it is not to deny itself, must insist upon the properly factual character of its basic affirmations. The reason for reaffirming this position, which has always been taken for granted by the religious mind, is brought out by considering the alternatives now being proposed. A growing number of contemporary philosophers have concluded that religious language is (apart from its empirical–historical elements) non-cognitive. It seems clear to them that whatever may be the legitimate point of, for example, 'God loves mankind', that point cannot be to assert a fact, since there are and can be no facts of this kind to be asserted. They have accordingly considered what function such a sentence may perform. Perhaps, for example, it expresses a way of looking at the natural world (John Wisdom, J. H. Randall, Peter Munz); or perhaps it declares an intention to live in a certain way (R. B. Braithwaite, T. R. Miles); or perhaps it is a 'convictional' statement, this being an utterance of a type which is to be classified as non-indicative (W. Zuurdeeg).

Possibly the clearest recent expression of the conception of religion as exclusively a phase of human culture is that of J. H. Randall. He argues, with impressive force and clarity, that religion is to be identified as 'a distinctive human enterprise with a socially indispensable function'.[3] Enlightened religion should have nothing to do with the superstitious belief in a really existing divine Being. Rather theology is 'an imaginative and symbolic rendering of men's moral experience and ideals: all religious beliefs are symbolic'.[4] The function of religious symbols (in conjunction with their associated rituals and ceremonies) is fourfold: to stimulate the will to moral activity; to bind a community together through its common symbols; to communicate a quality of experience which can only be expressed by poetry and symbol; and to open our eyes to the 'order of splendour' in the world, comprising nature's more elusive depths and mysteries. On the one hand, then, Randall sees religion as an important and valuable enrichment of human life, and on the other hand as a purely intra-mundane concern in which the idea of a transcendent God has no proper place.

On the assumption – for which, in his book, Randall offers no reasons – that belief in the reality of God is absurd, and out of the question for twentieth-century man, there is much to be said for a religious naturalism of this kind. But it is important to see that this

initial assumption does not constitute merely an enlightened
revision of Christian tradition but spells the *obituary* of historic
Christianity. The faith embodied in the biblical writings, and the
faith of the Church as an extension of this, depend upon the
conviction that God exists, not merely as an idea in some men's
minds, but as the creator and sustainer of the universe, the
ultimate reality with whom we have inescapably to do and whose
self-disclosed purpose towards us is supremely good and loving.

II

Here I enter into dialogue with the contemporary neo-
Wittgensteinian approach to the philosophy of religion as represented by Professor Dewi Z. Phillips in *The Concept of Prayer* and
Faith and Philosophical Enquiry.[5] And against that approach I wish to
propound three theses:

My first thesis is that it is presupposed in the Christian scriptures, creeds, confessions, prayers, sermons and theologies that it
is a factual truth that God exists.

Phillips does not agree with this. For example [in *The Concept of
Prayer*], he says that 'To have the idea of God is to know God.'[6]
This seems to entail that for someone to have the idea of God is for
God to exist – or perhaps to exist 'for' the one who has the concept.
This in turn suggests that there is no proper question whether God
exists, in distinction from the question whether people have the
concept of God. Again, he says, 'What [the believer] learns is
religious language; a language which he participates in along with
other believers. What I am suggesting is that to know how to use
this language is to know God' (p. 50). Or yet again, consider
Phillips's discussion of the possibility of atheism. He says that the
only sort of atheism that is philosophically in order is 'the
recognition that religion means nothing to one; one is at a loss to
know what to make of prayer, worship, creeds and so on. It is the
form of atheism summed up in the phrases, "I shouldn't call
myself religious", "Religion has no meaning for me"' (p. 19).

If this is the only philosophically proper form of atheism then
one form that must be philosophically improper is that expressed
by: 'It is irrational to believe that there is a God', 'There are no
adequate grounds for believing in the reality of God', 'It is logically
impossible that God, as defined in Christianity, should exist, since

this particular concept of deity is radically incoherent', 'In view of considerations x, y, and z, it is more probable that there is not a God than that there is.' Presumably Phillips believes that the issue which such atheism professes to settle is not a genuine issue. And if this is a non-issue then the corresponding contrary conclusion that God does exist, or that it is rational to believe that God exists, or that there are adequate grounds for believing in the reality of God, etc., must also be philosophically out of order.

To rule out the question whether God exists as logically improper is by implication to deny that the core religious statements, such as 'God loves mankind' or 'God is guiding the universe to his own end for it', are factually true-or-false. The debate which Phillips here enters between cognitive and non-cognitive analyses of religious language constitutes, I believe, the central issue in the philosophy of religion today. It connects on the one hand with the notion (representing the valid deposit of logical positivism) that 'existence' is to be defined in the operational terms of making an experienceable difference; and on the other hand with the discovery of the immense variety of the uses of language and in particular of its manifold non-cognitive functions. The notions of the existence of God and of the factual truth of statements about him are bound up with the principle that any possible history of the universe which satisfies, for example, 'God loves mankind', must differ experientially from any possible history of the universe which does not satisfy it. On the one side of the debate are those who hold that the existence of God is ultimately a factual issue. And on the other side are those who hold that the function of, for example, 'God loves mankind', is not to assert an alleged matter of fact but to do something quite different, such as to express an emotion, attitude or intention. (The mutual tolerance between the two positions is asymmetrical. The 'cognitivist' can hold that in asserting a matter of fact one is also expressing emotion, etc., but the 'non-cognitivist' cannot hold that in expressing emotion, etc., one is also asserting a matter of fact – beyond, of course, the fact that one has that emotion or intention.)

In denying, in his treatment of atheism, that there is a proper question as to whether God exists, and declaring instead that the proper question is whether one wants to use religious language, Phillips assumes that the use of religious language does not itself involve belief in the existence of God. But it seems clear to me that such utterances as 'God is a very present help in time of trouble',

'The Lord God omnipotent reigneth', 'In the beginning was the Word, and the Word was with God . . .', 'O God, from whom all holy desires, all good counsels, and all just works do proceed . . .' entail (in the case of the statements) or presuppose (in the case of the prayer) that God exists; and it also seems clear to me that normal or typical users of such language have intended this entailment or presupposition. That is to say, if asked 'Are you assuming that there actually is a Being whom you are addressing (or referring to) and who is eternal, omnipotent, etc.?' the typical religious man would unhesitatingly reply, 'Yes, of course I am.' And if we pressed him further, in the light of modern discussions about the distinction between factual and non-factual statements, and asked 'Do you regard it as an objective fact that God exists – a fact which obtains whether or not any particular person knows it or believes it' he would still unhesitatingly say 'Yes.' In other words, Christian language, as the actual speech of a living community, presupposes the extra-linguistic reality of God.

My second thesis follows from the first: Since Christian discourse affirms the factual reality of God, it gives rise to an entirely proper question concerning the truth or otherwise of this affirmation. For it is always logically in order, in face of a factual claim, to ask whether that claim is justified. There is always a proper question whether an indicative statement is true. It would be illogical to say that the central religious assertions are factually true or false, but that there is nevertheless no proper question *whether* they are true.

However, Phillips apparently admits no such question. In an important passage on pp. 22–3 of *The Concept of Prayer* he says:

To ask a question, then, about the reality of the physical world, is not to ask whether the physical world exists (what would that mean?) but to ask for an elucidation of the concept of reality in question. Similarly, the question of the reality of God which is of interest to the philosopher is a question about a *kind of reality*; a question about the possibility of giving an account of the distinction between truth and falsity, sense and nonsense, in religion. This is not a question of experimentation any more than the question of the reality of the physical world, but a question of conceptual elucidation; that is, the philosophers want to know what is meant by 'real' ('exists') in the statement God is real (exists).

The argument here seems to be: the user of physical-object language cannot meaningfully ask whether the physical world exists, though he can seek as a philosopher to elucidate the *kind* of reality it has. Similarly the user of theistic language cannot meaningfully ask whether God exists; though he can as a philosopher seek to elucidate the kind of reality God has. But this is a question-begging parallel. Whereas everyone is a user of physical-object language, so that there is no one in a position to ask seriously whether the physical world exists, by no means everyone is a user of theistic language, and there are many who ask seriously whether God exists. In the context of universal agreement that there is a material world, the question about its existence or reality is (as Phillips rightly says) a conceptual question asking for an elucidation of the notion of a material object. But in the quite different context of dispute as to whether God exists the question about the reality of God is not only a conceptual question but also a question of fact and existence. To ask 'What kind of reality has that which is spoken about in material-object language?' and 'What kind of reality has that which is spoken about in theistic language?' is to embark upon two very diverse kinds of inquiry.

At this point, however, Phillips would perhaps want to refer to Malcolm's discussion of the second form of the ontological argument, presented in Anselm's *Proslogion* 3 and in his *Reply* to Gaunilon. In his much discussed article, 'Anselm's Ontological Arguments' (*Philosophical Review*, January 1960), of which Phillips makes frequent use, Malcolm shows that the concept of God is such that it is not a contingent question whether God exists. God can neither contingently exist nor contingently fail to exist; divine existence must be either necessary or impossible. He further believes that the second case, equivalent to the necessary non-existence of God, can be excluded, thereby proving that God necessarily exists. I have criticised this argument in detail elsewhere.[7] But the point at the moment is that the concept of God is such that God's existing or not existing is not a contingent existing or not existing. That is to say, God is conceived as being without beginning or end and as without dependence for his existence upon anything other than himself. But it does not follow from this, as Phillips seems to suppose, that there is no question *whether* there is such an eternal independent Being. There is, to be sure, no question whether God contingently exists. But there is a question whether he eternally and independently (i.e. necessarily) exists, in distinction from eternally not existing. Even if Phillips were to claim that this question can be definitively settled by philosophical reasoning (as Malcolm perhaps and Hartshorne certainly claim), the question thus settled would still be a perfectly good question.

This leads me to my third thesis: Philosophical considerations are relevant to a decision as to whether or not it is reasonable to believe that God exists.

Here it seems that Phillips would accept the negative contention that philosophical criticism may render an existing belief untenable,[8] but would deny to philosophy any converse positive office. He says:

> The whole conception, then, of religion standing in need of justification is confused. Of course, epistemologists will seek to clarify the meaning of religious statements, but, as I have said, this means clarifying what is already there awaiting such clarification. Philosophy is neither for nor against religion: 'it leaves everything as it is'. This fact distinguishes philosophy from apologetics. It is not the task of the philosopher to decide whether there is a God or not, but to ask what it means to affirm or deny the existence of God.[9]

I should like to raise some questions about this passage. Certainly, philosophy in general is neither for nor against religion; but does it follow that there cannot be philosophical arguments for and against the belief-worthiness of religious claims, such as the claim that there is an infinite personal being who has created everything that exists other than himself? Again, certainly philosophy leaves everything as it is; but does it follow that it may not help us to discern how things are? Certainly, again, philosophy cannot decide whether God exists in the sense of determining whether he shall exist or not; but may philosophy not nevertheless help us to decide whether it is reasonable to believe that God exists; and may it not do this along precisely the path that Phillips indicates, namely by clarifying what it means to affirm or deny the existence of God? For example, given Yuri Gagarin's concept of God as an object that he would have observed, had it existed, during his first space flight, may one not put two and two together and conclude that it is unreasonable to believe that God, so conceived, exists? Of course, this latter operation of drawing conclusions concerning the truth or falsity of a belief is very much harder in the case of more sophisticated concepts of God; and if Phillips is saying just this, well and good. But that philosophy clarifies concepts, such as the concept of deity, does not entail that it can have nothing to say about whether there (logically) *can* be and, if so, whether it is reasonable to believe that there actually *is*, a reality answering to the concept. Nevertheless Phillips evidently holds, as a matter of definition, that it is properly philosophical to note what people say and to extract therefrom the concepts they are using, but not to consider reasons for and against believing what they say. The philosopher of religion is thus given the role of an observer who seeks to understand how religious persons talk and to discern the 'logic' of their language. He is committed as a spectator (or auditor) to noting, though not to accepting or rejecting, their religious beliefs and presuppositions. It is thus not open to him to conclude, either rightly or wrongly, that there cannot be a divine being such as religious people suppose there to be, and that they are therefore fundamentally mistaken. The philosopher, it would seem, is in this respect like an anthropologist or a sociologist who studies a living society, describing its structure and dynamics, but who does not in his capacity as anthropologist or sociologist form moral judgements about its life or truth-valuations about its beliefs. He accepts the society he is studying as a going concern, a part of the total phenomenon of human life, and he is not concerned to promote or oppose, praise or condemn, but simply to describe and understand it.

This conception of the philosophy of religion would cut out many of the topics that are normally discussed under that name. In excluding the critical consideration of possible grounds for believing or disbelieving in the reality of God it excludes study of the traditional theistic arguments; of the question of the cognitive value of religious experience and mysticism; of the relation between religious and scientific beliefs; of the apparently competing truth-claims of different religions; of naturalistic theories of the nature of religion; of the problem of evil considered as a challenge to theistic faith; of the alleged incoherences in the concept of God. Alas, some of us are not only profoundly interested in these questions but also earn our living by discussing them!

However, if some of us have a vested interest in traditional philosophy of religion and others haven't, this in itself hardly constitutes a philosophical issue. If a thinker prefers to omit certain

topics from his range of interest, or even to adopt a definition of
'philosophy' which excludes them, this is his own business. It may
appear to some of us as a needlessly quixotic act of self-denial, and
we may be inclined to congratulate Phillips when in practice he
infringes it by the interest that he shows in the ontological
argument. But if there is nothing more to it than an individual
preference there seems little more to be said.

There still remains, however, what *may* be a genuine difference
of religious attitude and understanding. Phillips seems to think
that there is such a difference, and he expresses it as follows:

> There are some people the truth of whose religion depends on
> the way things go in their lives. Things may not go well here and
> now, but unless the ultimate facts, the eschatological situation,
> are favourable in some sense or other, faith has been a hoax and
> a failure. For Hick, the kind of difference religion makes to life is
> the difference between a set of empirical facts being or not being
> the case. This belief is illustrated by a comment I heard a mother
> make about her mentally handicapped child: 'Only my religious
> faith keeps me going. Of one thing I am sure: my child's place in
> heaven is secure.' On Hick's account, the mother would be
> saying, 'It is terrible for my child at the moment, but he is to be
> compensated later on.' Her hope is in certain facts being
> realized.
>
> Although I sympathize with the mother's hope, I do not find it
> impressive religiously. Indeed, I should want to go further and
> say that it has little to do with religion, being much closer to
> superstition. Two other mothers of mentally handicapped chil-
> dren expressed what their religious faith meant to them in very
> different terms. One of them discussed the view that there is a
> *prima facie* incompatibility between belief in God and the terrible-
> ness of having a mentally handicapped child. People kept asking
> her why such a thing should have happened to her, to which she
> replied, 'Why shouldn't it have happened to me?' I found this
> answer extremely impressive, although I suspect that it needs a
> certain kind of religious belief to find it so. . . .[10]

I am not sure whether this points to a real religious difference or
not. I, for one, have no inclination whatever to regard religion as an
explanatory hypothesis. I regard it rather as consciousness of God
and as living on the basis of that consciousness. Contained within

it – though varying in degree of explication in different minds – are a number of beliefs, including the belief that God is real and that the whole universe is ultimately under the sovereignty and within the providence of divine love. This means, in the case of the two mothers of mentally handicapped children, that those children, whom they love and whose development as persons is stunted by a defective brain or mind, are objects of God's care and will in the end participate in the 'good *eschaton*' of his creation. It is this that we call symbolically the Kingdom of Heaven, in which 'all shall be well, and all shall be well, and all manner of thing shall be well'. One of the two mothers may not spell out at all in her own mind the implications of this Christian hope; she may simply be conscious of the reality and presence of God in her situation. And those who are least inclined to try to spell out the implications of their faith may be the ones who are living most firmly on the basis of it. (Perhaps this is what Phillips is concerned to emphasise.) But any faith that is recognisably continuous with that of the New Testament has an eschatological aspect of it. This is not a matter of 'pie in the sky' – any more than was Jesus' own awareness of God's sovereignty as ensuring the eventual triumph of the divine purpose for the whole creation. It was rather a sense of the *reality* of God and of the ultimate sovereignty of the divine love in relation to the temporal process.

III

In his paper on 'Religious Beliefs and Language Games'[11] Phillips faces the charge made by a number of writers (he cites Ronald Hepburn, Kai Nielsen and myself) that to regard religious language as a language-game with its own internal criteria of meaning and validity is to treat it as a form of protected discourse. As such it would be invulnerable to external criticism but, as the price of such invulnerability, of significance only to those who chose to play this 'game'. The teaching of Jesus, for example, could then no longer be seen as declaring in common human language truths which are of infinite importance to mankind but which are also capable of being questioned from an agnostic or atheist standpoint.

In facing this criticism (made, for example, in the previous section of this chapter) Phillips writes, he says, 'as one who has talked of religious beliefs as language-games, but also as one who has come to feel misgivings in some respects about doing so'.[12] And in the course of the paper he goes quite a long way in acknowledging that religious language cannot be an autonomous language-game, discontinuous with the rest of our speech and immune from the possibility of conflict with our other beliefs. 'So far', he says, 'from it being true that religion can be thought of as an isolated language-game, cut off from all other forms of life, the fact is that religious beliefs cannot be understood at all unless their relation to other modes of life is taken into account.'[13] Again, 'one must stress the connection between religious beliefs and the world, not only in bringing out the force which these beliefs have, but also in bringing out the nature of the difficulties which the belief may occasion. If religion were an isolated language-game, cut off from everything which is not formally religious, how could there be any of the characteristic difficulties connected with religious belief?'[14]

This is a welcome clarification of Phillips's position, developing it in what is, I believe, the right direction. But I want to suggest that having set out on this path it is necessary to go a great deal further. For religious beliefs not only have connections with this familiar world, and with all our life within it, but also with aspects of reality transcending this world and our present earthly life. An obvious example is the religious faith in God's purpose to raise us to life again after death. So far as Christian language is concerned, it would be utterly arbitrary and dogmatic to cut out all references to resurrection, the life to come, heaven and hell, immortality, the fulfilment of God's purpose for men and women beyond as well as within this world. Further, there is a manifest connection between this area of religious belief and expectations concerning the future course of human experience after death. But faced with this particular connection between language and fact, Phillips reverts to the autonomy-of-religious-language thesis and refuses to admit the connections which the language itself claims. Thus in *Death and Immortality*, after expounding the standard philosophical arguments against the intelligibility of the idea of personal survival after death, he offers his own this-wordly reinterpretation of the language of immortality. 'Eternity', he says, 'is not *more* life, but this life seen under certain moral and religious modes of thought.'[15]

The religious truth which lies in the offing is that eternal life, in its fullness, is a quality of life, a life that is not only lived for ever but is above all *worth* living for ever, and that this quality of life may be entered upon now in the midst of this earthly existence. But the untruth of Phillips's position lies in its unfaithfulness to actual religious language, by cutting off its implications concerning 'what there is' and 'how things are'. Consider the connection between belief in the love of God for all his human creatures and belief in the final perfecting of human life after bodily death. In the context of Christian faith, God's love for mankind is not an isolated unit of language, devoid of concrete implications, but refers to the creative divine purpose of bringing men and women to enjoy the supreme quality of life, in community with one another and in conscious dependence upon God, that is symbolised as the Kingdom of Heaven. In so far as human beings live in the misery of fear, hatred, jealousy, suspicion, anxiety, ignorance, oppression and frustrated potentiality, God's love for them is defeated and his loving purpose unfulfilled. Phillips ignores the thousands of millions of people down the ages for whom God's good purpose has not in fact been fulfilled in this earthly life, and develops his theories in terms of the more fortunate minority who have been able to find God in the midst of oppression or calamity, pain or failure. It is happily true that suffering does sometimes ennoble and deepen the human personality and bring one nearer to God. But it would be unrealistic to think that this is always or even usually the case. Phillips looks at the problem of evil through the eyes of such writers as Simone Weil, Kierkegaard, some of Dostoevsky's heroes, and saintly individuals who have found God in the midst of suffering. But the result is a spiritually élitist view which disregards the large and very imperfect mass of humanity. God's love enfolds sinners as well as saints, ordinary struggling and failing mortals as well as spiritual giants. For very many ordinary people God's loving purpose is manifestly not brought to completion in a world in which the majority of the human beings who have ever been born have died in infancy; and in which the majority of those who have survived to adulthood have lived in poverty, undernourishment and ill-health, in slavery or oppression and lack of freedom, and without any possibility of being enlarged by the emotional and intellectual riches opened up by literature and the arts, science and philosophy. Thus if we think of God's love in concrete terms, as a creative purpose seeking an authentically human existence for every individual, we are led to see life in a much larger context than this earth. For on this earth God's loving purpose succeeds only very partially. If babies who die in infancy, and the multitude of the oppressed in all ages, and the many who are defeated rather than elevated by suffering and injustice are ever to participate in the fulfilment of the divine intention there must be a further life to come; and accordingly talk of the love of God must have implications for the future course of human experience beyond bodily death.

I therefore suggest that having recognised in principle that religious beliefs do not constitute an autonomous language-game, but ramify out to connect with the whole of reality, one must accept the implications of belief in a loving God. If the word 'loving' has any meaning when applied to God it must bear the kind of positive analogy to human love that is indicated in so many of Jesus' sayings and parables. For *God*, the Creator and Lord of the universe, to be loving entails that evil is not ultimate and that infinite good will, however slowly and painfully, be brought out of it. And this in turn entails the completion of God's good purpose for human beings beyond this earthly life.

What is at issue here is not compensation in another life for men's sufferings in this, but the fulfilment of God's purpose for his creation. If that purpose involves that all his human children shall eventually be drawn into the divine life, this purpose has unavoidable implications concerning the structure and process of the universe. Expressions of Christian faith are thus also, by implication, expressions of belief about the character of our total environment. This is, as I have been suggesting, brought home to us when we confront the theological problem of evil [see Ch. 6].

NOTES

1. Bertrand Russell, *Why I am not a Christian* (London: Allen and Unwin, 1957) p. 172, (New York: Simon and Schuster, 1957) p. 197.
2. *The Christian Century*, 21 Dec 1960, p. 1497.
3. J. H. Randall, *The Role of Knowledge in Western Religion* (Boston, Mass.: Starr King Press, 1958) p. 6.
4. Ibid., p. 9.
5. D. Z. Phillips, *Faith and Philosophical Inquiry* (London: Routledge and Kegan Paul, 1970).
6. D. Z. Phillips, *The Concept of Prayer* (London: Routledge and Kegan Paul, 1965) p. 18.
7. John Hick and Arthur McGill (eds), *The Many-Faced Argument* (New York: Macmillan, 1967; London: Macmillan, 1968) ch. 19.
8. Phillips, *Faith and Philosophical Inquiry*, ch. 13.

9. Phillips, *The Concept of Prayer*, p. 10.
10. Phillips, *Faith and Philosophical Inquiry*, pp. 127–8.
11. Ibid., ch. 5.
12. Ibid., p. 78.
13. Ibid., p. 97.
14. Ibid., p. 90.
15. D. Z. Phillips, *Death and Immortality* (London: Macmillan; New York: St Martin's Press, 1970) p. 49.

3

Religious Faith as Experiencing-as

The particular sense or use of the word 'faith' that I am seeking to understand is that which occurs when the religious man, and more specifically the Christian believer, speaks of 'knowing God' and goes on to explain that this is a knowing of God by faith. Or again, when asked how he professes to know that God, as spoken about in Christianity, is real, his answer is 'by faith'. Our question is: what does 'faith' mean in these contexts? And what I should like to be able to do is to make a descriptive (or if you like phenomenological) analysis that could be acceptable to both believers and non-believers. A Christian and an atheist or agnostic should equally be able to say, Yes, that is what, phenomenologically, faith is – though they would of course then go on to say radically different things about its value.

The modes of cognition have been classified in various ways. But the distinction that is most relevant to our present purpose is that between what I shall call cognition in presence and cognition in absence; or acquaintance (using this term less restrictedly than it was used by Russell) and holding beliefs-about. We cognise things that are present before us, this being called perception; and we also cognise things in their absence, this being a matter of holding beliefs about them. And the astonishing fact is that while our religious literature – the Bible, and prayers, hymns, sermons, devotional meditations and so on – confidently presupposes a cognition of God by acquaintance, our theological literature in contrast recognises for the most part only cognition in absence. That is to say, whereas the Bible itself, and other writings directly expressing the life of faith, are full of men's encounters with God and men's personal dealings with the divine Thou, the dominant systems of Christian theology nevertheless treat faith as belief, as a propositional attitude. In the Catholic tradition deriving from St Thomas, and no less in the Protestant orthodoxy that supervened

34

upon the Reformation movement, faith has been quite explicitly
defined as believing on God's authority certain truths, i.e. propositional truths, that he has revealed. Thus faith, instead of being seen
as a religious response to God's redemptive action in the life of
Jesus of Nazareth, has been seen instead as primarily an assent to
theological truths. For good or ill this was a very major and radical
step, taken early on in the Church's history and displaying its
implications over the centuries in many different aspects of the life
of Christendom. I believe that it was a wrong step, which the
Reformers of the sixteenth century sought to correct. If this is so,
we want to find a viable way, or perhaps even ways (in the plural),
of thinking of faith as a form of cognition by acquaintance or
cognition in presence. Instead of assimilating faith to propositional
belief – whether such belief be produced by reasoning or act of will
or both – we must assimilate it to perception. I therefore want to
explore the possibility that the cognition of God by faith is more
like perceiving something, even perceiving a physical object, that
is present before us than it is like believing a statement about some
absent object, whether because the statement has been proved to
us or because we want to believe it.

But surely – if I may myself at once voice an inevitable protest –
the cognition of God can no more be like sense perception than
God is like a physical object. It is true that Christian tradition tells
of an ultimate beatific vision of God, but we are not now speaking
of this but of the ordinary believer's awareness of God in our
present earthly life. And this is not a matter of perceiving him, but
of believing, without being able to perceive him, that he nevertheless exists. It is in fact, as it has traditionally been held to be, a case
of cognition in absence, or of holding beliefs-about.

However the hypothesis that we want to consider is not that
religious faith *is* sense perception, but that as a form of cognition
by acquaintance it is *more like* sense perception than like propositional belief. That propositions may be validly founded upon the
awareness of God, and that they then play an indispensable and
immensely valuable part in the religious life, is not in question. But
what we are interested in now is the awareness of God itself; for
this is faith – that is to say, distinctively religious cognition – in its
primary sense.

It is today hardly a contentious doctrine requiring elaborate
argumentation that seeing – to confine ourselves for the moment to
this one mode of perceiving – is not a simple straightforward

matter of physical objects registering themselves on our retinas and thence in our conscious visual fields. There are complexities, and indeed a complex variety of complexities. The particular complexity that concerns us now was brought to the attention of philosophers by Wittgenstein's discussion of seeing-as in the *Philosophical Investigations*. Wittgenstein pointed to puzzle pictures and ambiguous diagrams of the kind that are found in abundance in some of the psychological texts – for instance the Necker cube, Jastrow's duck–rabbit, and Köhler's goblet–faces. The cube diagram, for instance, can be seen as a cube viewed either from below or from above, and the perceiving mind tends to alternate between these two perspectives. The goblet–faces diagram can be seen as the outline of a goblet or vase or as the outlines of two faces looking straight into each other's eyes. The duck–rabbit can be seen as the representation of a rabbit's head facing to the left or of a duck's head facing to the right. In these cases every line of the diagram plays its part in both aspects (as Wittgenstein called them) and has equal weight in each: these may accordingly be called cases of total ambiguity. Another sort, artistically more complex, might be called cases of emergent pattern; for example, those puzzle pictures in which you are presented with what at first seems to be a random and meaningless scattering of lines and dots, but in which as you look at it you come to see, say, a face; or again, as another example, the well-known 'Christ in the snow' picture. And in between there are various other sorts of intermediate cases which we need not however take account of here. We speak of seeing-as when that which is objectively there, in the sense of that which affects the retina, can be consciously perceived in two different ways as having two different characters or natures or meanings or significances; and very often, in these two-dimensional instances, we find that the mind switches back and forth between the alternative ways of seeing-as.

Let us at this point expand the notion of seeing-as into that of experiencing-as. The elements of experiencing-as are the purely visual seeing-as which we have thus far been discussing, plus its equivalents for the other senses. For as well as seeing a bird as a bird, we may hear it as a bird – hear the bird's song as a bird's song, hear the rustle of its wings as a bird in flight, hear the rapping of the woodpecker as just that; and so on. Again, a carpenter may not only see the wood as mahogany but also feel it as mahogany; he may recognise it tactually as well as visually. Or again, we may taste the wine as Burgundy and smell the cheese as Gorgonzola. Not of course that the different senses normally function in isolation. We perceive and recognise by means of all the relevant senses co-operating as a single complex means of perception; and I suggest that we use the term 'experiencing-as' to refer to the end-product of this in consciousness.

The next step is from these two-dimensional pictures and diagrams to experiencing-as in real life – for example, seeing the tuft of grass over there in the field as a rabbit, or the shadows in the corner of the room as someone standing there. And the analogy to be explored is with two contrasting ways of experiencing the events of our lives and of human history, on the one hand as purely natural events and on the other hand as mediating the presence and activity of God. For there is a sense in which the religious man and the atheist both live in the same world and another sense in which they live consciously in different worlds. They inhabit the same physical environment and are confronted by the same changes occurring within it. But in its actual concrete character in their respective 'streams of consciousness' it has for each a different nature and quality, a different meaning and significance; for one does and the other does not experience life as a continual interaction with the transcendent God. Is there then any true analogy or parallel between, on the one hand, these two ways of experiencing human life, *as* an encounter with God or *as* an encounter only with a natural order, and on the other hand the two ways of seeing the distant shape, *as* a rabbit or *as* a tuft of grass?

An immediate comment might be: if there is any such analogy, so much the worse for religious cognition! For does not the analogy between seeing a puzzle picture in a certain way and experiencing human life in a certain way underline once again the purely subjective and gratuitous character of religious knowledge-claims in contrast with the compelling objectivity of ordinary sense perception?

So far as the argument has thus far gone, perhaps it does. But the next point to be introduced must considerably affect the upshot of what has gone before. This is the thesis that *all* experiencing is experiencing-as – not only, for example, seeing the tuft of grass, erroneously, as a rabbit, but also seeing it correctly as a tuft of grass. On the face of it this sounds paradoxical. One might put the difficulty in this way: we may if we like speak of seeing the tuft of grass *as* a tuft of grass because it is evidently possible to misperceive it as a sitting rabbit. But what about something utterly familar and unmistakable? What about the fork on the table? Would it not be absurd to say that you are seeing it *as* a fork? It must be granted that this particular locution would be distinctly odd in most circumstances. However we have more acceptable names for ordinary seeing-as in real life; we call it 'recognising' or 'identifying'. Of course we are so familiar with forks that normally we recognise one without encountering even enough difficulty to make us notice that we are in fact performing an act of recognition. But if the fork were sufficiently exotic in design I might have occasion to say that I can recognise the thing before me on the table as a fork – that is, as a man-made instrument for conveying food into the mouth. And, going further afield, a Stone Age savage would not be able to recognise it at all. He might identify it instead as a marvellously shining object which must be full of *mana* and must not be touched; or as a small but deadly weapon; or as a tool for digging; or just as something utterly baffling and unidentifiable. But he would not have the concept of a fork with which to identify it as a fork. Indeed to say that he does not have this concept and that he cannot perform this act of recognition are two ways of saying the same thing. That there is no ambiguity or mystery about forks for you or me is simply due to the contingent circumstance that forks are familiar parts of the apparatus of our culture. For the original nature or meaning of an artefact is determined by the purpose for which it has been made, and this purpose necessarily operates within a particular cultural context. But simply as a physical object of a certain size and shape an artefact does not bear its meaning stamped upon it. To recognise or identify is to experience-as in terms of a concept; and our concepts are social products having their life within a particular linguistic environment.

Further, this is as true of natural objects as it is of artefacts. Here, too, to recognise is to apply a concept; and this is always to cognise the thing as being much more than is currently perceptible. For example, to identify a moving object in the sky as a bird is not only to make implicit claims about its present shape, size, and structure beyond what we immediately observe but also about its past (for instance, that it came out of an egg, not a factory), about its future (for instance, that it will one day die), and about its behaviour in various hypothetical circumstances (for instance, that it will tend to be frightened by loud noises). When we thus equate experiencing-as with recognising it is I think no longer a paradoxical doctrine that all conscious experiencing is experiencing-as.

But – if I may raise a possible objection – is it not the case that 'He recognises x' entails that the thing recognised is indeed x, while 'He is experiencing a as x' does not entail that a is indeed x: and must we not therefore acknowledge a distinction between recognising and experiencing-as? As a matter of the ordinary use of these words the objection is, I think, in order. But what it indicates is that we lack a term to cover both recognition and misrecognition. We are accordingly driven to use 'recognition' generically, as 'knowledge' in 'theory of knowledge' is used to cover error as well as knowledge, or as 'morality' in 'theory of morality' is used to cover immorality also. I have been using 'recognition' here in an analogous way to include unjustified as well as justified identification assertions.

I proceed, then, from the proposition that all conscious experiencing involves recognitions which go beyond what is given to the senses and is thus a matter of experiencing-as. This means that ordinary secular perceiving shares a common epistemological character with religious experiencing. We must accordingly abandon the view – if we ever held it – that sense perception at the highly sophisticated human level is a mere automatic registering by the mind of what is on the retina, while religious perception is, in contrast, a subjective response which gratuitously projects meanings into the world. We find instead that all conscious perceiving goes beyond what the senses report to a significance which has not as such been given to the senses. And the religious experience of life as a sphere in which we have continually to do with God and he with us is likewise an awareness in our experience as a whole of a significance which transcends the scope of the senses. In both cases, in a classic statement of John Oman's, 'knowing is not knowledge as an effect of an unknown external cause, but is knowledge as we so interpret that our meaning is the actual meaning of our environment'.[1] And, as Oman also taught, the claim of the religious believer is that in his religious commitment he is relating himself to his total environment in its most ultimate meaning.

The conclusion that *all* experiencing is experiencing-as enables us to meet a fundamental objection that might be made against the analogy between experiencing-as in ordinary life and in religious awareness. It might be pointed out that it is only possible to see, let us say, a tuft of grass as a rabbit if one has previously seen real rabbits; and that in general to see *A* as a *B* presupposes acquaintance with *B*s. Analogously, in order to experience some event, say a striking escape from danger or a healing, as an act of God it would seem that we must first know by direct acquaintance what an act of God is like. However all that has ever been witnessed in the way of divine actions is earthly events which the religious mind has seen as acts of God but which a sceptical observer could see as having a purely natural explanation. In other words, we never have before us unambiguously divine acts, but only ambiguous events which are capable of taking on religious significance to the eyes of faith. But in that case, it will be said, we have no unproblematic cases of divine actions available to us, as we have in abundance unproblematic instances of rabbits and forks; and consequently we can never be in a position to recognise any of these ambiguous events *as* acts of God. Just as it would be impossible for one who had never seen rabbits to see anything *as* a rabbit, so it must be impossible for us who have never seen an undeniable act of God, to see an event *as* an act of God. This seems on the face of it to be a conclusive objection.

However the objection collapses if, as I have been arguing, *all* experiencing, involving as it does the activity of recognising, is to be construed as experiencing-as. For although the process of recognising is mysterious, there is no doubt that we do continually recognise things, and further that we can learn to recognise. We have learned, starting from scratch, to identify rabbits and forks and innumerable other kinds of thing. And so there is thus far in principle no difficulty about the claim that we may learn to use the concept 'act of God', as we have learned to use other concepts, and acquire the capacity to recognise exemplifying instances.

But of course – let it at once be granted – there are very obvious and indeed immense differences between the concept of a divine act and such concepts as rabbit and fork. For one thing, rabbits and forks are objects – substances, if you like – whereas a divine act is an event. This is already a considerable conceptual contrast. And we must proceed to enlarge it still further. For the cognition of God recorded in the Bible is much wider in scope than an awareness of particular isolated events as being acts of God. Such divine acts are but points of peculiarly intense focus within a much wider awareness of existing in the presence of God. Indeed the biblical cognition of God is typically mediated through the whole experience of the prophet or apostle after his call or conversion, even though within this totality there are specially vivid moments of awareness of God, some of which are evoked by striking or numinous events which thereby become miracles or theophanies. However, we are primarily concerned here with the wider and more continuous awareness of living within the ambience of the unseen God – with the sense of the presence of God – and this is surely something very unlike the awareness of forks and rabbits.

But although the sense of the presence of God is indeed very far removed from the recognition of forks and rabbits, it is already, I think, clear that there are connecting links in virtue of which the religious awareness need not be completely unintelligible to us. In its epistemological structure it exhibits a continuity with our awareness in other fields.

In seeking further to uncover and investigate this continuity we must now take note of another feature of experiencing-as, namely the fact that it occurs at various levels of awareness. By this I mean that as well as there being values of x and y such that to experience A as x is incompatible with experiencing it as y, because x and y are mutually exclusive alternatives, there are also values of x and y such that it is possible to experience A as simultaneously x and y. Here y is supplementary to x, but on a different level. What is meant by 'levels' in this context? That y is on a higher level than x means that the experiencing of A as y presupposes but goes beyond the experiencing of it as x. One or two examples may be useful at this point. As an example, first, of mutually exclusive experiencings-as, one cannot see the tuft of grass simultaneously as a tuft of grass and as a rabbit; or the person whose face we are watching as both furiously angry and profoundly delighted. On the other hand, as an example of supplementary experiencings-as, we may see what is moving above us in the sky as a bird; we may further see it as a hawk; and we may further see it as a hawk engaged in searching for prey; and if we are extremely expert bird watchers we may even see it as a hawk about to swoop down on something on the far side of that low hump of ground. These are successively higher-level recognitions in the sense that each later member of the list presupposes and goes beyond the previous one.

Now let us call the correlate of experiencing-as 'significance', defining this by means of the notion of appropriate response. That is to say, to recognise what is before us as an x involves being in a dispositional state to act in relation to it in a certain distinctive way or range of ways. For example, to recognise the object on the table as a fork is to be in a different dispositional state from that in which one is if one recognises it as a fountain pen. One is prepared in the two cases for the object to display different characteristics, and to be surprised if it doesn't; and one is prepared to use it in different ways and on different occasions, and so on; and in general to recognise something *as* a this or a that (i.e. as significant in this way or in that way) involves being in a certain dispositional state in relation to it.

Our next step must be to shift attention from isolated objects as units of significance to larger and more complex units, namely situations.

A situation is composed of objects; but it is not simply any random collocation of objects. It is a group of objects which, when attended to as a group, has its own distinctive significance over and above the individual significances of its constituent members. That is to say, the situation evokes its own appropriate dispositional response.

As in the case of object-significance there can be different levels of situational significance, with higher levels presupposing lower. An example that is directly relevant is the relation between the ethical significance of a human situation and its purely natural or physical significance. Think of any situation involving an element of moral obligation. Suppose, for example, that someone is caught at the foot of a steep cliff by an incoming tide and I at the top hear his cries for help. He asks me to run to the nearest telephone, ring the police and ask them to call out the lifeboat to rescue him. Consider this first at the purely natural or physical level. There are the cliff and the sea, a human creature liable in due course to be submerged by the rising tide, and his shouted appeals for help. And, morality apart, that is all that there is – just this particular pattern of physical events. However as moral beings we are aware of more than that. As well as experiencing the physical events as physical events we also experience them as constituting a situation of moral claim upon ourselves. We experience the physical pattern as having ethical significance; and the dispositional response that it renders appropriate is to seek to help the trapped person in whatever way seems most practicable. We can, however, conceive of someone with no moral sense at all, who simply fails to be aware of the ethical significance of this situation. He would be interpreting or recognising or experiencing-as only at the physical level of significance. And there would be no way of proving to someone who was thus morally defective that there is any such thing as moral obligation. No doubt an amoral creature could be induced by threats and promises to conform to a socially desirable pattern of behaviour, but he could never by turned by these means into a moral being. In the end we can only say, tautologously, that a person is aware of the ethical significance of situations because he is a moral being; he experiences in moral terms because he is built that way.

The ethical is experienced as an order of significance which supervenes upon, interpenetrates, and is mediated through the physical significance which it presupposes. And if on some occasion the moral character of a situation is not at first apparent to us, but dawns upon as we contemplate it, something happens that is comparable to the discovery of an emergent pattern in a puzzle picture. As the same lines and marks are there, but we have now come to see them as constituting an importantly new pattern, so the social situation is there with the same describable features, but we have now come to be aware of it as laying upon us an inescapable moral claim.

Now consider religious significance as a yet higher level of significance. It is a higher level of significance, adding a new dimension which both includes and transcends that of moral judgement, and yet on the other hand it does not form a simple continuation of the pattern we have already noted. As between natural and ethical significance it is safe to say that every instance of the latter presupposes some instance of the former; for there could be no moral situations if there were no physical situations to have moral significance. But as between ethical and religious significance the relationship is more complex. Not every moment of religious awareness is superimposed upon some occasion of moral obligation. Very often – and especially in the prophetic type of religion that we know in Judaism and Christianity – the sense of the presence of God does carry with it some specific or general moral demand. But we may also be conscious of God in solitude, surrounded only by the natural world, when the divine presence is borne in upon us by the vastness of the starry heavens above or the majestic beauty of a sunrise or a mountain range or some lake or forest scene, or other aspect of earth's marvellously varied face. Again, the sense of the presence of God may occur without any specific environmental context, when the mind is rapt in prayer or meditation; for there is a contemplative and mystical awareness of God which is relatively independent of external circumstances. And indeed even within the prophetic type of religious experience there are also moments of encounter with God in nature and through solitary prayer as well as in the claims of the personal world. But on the other hand even when the sense of the presence of God has dawned upon us in solitude it is still normally true that it leads us back to our neighbours and often deepens the ethical significance of our relations with them. Thus the dispositional response which is part of the awareness of God is a response in terms of our involvement with our neighbours within our common environment. Even the awareness of God through nature and mystical contemplation leads eventually back to the service of God in the world.

Let us then continue to think here primarily of the prophetic awareness of God, since although this is not the only form of religious cognition it is the typically Judaic–Christian form. And let us test the notion of faith as religious experiencing-as by applying it to the particular history of faith which is reflected in the biblical records.

The Old Testament prophets were vividly conscious of Yahveh as acting in relation to the people of Israel in certain of the events of their time. Through the writings which recall their words and deeds we feel their overwhelmingly vivid consciousness of God as actively present in their contemporary history. It was God who, in the experience of Amos, was threatening selfish and complacent Israel with Assyrian conquest, while also offering mercy to such as should repent. It was God in his holy anger who, in the experience of Jeremiah, was bringing up the Babylonian army against Jerusalem and summoning his people to turn from their greed and wickedness. It is equally true of the other great prophets of the Old Testament that they were experiencing history, as it was taking place around them, as having a distinctively religious significance. Humanly explicable events were experienced as also acts of God, embodying his wrath or his mercy or his calling of the Jewish nation into covenant with him. The prophets experienced the religious significance of these events and declared it to the people; and this religious significance was always such that to see it meant being conscious of a sacred demand to behave in a new way towards one's neighbours.

It is, I think, important to realise that this prophetic interpretation of Hebrew history was not in the first place a philosophy of history, a theoretical pattern imposed retrospectively upon remembered or recorded events. It was in the first place the way in which the great prophets actually experienced and participated in these events at the time. Hosea did not *infer* Yahveh's mercy; second Isaiah did not *infer* his universal sovereignty; Jeremiah did not *infer* his holy righteousness – rather they were conscious of the Eternal as acting towards them, and towards their nation, in his mercy, in his holy righteousness, in his absolute sovereignty. They were, in other words, experiencing-as.

Again, in the New Testament, the primary instance of faith, the rock on which Christianity is based, consisted in seeing Jesus as the Christ. This was the faith of the disciples, epitomised in Peter's confession at Caesarea Philippi, whereby their experience of following Jesus was also an experience of being in the presence of God's personal purpose and claim and love. They may or may not at the time have used any of the terms that were later used in the New Testament writings to express this awareness – Messiah, Son of God, divine Logos. However, these terms point back to that original response, and the faith which they came to express must have been implicit within it. And once again this primary response of the first disciples to Jesus as Lord and Christ was not a theory about him which they adopted, but an experience out of which Christian language and theory later grew. That he was their Lord was a fact of experience given in their personal dealings with him. And the special character of their way of seeing and responding to him, in contrast to that of others who never found him to be their Lord, is precisely the distinctive essence of Christian faith.

The experiencing of Jesus of Nazareth as Lord – Jesus of Nazareth, that is to say, not as a theological symbol but in his historical concreteness, including his teaching concerning God and man – meant coming to share in some degree both his experiencing of life as the sphere of God's redemptive activity and his practical response to God's purposes in the world. What that involved for Jesus himself, as the one in whom men were to see the divine Logos made flesh, is spelled out in his life, and especially in the drama of his death. What it involves for Christians – for those who have begun to share Jesus' vision of the world in its relation to God – is indicated in his moral teaching. For this is simply a general description, with concrete examples drawn from the life of first-century Palestine, of the way in which someone tends spontaneously to behave who is consciously living in the presence of God as Jesus has revealed him.

I have now, I hope, offered at least a very rough outline of a conception of faith as the interpretative element within our cognitive religious experience. How is one to test such a theory, and how decide whether to accept or reject it? All that can be done is to spell out its consequences as fully as possible in the hope that the theory will then either founder under a weight of implausible corollaries, or else show its viability as it proceeds and float triumphantly on to acceptance. I have already tried to indicate its epistemological basis in the thesis that all experiencing is experiencing-as, and the way in which this thesis is relevant to the stream of distinctively religious experience recorded in the Bible. Let me now in conclusion sketch some of its lines of implication in other directions.

It suggests, as I have already mentioned, a view of the Christian ethic as the practical corollary of the distinctively Christian vision of the world. Taking a hint from the modern dispositional analysis of belief we may say that to experience the world as having a certain character is, among other things, to be in a dispositional state to live in it in the manner which such a character in our environment renders appropriate. And to experience it in a way derived from Christ's own experience is accordingly to tend to live in the kind of way that he both taught and showed forth in his own life.

Another implication of this theory of faith concerns the nature of revelation. For in Christian theology revelation and faith are correlative concepts, faith being a human response to the divine activity of self-revelation. If faith is construed as a distinctively religious experiencing of life as mediating God's presence and activity, this clearly fits and even demands a *heilsgeschichtliche* conception of revelation as consisting in divine actions in human history. God is self-revealingly active within the world that he has made. But his actions are not overwhelmingly manifest and unmistakable; for then men would have no cognitive freedom in relation to their Maker. Instead God always acts in such a way that man is free to see or fail to see the events in question as divine acts. The prophets were conscious of God at work in the happenings of their time; but many of their contemporaries were not. Again, the disciples were conscious of Jesus as the Christ; but the scribes and pharisees and the Romans were not. Thus revelation, as communication between God and man, only becomes actual when it meets an answering human response of faith; and the necessity for this response, making possible an uncompelled cognition of God's presence and activity, preserves the freedom and responsibility of the finite creature in relation to the infinite Creator.

This in turn suggests an understanding of the special character of the Bible and of its inspiration. The Bible is a record of the stream of revelatory events that culminated in the coming of the Christ. But it differs from a secular account of the same strand of history in that the Bible is written throughout from the standpoint of faith. It describes this history as it was experienced from within by the prophets and then by the apostles. And the faith of the writers, whereby they saw the revelatory events *as* revelatory, is their inspiration. The uniqueness of the Bible is not due to any unique mode or quality of its writing but to the unique significance of the events of which it is the original documentary expression, which became revelatory through the faith of the biblical writers. As such the Bible mediates the same revelation to subsequent generations and is thus itself revelatory in a secondary sense, calling in its own turn for a response of faith.

This theory of faith can also be used to throw light on the nature of the miraculous. For a miracle, whatever else it may be, is an event through which we become vividly and immediately conscious of God as acting towards us. A startling happening, even if it should involve a suspension of natural law, does not constitute for us a miracle in the religious sense of the word if it fails to make us intensely aware of being in God's presence. In order to be miraculous, an event must be experienced as religiously significant. Indeed we may say that a miracle is any event that is experienced as a miracle; and this particular mode of experiencing-as is accordingly an essential element in the miraculous.

Finally, yet another application of this theory of faith is to the sacraments. In the sacraments some ordinary material object, bread or wine or water, is experienced as a vehicle of God's grace and becomes a focus of specially intense consciousness of God's overshadowing presence and purpose. A sacrament has in fact the same religious quality as a miracle but differs from other miracles in that it occurs within a liturgical context and is a product of ritual. In themselves, apart from the sacramental context of worshipping faith, the bread and wine or the water are ordinary material things; they have no magical properties. What happens in the sacramental event is that they are experienced as channels of divine grace. They thus invite a peculiarly direct moment of religious experiencing-as, fulfilling for subsequent believers the faith-eliciting and faith-nourishing function of the person of Christ in the experience of the first disciples.

Now in conclusion may I repeat something that I said near the beginning. What I have been attempting to formulate is an epistemological analysis of religious faith, not an argument for the validity of that faith. Faith, I have been suggesting, is the interpretative element within what the religious man reports as his experience of living in the presence of God. But whether that experience is veridical or illusory is another question. My own view is that it is as rational for the religious man to treat his experience of God as veridical as it is for him and others to treat their experience of the physical world as veridical. But that requires another argument [see Ch. 4].

NOTE

1.   John Oman, *The Natural and the Supernatural* (Cambridge: Cambridge University Press, 1931) p. 175.

4

Rational Theistic Belief without Proofs

I THE RELIGIOUS REJECTION OF THE THEISTIC ARGUMENTS

The major theistic arguments are all open to serious philosophical objections, and there is a widespread consensus among contemporary philosophers that these arguments fail to do what they profess to do. Neither those which undertake strictly to demonstrate the existence of an absolute Being, nor those which profess to show divine existence to be probable, are able to fulfil their promise. It seems that it is impossible to demonstrate the reality of God by *a priori* reasoning, since such reasoning is confined to the realm of concepts; impossible to demonstrate it by *a posteriori* reasoning, since this would have to include a premise begging the very question at issue; and impossible to establish it as in a greater or lesser degree probable, since the notion of probability lacks any clear meaning in this context. A philosopher unacquainted with modern developments in theology might well assume that theologians would, *ex officio*, be supporters of the theistic proofs and would regard as a fatal blow this conclusion that there can be neither a strict demonstration of God's existence nor a valid probability argument for it. In fact however such an assumption would be true only of certain theological schools. It is true of the more traditional Roman Catholic theology,[1] of sections of conservative Protestantism,[2] and of most of those Protestant apologists who continue to work within the tradition of nineteenth-century idealism.[3] It has never been true, on the other hand, of Jewish religious thought;[4] and it is not true of that central stream of contemporary Protestant theology which has been influenced by the 'neo-orthodox' movement, the revival of Reformation studies and the 'existentialism' of Kierkegaard and his successors; or of the most significant contemporary Roman Catholic thinkers, who are

49

on this issue (as on so many others) in advance of the official teaching of the magisterium. Accordingly we have now to take note of this theological rejection of the theistic proofs, ranging from a complete lack of concern for them to a positive repudiation of them as being religiously irrelevant or even harmful. There are several different considerations to be evaluated.

1   It has often been pointed out that for the man of faith, as he is depicted in the Bible, no theistic proofs are necessary.[5] Philosophers in the rationalist tradition, holding that to know means to be able to prove, have been shocked to find that in the Bible, which is supposed to be the basis of Western religion, no attempt whatever is made to demonstrate the existence of God. Instead of professing to establish the divine reality by philosophical reasoning the Bible throughout takes this for granted. Indeed to the biblical writers it would have seemed absurd to try to establish by logical argumentation that God exists. For they were convinced that they were already having to do with him and he with them in all the affairs of their lives. They did not think of God as an inferred entity but as an experienced reality. Many of the biblical writers were (sometimes, though doubtless not at all times) as vividly conscious of being in God's presence as they were of living in a material world. It is impossible to read their pages without realising that to them God was not a proposition completing a syllogism, or an idea adopted by the mind, but the supreme experiential reality. It would be as sensible for a husband to desire a philosophical proof of the existence of the wife and family who contribute so much of the meaning and value of his life as for the man of faith to seek for a proof of the existence of the God within whose purpose he believes that he lives and moves and has his being.

As Cook Wilson wrote:

If we think of the existence of our friends; it is the 'direct knowledge' which we want: merely inferential knowledge seems a poor affair. To most men it would be as surprising as unwelcome to hear it could not be directly known whether there were such existences as their friends, and that it was only a matter of (probable) empirical argument and inference from facts which are directly known. And even if we convince ourselves on reflection that this is really the case, our actions prove that we have a confidence in the existence of our friends which can't be derived from an empirical argument (which can never be certain) for a man will risk his life for his friend. We don't want merely inferred friends. Could we possibly be satisfied with an inferred God?[6]

In other words the man of faith has no need of theistic proofs; for he has something which for him is much better. However it does not follow from this that there may not be others who do need a theistic proof, nor does it follow that there are in fact no such proofs. All that has been said about the irrelevance of proofs to the life of faith may well be true, and yet it might still be the case that there are valid arguments capable of establishing the existence of God to those who stand outside the life of faith.

2   It has also often been pointed out that the God whose existence each of the traditional theistic proofs professes to establish is only an abstraction from and a pale shadow of the living God who is the putative object of biblical faith. A First Cause of the Universe might or might not be a deity to whom an unqualified devotion, love and trust would be appropriate; Aquinas's *Et hoc omnes intelligunt Deum* ('and this all understand to be God') is not the last step in a logical argument but merely an exercise of the custom of overlooking a gap in the argument at this point. A Necessary Being, and indeed a being who is metaphysically absolute in every respect – omnipotent, omniscient, eternal, uncreated – might be morally good or evil. As H. D. Aitken has remarked, 'Logically, there is no reason why an almighty and omniscient being might not be a perfect stinker.'[7] A divine Designer of the world whose nature is read off from the appearances of nature might, as Hume showed, be finite or infinite, perfect or imperfect, omniscient or fallible, and might indeed be not one being but a veritable pantheon.[8] It is only by going beyond what is proved, or claimed to have been proved, and identifying the First Cause, Necessary Being, or Mind behind Nature with the God of biblical faith that these proofs could ever properly impel to worship. By themselves and without supplementation of content and infusion of emotional life from religious traditions and experiences transcending the proofs themselves they would never lead to the life of faith.

The ontological argument on the other hand is in this respect in a different category. If it succeeds it establishes the reality of a being so perfect in every way that no more perfect can be conceived. Clearly if such a being is not worthy of worship none ever could be. It would therefore seem that, unlike the other proofs, the ontological argument, if it were logically sound, would present the relatively few persons who are capable of appreciating such abstract reasoning with a rational ground for worship. On the other hand, however, whilst this is the argument that would accomplish most if it succeeded it is also the argument which is most absolutely incapable of succeeding; for it is, as we have seen, inextricably involved in the fallacy of professing to deduce existence from a concept.

3   It is argued by some religious writers that a logical demonstration of the existence of God would be a form of coercion and would as such be incompatible with God's evident intention to treat his human creatures as free and responsible persons. A great deal of twentieth-century theology emphasises that God as the infinite personal reality, having made man as person in his own image, always treats men as persons, respecting their relative freedom and autonomy. He does not override the human mind by revealing himself in overwhelming majesty and power, but always approaches us in ways that leave room for an uncompelled response of human faith. Even God's own entry into our earthly history, it is said, was in an 'incognito' that could be penetrated only by the eyes of faith. As Pascal put it, 'willing to appear openly to those who seek him with all their heart, and to be hidden from those who flee from him with all their heart, he so regulates the knowledge of himself that he has given indications of himself which are visible to those who seek him and not to those who do not seek him. There is enough light for those to see who only desire to see, and enough obscurity for those who have a contrary disposition'.[9] God's self-revealing actions are accordingly always so mediated through the events of our temporal experience that men only become aware of the divine presence by interpreting and responding to these events in the way which we call religious faith. For if God were to disclose himself to us in the coercive manner in which our physical environment obtrudes itself we should be dwarfed to nothingness by the infinite power thus irresistibly breaking open the privacy of our souls. Further, we should be spiritually blinded by God's perfect holiness and paralysed by his infinite energy; 'for human kind cannot bear very much reality'.[10]

Such a direct, unmediated confrontation breaking in upon us and shattering the frail autonomy of our finite nature would leave no ground for a free human response of trust, self-commitment and obedience. There could be no call for a man to venture upon a dawning consciousness of God's reality and thus to receive this consciousness as an authentic part of his own personal existence precisely because it has not been injected into him or clamped upon him by magisterial exercise of divine omnipotence.

The basic principle invoked here is that for the sake of creating a personal relationship of love and trust with his human creatures God does not force an awareness of himself upon them. And (according to the view which we are considering) it is only a further application of the same principle to add that a logically compelling demonstration of God's existence would likewise frustrate this purpose. For men – or at least those of them who are capable of following the proof – could then be forced to know that God is real. Thus Alasdair MacIntyre, when a Christian apologist, wrote:

> For if we could produce logically cogent arguments we should produce the kind of certitude that leaves no room for decision; where proof is in place, decision is not. We do not decide to accept Euclid's conclusions; we merely look to the rigour of his arguments. If the existence of God were demonstrable we should be as bereft of the possibility of making a free decision to love God as we should be if every utterance of doubt or unbelief was answered by thunderbolts from heaven.[11]

This is the 'religious coercion' objection to the theistic proofs.

To what extent is it a sound objection? We may accept the theological doctrine that for God to force men to know him by the coercion of logic would be incompatible with his purpose of winning the voluntary response and worship of free moral beings. But the question still remains whether the theistic proofs could ever do this. Could a verbal proof of divine existence compel a consciousness of God comparable in coerciveness with a direct manifestation of his divine majesty and power? Could anyone be moved and shaken in their whole being by the demonstration of a proposition, as men have been by a numinous experience of overpowering impressiveness? Would the things that have just been said about an overwhelming display of divine glory really apply to verbal demonstrations – that infinite power would be irresistibly breaking in upon the privacy of our souls and that we should be blinded by God's perfect holiness and paralysed by his infinite energy? Indeed could a form of words, culminating in the proposition that 'God exists', ever have power by itself to produce more than what Newman calls a notional assent in our minds?[12]

It is of course true that the effect of purely rational considerations such as those which are brought to bear in the theistic proofs are much greater in some minds than in others. The more rational the mind the more considerable is the effect to be expected. In many persons – indeed taking mankind as a whole, in the great majority – the effect of a theistic proof, even when no logical flaw is found in it, would be virtually nil! But in more sophisticated minds the effect must be greater, and it is at least theoretically possible that there are minds so rational that purely logical considerations can move them as effectively as the evidence of their senses. It is therefore conceivable that someone who is initially agnostic might be presented with a philosophical proof of divine existence – say the ontological argument, with its definition of God as that than which no more perfect can be conceived – and might as a result be led to worship the being whose reality has thus been demonstrated to him. This seems to be possible; but I believe that even in such a case there must, in addition to an intelligent appreciation of the argument, be a distinctively religious response to the idea of God which the argument presents. Some propensity to respond to unlimited perfection as holy and as rightly claiming a response of unqualified worship and devotion must operate, over and above the purely intellectual capacity for logical calculation.[13] For we can conceive of a purely or merely logical mind, a kind of human calculating machine, which is at the same time devoid of the capacity for numinous feeling and worshipping response. Such a being might infer that God exists but be no more existentially interested in this conclusion than many people are in, say, the fact that the Shasta Dam is 602 feet high. It therefore seems that when the acceptance of a theistic proof leads to worship, a religious reaction occurs which turns what would otherwise be a purely abstract conclusion into an immensely significant and moving fact. In Newman's terminology, when a notional assent to the proposition that God exists becomes a real assent, equivalent to an actual living belief and faith in God, there has been a free human response to an idea which could instead have been rejected by being held at the notional level. In other words, a verbal proof of God's existence cannot by itself break down our human freedom; it can only lead to a notional assent which has little or no positive religious value or substance.

I conclude, however, that the theological objections to the theistic proofs are considerably less strong than the philosophical ones; and that theologians who reject natural theology would therefore do well to do so primarily on philosophical rather than on theological grounds. These philosophical reasons are, as we have seen, very strong; and we therefore now have to consider whether, in the absence of any theistic proofs, it can nevertheless be rational to believe in the existence of God.

II   CAN THERE BE RATIONAL THEISTIC BELIEF WITHOUT PROOFS?

During the period dominated by the traditional theistic arguments the existence of God was often treated by philosophers as something to be discovered through reasoning. It was seen as the conclusion of an inference; and the question of the rationality of the belief was equated with that of the soundness of the inference. But from a religious point of view, as we have already seen, there has always been something very odd about this approach. The situation which it envisages is that of people standing outside the realm of faith, for whom the apologist is trying to build a bridge of rational inference to carry them over the frontier into that realm. But of course this is not the way in which religious faith has originally or typically or normally come about. When the cosmological, ontological, teleological and moral arguments were developed, theistic belief was already a functioning part of an immemorially established and developing form of human life. The claims of religion are claims made by individuals and communities on the basis of their experience – and experience which is none the less their own for occurring within an inherited framework of ideas. We are not dealing with a merely conceivable metaphysical hypothesis which someone has speculatively invented but which hardly anyone seriously believes. We are concerned, rather, with convictions born out of experience and reflection and living within actual communities of faith and practice. Historically, then, the philosophical 'proofs' of God have normally entered in to support

and confirm but not to create belief. Accordingly the proper
philosophical approach would seem to be a probing of the actual
foundations and structure of a living and operative belief rather
than of theoretical and non-operative arguments subsequently
formulated for holding those beliefs. The question is not whether it
is possible to prove, starting from zero, that God exists; the
question is whether the religious man, given the distinctively
religious form of human existence in which he participates, is
properly entitled as a rational person to believe what he does
believe.

At this point we must consider what we mean by a rational
belief. If by a belief we mean a proposition believed, then what we
are to be concerned with here are not rational beliefs but rational
believings. Propositions can be well-formed or ill-formed, and they
can be true or false, but they cannot be rational or irrational. It is
people who are rational or irrational, and derivately their states and
their actions, including their acts and states of believing. Further,
apart from the believing of analytic propositions, which are true by
definition and are therefore rationally believed by anyone who
understands them, the rationality of acts (or states) of believing has
to be assessed separately in each case. For it is a function of the
relation between the proposition believed and the evidence on the
basis of which the believer believes it. It might conceivably be
rational for Mr X to believe p but not rational for Mr Y to believe p,
because in relation to the data available to Mr X p is worthy of belief
but not in relation to the data available to Mr Y. Thus the question
of the rationality of belief in the reality of God is the question of the
rationality of a particular person's believing, given the data that he
is using; or that of the believing of a class of people who share the
same body of data. Or putting the same point the other way round,
any assessing of the belief-worthiness of the proposition that God
exists must be an assessing of it in relation to particular ranges of
data.

Now there is one area of data or evidence which is normally
available to those who believe in God, and that provides a very
important part of the ground of their believing, but which is
normally not available to and therefore not taken into account by
those who do not so believe; and this is religious experience. It
seems that the religious man is in part basing his believing upon
certain data of religious experience which the non-religious man is
not using because he does not have them. Thus our question

resolves itself into one about the theist's right, given his distinctively religious experience, to be certain that God exists. It is the
question of the rationality or irrationality, the well-groundedness
or ill-groundedness, of the religious man's claim to know God. The
theist cannot hope to prove that God exists; but despite this it may
nevertheless be possible for him to show it to be wholly reasonable
for him to believe that God exists.

What is at issue here is not whether it is rational for someone
else, who does not participate in the distinctively religious mode of
experience, to believe in God on the basis of the religious man's
reports. I am not proposing any kind of 'argument from religious
experience' by which God is inferred as the cause of the special
experiences described by mystics and other religious persons. It is
not the non-religious man's theoretical use of someone else's
reported religious experience that is to be considered, but the
religious man's own practical use of it. The question is whether he
is acting rationally in trusting his own experience and in proceeding to live on the basis of it.

In order to investigate this question we must consider what
counts as rational belief in an analogous case. The analogy that I
propose is that between the religious person's claim to be conscious of God and any man's claim to be conscious of the physical
world as an environment, existing independently of himself, of
which he must take account.

In each instance a realm of putatively cognitive experience is
taken to be veridical and is acted upon as such, even though its
veridical character cannot be logically demonstrated. So far as
sense experience is concerned this has emerged both from the
failure of Descartes' attempt to provide a theoretical guarantee that
our senses relate us to a real material environment, and from the
success of Hume's attempt to show that our normal non-solipsist
belief in an objective world of enduring objects around us in space
is neither a product of, nor justifiable by, philosophical reasoning
but is what has been called in some expositions of Hume's thought
(though the term does not seem to have been used by Hume
himself) a natural belief. It is a belief which naturally and indeed
inevitably arises in the normal human mind in response to normal
human perceptual experience. It is a belief on the basis of which we
live and the rejection of which, in favour of a serious adoption of
the solipsist alternative, would so disorient our relationship to
other persons within a common material environment that we

should be accounted insane. Our insanity would consist in the fact that we should no longer regard other people as independent centres of consciousness, with their own purposes and wills, with whom interpersonal relationships are possible. We should instead be living in a one-person world.

It is thus a basic truth in, or a presupposition of, our language that it is rational or sane to believe in the reality of the external world that we inhabit in common with other people, and irrational or insane not to do so.

What are the features of our sense experience in virtue of which we all take this view? They would seem to be twofold: the givenness or the involuntary character of this form of cognitive experience, and the fact that we can and do act successfully in terms of our belief in an external world. That is to say, being built and circumstanced as we are we cannot help initially believing as we do, and our belief is not contradicted, but on the contrary continuously confirmed, by our continuing experience. These characteristics jointly constitute a sufficient reason to trust and live on the basis of our perceptual experience in the absence of any positive reason to distrust it; and our inability to exclude the theoretical possibility of our experience as a whole being purely subjective does not constitute such a reason. This seems to be the principle on which, implicitly, we proceed. And it is, by definition, rational to proceed in this way. That is to say, this is the way in which all human beings do proceed and have proceeded, apart from a very small minority who have for that very reason been labelled by the majority as insane. This habitual acceptance of our perceptual experience is thus, we may say, part of our operative concept of human rationality.

We can therefore now ask whether a like principle may be invoked on behalf of a parallel response to religious experience. 'Religious experience' is of course a highly elastic concept. Let us restrict attention, for our present purpose, to the theistic 'sense of the presence of God', the putative awareness of a transcendent divine Mind within whose field of consciousness we exist and with whom therefore we stand in a relationship of mutual awareness. This sense of 'living in the divine presence' does not take the form of a direct vision of God, but of experiencing events in history and in our own personal life as the medium of God's dealings with us. Thus religious differs from non-religious experience, not as the awareness of a different world, but as a different way of experiencing the same world. Events which can be experienced as having a purely natural significance are experienced by the religious mind as having also and at the same time religious significance and as mediating the presence and activity of God.[14]

It is possible to study this type of religious experience either in its strongest instances, in the primary and seminal religious figures, or in its much weaker instances in ordinary adherents of the traditions originated by the great exemplars of faith. Since we are interested in the question of the claims which religious experience justifies it is appropriate to look at that experience in its strongest and purest forms. A description of this will accordingly apply only very partially to the ordinary rank-and-file believer either of today or in the past.

If then we consider the sense of living in the divine presence as this was expressed by, for example, Jesus of Nazareth, or by St Paul, St Francis, St Anselm or the great prophets of the Old Testament, we find that their 'awareness of God' was so vivid that he was as indubitable a factor in their experience as was their physical environment. They could no more help believing in the reality of God than in the reality of the material world and of their human neighbours. Many of the pages of the Bible resound with the sense of God's presence as a building might reverberate from the tread of some gigantic being walking through it. God was known to the prophets and apostles as a dynamic will interacting with their own wills; a sheerly given personal reality, as inescapably to be reckoned with as destructive storm and life-giving sunshine, the fixed contours of the land, or the hatred of their enemies and the friendship of their neighbours.

Our question concerns, then, one whose 'experience of God' has this compelling quality, so that he is no more inclined to doubt its veridical character than to doubt the evidence of his senses. Is it rational for him to take the former, as it is certainly rational for him to take the latter, as reliably cognitive of an aspect of his total environment and thus as knowledge in terms of which to act? Are the two features noted above in our sense experience – its givenness, or involuntary character, and the fact that we can successfully act in terms of it – also found here? It seems that they are. The sense of the presence of God reported by the great religious figures has a similar involuntary and compelling quality; and as they proceed to live on the basis of it they are sustained and confirmed by their further experiences in the conviction that they are living in relation, not to illusion, but to reality. It therefore seems *prima facie*, that the religious man *is* entitled to trust his religious experience and to proceed to conduct his life in terms of it.

The analogy operating within this argument is between our normal acceptance of our sense experience as perception of an objective external world, and a corresponding acceptance of the religious experience of 'living in God's presence' as the awareness of a divine reality external to our own minds. In each case there is a solipsist alternative in which one can affirm *solus ipse* to the exclusion of the transcendent – in the one case denying a physical environment transcending our own private consciousness and in the other case denying a divine Mind transcending our own private consciousness. It should be noted that this analogy is not grounded in the perception of particular material objects and does not turn upon the contrast between veridical and illusory sense perceptions, but is grounded in our awareness of an objective external world as such and turns upon the contrast between this and a theoretically possible solipsist interpretation of the same stream of conscious experience.

III RELIGIOUS AND PERCEPTUAL BELIEF

Having thus set forth the analogy fairly boldly and starkly I now want to qualify it by exploring various differences between religious and sensory experience. The resulting picture will be more complex than the first rough outline presented so far; and yet its force as supporting the rationality of theistic faith will not, I think, in the end have been undermined.

The most obvious difference is that everyone has and cannot help having sense experiences, whereas not everyone has religious experiences, at any rate of the very vivid and distinct kind to which we have been referring. As bodily beings existing in a material environment, we cannot help interacting consciously with that environment. That is to say, we cannot help 'having' a stream of sense experiences; and we cannot help accepting this as the perception of a material world around us in space. When we open our eyes in daylight we cannot but receive the visual experiences that come to us; and likewise with the other senses. And the world which we thus perceive is not plastic to our wishes but presents itself to us as it is, whether we like it or not. Needless to say, our senses do not coerce us in any sense of the word 'coerce' that implies unwillingness on our part, as when a policeman coerces an unwilling suspect to accompany him to the police station. Sense experience is coercive in the sense that we cannot when sane believe that our material environment is not broadly as we perceive it to be, and that if we did momentarily persuade ourselves that what we experience is not there we should quickly be penalised by the environment and indeed, if we persisted, destroyed by it.[15]

In contrast to this we are not obliged to interact consciously with a spiritual environment. Indeed it is a commonplace of much contemporary theology that God does not force an awareness of himself upon mankind but leaves us free to know him by an uncompelled response of faith. And yet once a man has allowed himself freely to become conscious of God – it is important to note – that experience is, at its top levels of intensity, coercive. It creates the situation of the person who *cannot help* believing in the reality of God. The apostle, prophet or saint may be so vividly aware of God that he can no more doubt the veracity of his religious awareness than of his sense experience. During the periods when he is living consciously in the presence of God, when God is to him the divine Thou, the question whether God exists simply does not arise. Our cognitive freedom in relation to God is not to be found at this point but at the prior stage of our coming to be aware of him. The individual's own free receptivity and responsiveness plays an essential part in his dawning consciousness of God; but once he *has* become conscious of God that consciousness can possess a coercive and indubitable quality.[16]

It is a consequence of this situation that whereas everyone perceives and cannot help perceiving the physical world, by no means everyone experiences the presence of God. Indeed only rather few people experience religiously in the vivid and coercive way reported by the great biblical figures. And this fact immediately suggests a sceptical question. Since those who enjoy a compelling religious experience form such a small minority of mankind, ought we not to suspect that they are suffering from a delusion comparable with that of the paranoiac who hears threatening voices from the walls or the alcoholic who sees green snakes?

This is of course a possible judgement to make. But this judgement should not be made *a priori*, in the absence of specific grounds such as we have in the other cases mentioned. And it would in fact be difficult to point to adequate evidence to support this hypothesis. On the contrary the general intelligence and exceptionally high moral quality of the great religious figures clashes with any analysis of their experience in terms of abnormal psychology. Such analyses are not indicated, as is the parallel view of paranoiacs and alcoholics, by evidence of general disorientation to reality or of incapacity to live a productive and satisfying life. On the contrary, Jesus of Nazareth, for example, has been regarded by hundreds of millions of people as the fulfilment of the ideal possibilities of human nature. A more reasonable negative position would therefore seem to be the agnostic one that whilst it is proper for the religious man himself, given his distinctive mode of experience, to believe firmly in the reality of God, one does not oneself share that experience and therefore has no ground upon which to hold that belief. Theism is then not positively denied, but is on the other hand consciously and deliberately not affirmed. This agnostic position must be accepted by the theist as a proper one. For if it is reasonable for one man, on the basis of his distinctively religious experience, to affirm the reality of God it must also be reasonable for another man, in the absence of any such experience, not to affirm the reality of God.

The next question that must be raised is the closely connected one of the relation between rational belief and truth. . . . By a rational belief we shall mean a belief which it is rational for the one who holds it to hold, given the data available to him. Clearly such beliefs are not necessarily or always true. It is sometimes rational for an individual to have, on the basis of incomplete data, a belief which is in fact false. For example, it was once rational for people to believe that the sun revolves round the earth; for it was apparently perceived to do so, and the additional theoretical and observational data were not yet available from which it has since been inferred that it is the earth which revolves round the sun. If, then, a belief may be rational and yet false, may not the religious man's belief be of this kind? May it not be that when the data of religious experience are supplemented in the believer's mind by further data provided by the sciences of psychology or sociology, it ceases to be rational for him to believe in God? Might it not then be rational for him instead to believe that his 'experience of the presence of God' is to be understood as an effect of a buried infancy memory of his father as a benevolent higher power; or of the pressure upon him of the human social organism of which he is a cell; or in accordance with some other naturalistic theory of the nature of religion?

Certainly this is possible. Indeed we must say, more generally, that all our beliefs, other than our acceptance of logically self-certifying propositions, are in principle open to revision or retraction in the light of new data. It is always conceivable that something which it is now rational for us to believe, it may one day not be rational for us to believe. But the difference which this general principle properly makes to our present believing varies from a maximum in relation to beliefs involving a considerable theoretical element, such as the higher-level hypotheses of the sciences, to a minimum in relation to perceptual beliefs, such as the belief that I now see a sheet of paper before me. And I have argued that so far as the great primary religious figures are concerned, belief in the reality of God is closer to the latter in that it is analogous to belief in the reality of the perceived material world. It is not an explanatory hypothesis, logically comparable with those developed in the sciences, but a perceptual belief. God was not, for Amos or Jeremiah or Jesus of Nazareth, an inferred entity but an experienced personal presence. If this is so, it is appropriate that the religious man's belief in the reality of God should be no more provisional than his belief in the reality of the physical world. The situation is in each case that, given the experience which he has and which is part of him, he cannot help accepting as 'there' such aspects of his environment as he experiences. He cannot help believing either in the reality of the material world which he is conscious of inhabiting, or of the personal divine presence which is overwhelmingly evident to him and to which his mode of living is a free response. And I have been suggesting that it is *as* reasonable for him to hold and to act upon the one belief as the other.

IV   THE PROBLEM OF CONFLICTING RELIGIOUS BELIEFS

We must now take note of another circumstance which qualifies and threatens to erode our analogy. What are we to make of the immense variety of the forms of religious experience, giving rise as they do to apparently incompatible beliefs? In contrast to this, human sense experience reveals a world which is public in that normally the perceptions of any two individuals can readily be correlated in terms of the hypothesis of a common world which they jointly inhabit.

The variety commonly brought under the name of religion is indeed as wide as the range of man's cultural and psychological diversities. By no means all religious experience is theistic; ultimate reality is apprehended as non-personal and as multi-personal as well as unipersonal. And if we choose to extend the notion of religious experience, as Abraham Maslow has recently done by his concept of peak-experiences,[17] the variety is multiplied again. But even apart from this last expansion of the field it is clearly true that religious experience is bewilderingly varied in content and that the different reports to which it gives rise cannot easily be correlated as alternative accounts of the same reality. And therefore since one could restate the argument of the earlier part of this chapter from the point of view of many different religions, with their different forms of religious experience and belief, the question arises whether the argument does not prove too much. In establishing the rationality of the Judaic–Christian theist's belief in the reality of God, must it not also and equally establish the rationality of the Buddhist's belief, arising out of *his* own coercive religious experience, and likewise of Hindu belief and of Islamic belief, and so on?

We need, I think, have no hesitation in accepting this implication. The principle which I have used to justify as rational the faith of a Christian who on the basis of his own religious experience cannot help believing in the reality of 'the God and Father of our Lord Jesus Christ', also operates to justify as rational the faith of a Muslim who on the basis of *his* religious experience cannot help believing in the reality of Allah and his providence; and the faith of the Buddhist who on the basis of *his* religious experience cannot help accepting the Buddhist picture of the universe; and so on.

But this is not the end of the matter. Various possibilities now open before us. I can only in conclusion attempt a small-scale map of the different paths that may be taken, showing in what direction they each lead and forecasting to some extent the kind of difficulties that are to be expected if one chooses to travel along them.

The first fork in the road is constituted by the alternative possibilities that the truth concerning the nature of the universe will, and that it will not, ultimately be a matter of public knowledge. The question is whether there will eventually be a situation in which all rational persons will find themselves obliged to agree, on the basis of a common body of experience, that the universe has this or that specific character. The issue, in other words, is that of the ultimate public verifiability and falsifiability of religious faiths.

On the one hand, in one conceivable picture of the universe it is possible for adherents of different and incompatible faiths to remain, so long as they continue to exist and to hold beliefs, under the impression that their own understanding of the universe is true; for they never meet an experiential crux which either verifies or falsifies their faith. This is a not always acknowledged feature of the pictures adopted both by the non-eschatological religions and by most atheistic and naturalistic theories. On the other hand, in another possible picture of the universe, or rather family of pictures painted by the different eschatological religions, the future development of human experience will narrow down the options until eventually only one faith is compatible with the facts and it becomes irrational to hold any contrary view. Thus it is affirmed in Christianity, in Islam, in one type of Judaism and perhaps in one type of Buddhism that the universe has a certain definite structure and is moving towards a certain definite fulfilment such that in the light of that fulfilment it will be beyond rational doubt that the universe has the particular character that it has.

Both types of universe are logically possible. If Christianity is true we are living in a universe of the latter type, in which religious faith is ultimately verified; and since we are now investigating the rationality of the Christian belief in God we shall want at this first fork to take the verifiability-of-faiths option in order to explore it further and to see where it leads.

Travelling along this path, then, we now meet a second fork in the road, offering two rival conceptions of the relations between the different religions. Along one path we affirm the ultimate compatibility of the plurality of religious faiths, whilst along the other path we deny this. The latter, incompatibility thesis leads us to the following picture: it is at the moment rational for adherents of different religions, whose experience is such that they cannot help believing as they do, to hold their respective beliefs. But – still assuming the verifiability-of-faiths thesis – it will eventually cease to be possible for rational persons to adhere to rival and incompatible understandings of the universe. For according to this option in its strongest form, there is one true faith and many false ones – this view corresponding of course to the traditional dogmatic stances of the eschatological religions, such as Christianity and Islam. There is however a specifically Christian reason for abandoning this stance. This is that belief in the redeeming love of God for all his human creatures makes it incredible that the divine activity in relation to mankind should have been confined to those within the reach of the influence of the Christian revelation. The majority of the human beings who have existed since man began have lived either before or outside the historical influence of Jesus of Nazareth. Thus the doctrine that there is no salvation outside historic Christianity would in effect deny the universal love and redeeming activity of God.

Any modification of that traditional claim soon leads us over onto the alternative path, at the end of which lies the conclusion that the different forms of religious experience, giving rise to the different religions of the world, are properly to be understood as experiences of different aspects of one immensely complex and rich divine reality. If this is so, the beliefs of the different religions will be related to a larger truth as the experiences which gave rise to those beliefs are related to a larger reality.

The further exploration of this possibility would take us beyond our present necessarily limited inquiry. I have argued that when on the basis of his own compelling religious experience someone believes in the reality of God, he is believing rationally; and I have added the rider that when we set alongside this argument the fact of the plurality of religions and their forms of religious experience, we are led to postulate a divine reality of which the different religions of the world represent different partial experiences and partial knowledge. This latter possibility [requires the development of a philosophy of religious pluralism, for which see Chapter 10].

NOTES

1. For a modern papal reaffirmation of the position that 'human reason can, without the help of divine revelation and grace, prove the existence of a personal God by arguments drawn from created things', see Pope Pius XII's encyclical *Humani Generis* (1940), esp. paras 2, 3, 25 and 29.

2. See, for example, J. Oliver Buswell, *What is God?* (Grand Rapids, Mich.: Zondervan, 1937); and Robert E. D. Clark, *The Universe: Plan or Accident?* (Philadelphia: Muhlenberg Press; London: Paternoster Press, 1961).

3. For example, W. R. Matthews, *Studies in Christian Philosophy*, 2nd edn (London: Macmillan, 1928); and 'Theism', in *Encyclopaedia Britannica* (1949) xxii, 50.

4. See Abraham Heschel, *God in Search of Man: A Philosophy of Judaism* (New York: Jewish Publication Society of America, 1955) pp. 246f.;

Martin Buber, *Eclipse of God* (New York: Harper and Row, 1952; and London: Gonancy, 1953) ch. 8.

5. For example, John Baillie, *Our Knowledge of God* (London: Oxford University Press, 1939) ch. 3, section 10.

6. J. Cook Wilson, *Statement and Inference* (London: Oxford University Press, 1926) II, 853.

7. H. D. Aitken, 'God and Evil: A Study of Some Relations between Faith and Morals', *Ethics*, Jan. 1958, p. 82.

8. David Hume, *Dialogues concerning Natural Religion*, v.

9. Pascal, *Pensées*, ed. Leon Brunschvicg, trs. W. F. Trotter (London: J. M. Dent, 1931) no. 430.

10. T. S. Eliot, *Burnt Norton*, I.

11. Alasdair MacIntyre, *Metaphysical Beliefs* (London: SCM Press; New York: Allenson, 1957) p. 197. MacIntyre makes the same point in *Difficulties in Christian Belief* (London: SCM Press, 1960) p. 77.

12. J. H. Newman, *A Grammar of Assent* (1870) ch. 4.

13. The exercise of this capacity is well described by C. S. Peirce as the unfolding of what he calls 'the humble argument' for the reality of God. See his *Collected Papers* (Cambridge, Mass.: Harvard University Press, 1934) VI, 467, 486.

14. This view is developed in my *Faith and Knowledge*, 2nd edn (Ithaca, NY: Cornell University Press, 1966; London: Macmillan, 1967). [In the present volume, see Ch. 5.]

15. For a discussion of the notion of 'coerciveness' in sense experience and religious experience, see Donald F. Henze, 'Faith, Evidence, and Coercion', *Philosophy*, Jan. 1967; and John Hick, 'Faith and Coercion', *Philosophy*, July 1967; and D. R. Duff-Forbes, 'Faith, Evidence, Coercion', *Australasian Journal of Philosophy*, Aug. 1969.

16. This is developed more fully in my 'Sceptics and Believers', in John Hick (ed.), *Faith and the Philosophers* (London: Macmillan; New York: St Martin's Press, 1964).

17. Abraham H. Maslow, *Religions, Values, and Peak-Experiences* (Columbus, Ohio: Ohio State University Press, 1964).

5

Theology and Verification

To ask 'Is the existence of God verifiable?' is to pose a question which is too imprecise to be capable of being answered. There are many different concepts of God, and it may be that statements employing some of them are open to verification or falsification while statements employing others of them are not. Again, the notion of verifying is itself by no means perfectly clear and fixed; it may be that on some views of the nature of verification the existence of God is verifiable whereas on other views it is not.

Instead of seeking to compile a list of the various different concepts of God and the various possible senses of 'verify', I wish to argue with regard to one particular concept of deity, namely the Christian concept, that divine existence is in principle verifiable; and as the first stage of this argument I must indicate what I mean by 'verifiable'.

I

The central core of the concept of verification, I suggest, is the removal of ignorance or uncertainty concerning the truth of some proposition. That p is verified (whether p embodies a theory, hypothesis, prediction, or straightforward assertion) means that something happens which makes it clear that p is true. A question is settled so that there is no longer room for rational doubt concerning it. The way in which grounds for rational doubt are excluded varies of course with the subject matter. But the general feature common to all cases of verification is the ascertaining of truth by the removal of grounds for rational doubt. Where such grounds are removed, we rightly speak of verification having taken place.

To characterise verification in this way is to raise the question whether the notion of verification is purely logical or is both logical and psychological. Is the statement that p is verified simply the statement that a certain state of affairs exists (or has existed), or is it the statement also that someone is aware that this state of affairs exists (or has existed) and notes that its existence establishes the truth of *p*? A geologist predicts that the earth's surface will be covered with ice in 15 million years time. Suppose that in 15 million years time the earth's surface *is* covered with ice, but that in the meantime the human race has perished, so that no one is left to observe the event or to draw any conclusion concerning the accuracy of the geologist's prediction. Do we now wish to say that his prediction has been verified, or shall we deny that it has been verified on the ground that there is no one left to do the verifying?

The use of 'verify' and its cognates is sufficiently various to permit us to speak in either way. But the only sort of verification of theological propositions which is likely to interest us is one in which human beings participate. We may therefore, for our present purpose, treat verification as a logico-psychological rather than as a purely logical concept. I suggest then that 'verify' be construed as a verb which has its primary uses in the active voice: I verify, you verify, we verify, they verify or have verified. The impersonal passive, it is verified, now becomes logically secondary. To say that *p* has been verified is to say that (at least) someone has verified it, often with the implication that his or their report to this effect is generally accepted. But it is impossible, on this usage, for *p* to have been verified without someone having verified it. 'Verification' is thus primarily the name for an event which takes place in human consciousness.[1] It refers to an experience, the experience of ascertaining that a given proposition or set of propositions is true. To this extent verification is a psychological notion. But of course it is also a logical notion. For needless to say, not *any* experience is rightly called an experience of verifying *p*. Both logical and psychological conditions must be fulfilled in order for verification to have taken place. In this respect, 'verify' is like 'know'. Knowing is an experience which someone has or undergoes, or perhaps a dispositional state in which someone is, and it cannot take place without someone having or undergoing it or being in it; but not by any means every experience which people have, or every dispositional state in which they are, is rightly called knowing.

With regard to this logico-psychological concept of verification, such questions as the following arise. When A, but nobody else, has ascertained that *p* is true, can *p* be said to have been verified; or is it required that others also have undergone the same ascertainment? How public, in other words, must verification be? Is it necessary that p could in principle be verified by anyone without restriction even though perhaps only A has in fact verified it? If so, what is meant here by 'in principle'; does it signify, for example, that p must be verifiable by anyone who performs a certain operation; and does it imply that to do this is within everyone's power?

These questions cannot, I believe, be given any general answer applicable to all instances of the exclusion of rational doubt. The answers must be derived in each case from an investigation of the particular subject matter. It will be the object of subsequent sections of this article to undertake such an investigation in relation to the Christian concept of God.

Verification is often construed as the verification of a prediction. However verification, as the exclusion of grounds for rational doubt, does not necessarily consist in the proving correct of a prediction; a verifying experience does not always need to have been predicted in order to have the effect of excluding rational doubt. But when we are interested in the verifiability of propositions as the criterion for their having factual meaning, the notion of prediction becomes central. If a proposition contains or entails predictions which can be verifed or falsified, its character as an assertion (though not of course its character as a true assertion) is thereby guaranteed.

Such predictions may be and often are conditional. For example, statements about the features of the dark side of the moon are rendered meaningful by the conditional predictions which they entail to the effect that if an observer comes to be in such a position in space, he will make such-and-such observations. It would in fact be more accurate to say that the prediction is always conditional, but that sometimes the conditions are so obvious and so likely to be fulfilled in any case that they require no special mention, while sometimes they require for their fulfilment some unusual expedition or operation. A prediction, for example, that the sun will rise within twenty-four hours is intended unconditionally, at least as concerns conditions to be fulfilled by the observer; he is not required by the terms of the prediction to perform any special operation. Even in this case however there is an implied negative condition that he shall not put himself in a situation (such as immuring himself in the depths of a coal mine) from which a sunrise would not be perceptible. Other predictions however are explicitly conditional. In these cases it is true for any particular individual that in order to verify the statement in question he must go through some specified course of action. The prediction is to the effect that if you conduct such an experiment you will obtain such a result; for example, if you go into the next room you will have such-and-such visual experiences, and if you then touch the table which you see you will have such-and-such tactual experiences, and so on. The content of the 'if' clause is always determined by the particular subject matter. The logic of 'table' determines what you must do to verify statements about tables; the logic of 'molecule' determines what you must do to verify statements about molecules; and the logic of 'God' determines what you must do to verify statements about God.

In those cases in which the individual who is to verify a proposition must himself first perform some operation, it clearly cannot follow from the circumstances that the proposition is true that everybody has in fact verified it, or that everybody will at some future time verify it. For whether or not any particular person performs the requisite operation is a contingent matter.

II

What is the relation between verification and falsification? We are all familiar today with the phrase, 'theology and falsification'. Antony Flew[2] and others have raised instead of the question, 'What possible experiences would verify "God exists"?' the matching question 'What possible experiences would falsify "God exists"? What conceivable state of affairs would be incompatible with the existence of God?' In posing the question in this way it was apparently assumed that verification and falsification are symmetrically related, and that the latter is apt to be the more accessible of the two.

In the most common cases, certainly, verification and falsification are symmetrically related. The logically simplest case of verification is provided by the crucial instance. Here it is integral to a given hypothesis that if, in specified circumstances, A occurs, the hypothesis is thereby shown to be true, whereas if B occurs the hypothesis is thereby shown to be false. Verification and falsification are also symmetrically related in the testing of such a proposition as 'There is a table in the next room'. The verifying experiences in this case are experiences of seeing and touching, predictions of which are entailed by the proposition in question, under the proviso that one goes into the next room; and the absence of such experiences in those circumstances serves to falsify the proposition.

But it would be rash to assume, on this basis, that verification and falsification must always be related in this symmetrical fashion. They do not necessarily stand to one another as do the two sides of a coin, so that once the coin is spun it must fall on one side or the other. There are cases in which verification and falsification each correspond to a side on a different coin, so that one can fail to verify without this failure constituting falsification.

Consider, for example, the proposition that 'there are three successive sevens in the decimal determination of π'. So far as the value of π has been worked out, it does not contain a series of three sevens, but it will always be true that such a series may occur at a point not yet reached in anyone's calculations. Accordingly, the proposition may one day be verified if it is true, but can never be falsified it it is false.

The hypothesis of continued conscious existence after bodily death provides an instance of a different kind of such asymmetry, and one which has a direct bearing upon the theistic problem. This hypothesis has built into it a prediction that one will after the date of one's bodily death have conscious experiences, including the experience of remembering that death. This is a prediction which will be verified in one's own experience if it is true, but which cannot be falsified if it is false. That is to say, it can be false, but *that* it is false can never be a fact which anyone has experientially verified. But this circumstance does not undermine the meaningfulness of the hypothesis, since it is also such that if it be true, it will be known to be true.

It is important to remember that we do not speak of verifying logically necessary truths, but only propositions concerning matters of fact. Accordingly verification is not to be identified with the concept of logical certification or proof. The exclusion of rational doubt concerning some matter of fact is not equivalent to the exclusion of the logical possibility of error or illusion. For truths concerning fact are not logically necessary. Their contrary is never self-contradictory. But at the same time the bare logical possibility of error does not constitute ground for rational doubt as to the veracity of our experience. If it did, no empirical proposition could ever be verified, and indeed the notion of empirical verification would be without use and therefore without sense. What we rightly seek, when we desire the verification of a factual proposition, is not a demonstration of the logical impossibility of the proposition being false (for this would be a self-contradictory demand), but such kind and degree of evidence as suffices, in the type of case in question, to exclude rational doubt.

III

These features of the concept of verification – that verification consists in the exclusion of grounds for rational doubt concerning the truth of some proposition; that this means its exclusion from particular minds; that the nature of the experience which serves to exclude grounds for rational doubt depends upon the particular subject matter; that verification is often related to predictions and that such predictions are often conditional; that verification and falsification may be asymmetrically related; and finally, that the verification of a factual proposition is not equivalent to logical certification – are all relevant to the verification of the central religious claim, 'God exists.' I wish now to apply these discriminations to the notion of eschatological verification, which has been briefly employed by Ian Crombie in his contribution to *New Essays in Philosophical Theology*,[3] and by myself in *Faith and Knowledge*.[4] This suggestion has on each occasion been greeted with disapproval by both philosophers and theologians. I am, however, still of the opinion that the notion of eschatological verification is sound; and further, that no viable alternative to it has been offered to establish the factual character of theism.

The strength of the notion of eschatological verification is that it is not an *ad hoc* invention but is based upon an actually operative religious concept of God. In the language of Christian faith, the word 'God' stands at the centre of a system of terms, such as Spirit, grace, Logos, incarnation, Kingdom of God, and many more; and the distinctly Christian conception of God can only be fully grasped in its connection with these related terms.[5] It belongs to a complex of notions which together constitute a picture of the universe in which we live, of man's place therein, of a comprehensive divine purpose interacting with human purposes, and of the general nature of the eventual fulfilment of that divine purpose. This Christian picture of the universe, entailing as it does certain distinctive expectations concerning the future, is a very different picture from any that can be accepted by one who does not believe that the God of the New Testament exists. Further, these differences are such as to show themselves in human experience. The possibility of experiential confirmation is thus built into the Christian concept of God; and the notion of eschatological verification seeks to relate this fact to the problem of theological meaning.

Let me first give a general theological indication of this suggestion, by repeating a parable which I have related elsewhere,[6] and then try to make it more precise and eligible for discussion. Here, first, is the parable.

Two men are travelling together along a road. One of them believes that it leads to a Celestial City, the other that it leads nowhere; but since this is the only road there is, both must travel it. Neither has been this way before, and therefore neither is able to say what they will find around each next corner. During their journey they meet both with moments of refreshment and delight, and with moments of hardship and danger. All the time one of them thinks of his journey as a pilgrimage to the Celestial City and interprets the pleasant parts as encouragements and the obstacles as trials of his purpose and lessons in endurance, prepared by the king of that city and designed to make of him a worthy citizen of the place when at last he arrives there. The other, however, believes none of this and sees their journey as an unavoidable and aimless ramble. Since he has no choice in the matter, he enjoys the good and endures the bad. But for him there is no Celestial City to be reached, no all-encompassing purpose ordaining their journey; only the road itself and the luck of the road in good weather and in bad.

During the course of the journey the issue between them is not an experimental one. They do not entertain different expectations about the coming details of the road, but only about its ultimate destination. And yet when they do turn the last corner it will be apparent that one of them has been right all the time and the other wrong. Thus although the issue between them has not been experimental, it has nevertheless from the start been a real issue. They have not merely felt differently about the road; for one was feeling appropriately and the other inappropriately in relation to the actual state of affairs. Their opposed interpretations of the road constituted genuinely rival assertions, though assertions whose assertion-status has the peculiar characteristic of being guaranteed retrospectively by a future crux.

This parable has of course (like all parables) strict limitations. It is designed to make only one point: that Christian doctrine post-ulates an ultimate unambiguous state of existence *in patria* as well as our present ambiguous existence *in via*. There is a state of having arrived as well as a state of journeying, an eternal heavenly life as well as an earthly pilgrimage. The alleged future experience of this state cannot, of course, be appealed to as evidence for theism as a present interpretation of our experience; but it does suffice to render the choice between theism and atheism a real and not a merely empty or verbal choice. And although this does not affect the logic of the situation, it should be added that the alternative interpretations are more than theoretical, for they render different practical plans and policies appropriate now.

The universe as envisaged by the theist, then, differs as a totality from the universe as envisaged by the atheist. This difference does not, however, from our present standpoint within the universe, involve a difference in the objective content of each or even any of its passing moments. The theist and the atheist do not (or need not) expect different events to occur in the successive details of the temporal process. They do not (or need not) entertain divergent expectations of the course of history viewed from within. But the theist does and the atheist does not expect that when history is completed it will be seen to have led to a particular end-state and to have fulfilled a specific purpose, namely that of creating 'children of God'.

IV

The idea of an eschatological verification of theism can make sense, however, only if the logically prior idea of continued personal existence after death is intelligible. A desultory debate on this topic has been going on for several years in some of the philosophical periodicals. C. I. Lewis has contended that the hypothesis of immortality 'is an hypothesis about our own future experience. And our understanding of what would verify it has no lack of clarity'.[7] And Morris Schlick agreed, adding, 'We must conclude that immortality, in the sense defined [i.e. "survival after death", rather than "never-ending life"], should not be regarded as a "metaphysical problem", but is an empirical hypothesis, because it possesses logical verifiability. It could be verified by following the prescription: "Wait until you die!"[8] However, others have challenged this conclusion, either on the ground that the phrase 'surviving death' is self-contradictory in ordinary language or, more substantially, on the ground that the traditional distinction between soul and body cannot be sustained.[9] I should like to address myself to this latter view. The only self of which we know, it is said, is the empirical self, the walking, talking, acting, sleeping individual who lives, it may be, for some sixty to eighty years and then dies. Mental events and mental characteristics are analysed into the modes of behaviour and behavioural dispositions of this empirical self. The human being is described as an organism capable of acting in the 'high-level' ways which we characterise as intelligent, thoughtful, humorous, calculating, and the like. The concept of mind or soul is thus not the concept of a 'ghost in the machine' (to use Gilbert Ryle's loaded phrase[10]) but of the more flexible and sophisticated ways in which human beings behave and have it in them to behave. On this view there is no room for the notion of soul in distinction from body; and if there is no soul in distinction from body there can be no question of the soul surviving the death of the body. Against this philosophical background the specifically Christian (and also Jewish) belief in the resurrection of the flesh or body, in contrast to the Hellenic notion of the survival of a disembodied soul, might be expected to have attracted more attention than it has. For it is consonant with the conception of man as an indissoluble psycho-physical unity, and yet it also offers the possibility of an empirical meaning for the idea of 'life after death'.

Paul is the chief biblical expositor of the idea of the resurrection of the body.[11] His view, as I understand it, is this. When someone has died he is, apart from any special divine action, extinct. A human being is by nature mortal and subject to annihilation by death. But in fact God, by an act of sovereign power, either sometimes or always resurrects or (better) reconstitutes or re-creates him – not, however, as the identical physical organism that he was before death, but as a *soma pneumatikon* ('spiritual body') embodying the dispositional characteristics and memory traces of the deceased physical organism, and inhabiting an environment with which the *soma pneumatikon* is continuous as the *ante mortem* body was continuous with our present world. In discussing this notion we may well abandon the word 'spiritual', as lacking today any precise established usage, and speak of 'resurrection bodies' and of 'the resurrection world'. The principal questions to be asked concern the relation between the physical world and the resurrection world, and the criteria of personal identity which are operating when it is alleged that a certain inhabitant of the resurrection world is the same person as an individual who once inhabited this present world. The first of these questions turns out on investigation to be the more difficult of the two, and I shall take the easier one first.

Let me sketch a very odd possibility (concerning which, however, I wish to emphasise not so much its oddness as its possibility!), and then see how far it can be stretched in the direction of the notion of the resurrection body. In the process of stretching it will become even more odd than it was before; but my aim will be to show that, however, odd, it remains within the bounds of the logically possible. This progression will be presented in three pictures, arranged in a self-explanatory order.

First picture: Suppose that at some learned gathering in this country one of the company were suddenly and inexplicably to disappear, and that at the same moment an exact replica of him were suddenly and inexplicably to appear at some comparable meeting in Australia. The person who appears in Australia is exactly similar, as to both bodily and mental characteristics, with the person who disappears in America. There is continuity of memory, complete similarity of bodily features, including even fingerprints, hair and eye coloration and stomach contents, and also of beliefs, habits, and mental propensities. In fact there is everything that would lead us to identify the one who appeared with the one who disappeared, except continuity of occupancy of space. We may suppose, for example, that a deputation of the colleagues of the man who disappeared fly to Australia to interview the replica of him which is reported there, and find that he is in all respects but one exactly as though he had travelled from say, Princeton to Melbourne, by conventional means. The only difference is that he describes how, as he was sitting listening to Dr Z reading a paper, on blinking his eyes he suddenly found himself sitting in a different room listening to a different paper by an Australian scholar. He asks his colleagues how the meeting had gone after he ceased to be there, and what they had made of his disappearance, and so on. He clearly thinks of himself as the one who was present with them at their meeting in the United States. I suggest that faced with all these circumstances his colleagues would soon, if not immediately, find themselves thinking of him and treating him as the individual who had so inexplicably disappeared from their midst. We should be extending our normal use of 'same person' in a way which the postulated facts would both demand and justify if we said that the one who appears in Australia is the same person as the one who disappears in America. The factors inclining us to identify them would far outweigh the factors disinclining us to do this. We should have no reasonable alternative but to extend our usage of 'the same person' to cover the strange new case.

Second picture: Now let us suppose that the event in America is not a sudden and inexplicable disappearance, and indeed not a disappearance at all, but a sudden death. Only, at the moment when the individual dies, a replica of him as he was at the moment before his death, complete with memory up to that instant, appears in Australia. Even with the corpse on our hands, it would still, I suggest, be an extension of 'same person' required and warranted by the postulated facts, to say that the same person who died has been miraculously re-created in Australia. The case would be considerably odder than in the previous picture, because of the existence of the corpse in America contemporaneously with the existence of the living person in Australia. But I submit that, although the oddness of this circumstance may be stated as strongly as you please, and can indeed hardly be overstated, yet it does not exceed the bounds of the logically possible. Once again we must imagine some of the deceased's colleagues going to Australia to interview the person who has suddenly appeared there. He would perfectly remember them and their meeting, be interested in what had happened, and be as amazed and dumbfounded about it as anyone else; and he would perhaps be worried about the possible legal complications if he should return to America to claim his property; and so on. Once again, I believe, they would soon find themselves thinking of him and treating him as the same person as the dead Princetonian. Once again the factors inclining us to say that the one who died and the one who appeared are the same person would outweigh the factors inclining us to say that they are different people. Once again we should have to extend our usage of 'the same person' to cover this new case.

Third picture: My third supposal is that the replica, complete
with memory, etc., appears, not in Australia, but as a resurrection
replica in a different world altogether, a resurrection world inhabited by resurrected persons. This world occupies its own space,
distinct from the space with which we are now familiar.[12] That is to
say, an object in the resurrection world is not situated at any
distance or in any direction from an object in our present world,
although each object in either world is spatially related to each
other object in the same world.

Mr X, then, dies. A Mr X replica, complete with the set of
memory traces which Mr X had at the last moment before his
death, comes into existence. It is composed of other material than
physical matter, and is located in a resurrection world which does
not stand in any spatial relationship with the physical world. Let
us leave out of consideration St Paul's hint that the resurrection
body may be as unlike the physical body as is a full grain of
wheat from the wheat seed, and consider the simpler picture in
which the resurrection body has the same shape as the physical
body.[13]

In these circumstances, how does Mr X know that he has been
resurrected or re-created? He remembers dying; or rather he
remembers being on what he took to be his death-bed, and
becoming progressively weaker until, presumably, he lost consciousness. But how does he know that (to put it Irishly) his 'dying'
proved fatal; and that he did not, after losing consciousness, begin
to recover strength, and has now simply waked up?

The picture is readily enough elaborated to answer this question.
Mr X meets and recognises a number of relatives and friends and
historical personages whom he knows to have died; and from the
fact of their presence, and also from their testimony that he has
only just now appeared in their world, he is convinced that he has
died. Evidences of this kind could mount up to the point at which
they are quite as strong as the evidence which, in pictures one and
two, convince the individual in question that he has been miraculously translated to Australia. Resurrected persons would be
individually no more in doubt about their own identity than we are
now, and would be able to identify one another in the same kinds
of ways, and with a like degree of assurance, as we do now.

If it be granted that resurrected persons might be able to arrive at
a rationally founded conviction that their existence is *post mortem*,
how could they know that the world in which they find themselves

is in a different space from that in which their physical bodies were? How could such a one know that he is not in a like situation with the person in picture number two, who dies in America and appears as a full-blooded replica in Australia, leaving his corpse in the USA – except that now the replica is situated, not in Australia, but on a planet of some other star?

It is of course conceivable that the space of the resurrection world should have properties which are manifestly incompatible with its being a region of physical space. But on the other hand, it is not of the essence of the notion of a resurrection world that its space should have properties different from those of physical space. And supposing it not to have different properties, it is not evident that a resurrected individual could learn from any direct observations that he was not on a planet of some sun which is at so great a distance from our own sun that the stellar scenery visible from it is quite unlike that which we can now see. The grounds that a resurrected person would have for believing that he is in a different space from physical space (supposing there to be no discernible difference in spatial properties) would be the same as the grounds that any of us may have now for believing this concerning resurrected individuals. These grounds are indirect and consist in all those considerations (e.g. Luke 16:26) which lead most of those who consider the question to reject as absurd the possibility of, for example, radio communication or rocket travel between earth and heaven.

<h2 style="text-align:center">V</h2>

In the present context my only concern is to claim that this doctrine of the divine creation of bodies, composed of a material other than that of physical matter, which bodies are endowed with sufficient correspondence of characteristics with our present bodies, and sufficient continuity of memory with our present consciousness, for us to speak of the same person being raised up again to life in a new environment, is not self-contradictory. If, then, it cannot be ruled out *ab initio* as meaningless, we may go on to consider whether and how it is related to the possible verification of Christian theism.

So far I have argued that a survival prediction such as is contained in the *corpus* of Christian belief is in principle subject to future verification. But this does not take the argument by any means as far as it must go if it is to succeed. For survival, simply as such, would not serve to verify theism. It would not necessarily be a state of affairs which is manifestly incompatible with the non-existence of God. It might be taken just as a surprising natural fact. The atheist, in his resurrection body, and able to remember his life on earth, might say that the universe has turned out to be more complex, and perhaps more to be approved of, than he had realised. But the mere fact of survival, with a new body in a new environment, would not demonstrate to him that there is a God. It is fully compatible with the notion of survival that the life to come be, so far as the theistic problem is concerned, essentially a continuation of the present life, and religiously no less ambiguous. And in this event, survival after bodily death would not in the least constitute a final verification of theistic faith.

I shall not spend time in trying to draw a picture of a resurrection existence which would merely prolong the religious ambiguity of our present life. The important question, for our purpose, is not whether one can conceive of after-life experiences which would *not* verify theism (and in point of fact one can fairly easily conceive them), but whether one can conceive of after-life experiences which *would* serve to verify theism.

I think that we can. In trying to do so I shall not appeal to the traditional doctrine, which figures especially in Catholic and mystical theology, of the beatific vision of God. The difficulty presented by this doctrine is not so much that of deciding whether there are grounds for believing it, as of deciding what it means. I shall not, however, elaborate this difficulty, but pass directly to the investigation of a different and, as it seems to me, more intelligible possibility. This is the possibility not of a direct vision of God, whatever that might mean, but of a *situation* which points unambiguously to the existence of a loving God. This would be a situation which, so far as its religious significance is concerned, contrasts in a certain important respect with our present situation. Our present situation is one which in some ways seems to confirm and in other ways to contradict the truth of theism. Some events around us suggest the presence of an unseen benevolent intelligence and others suggest that no such intelligence is at work. Our situation is religiously ambiguous. But in order for us to be aware of this fact we must already have some idea, however vague, of what it would be for our situation to be not ambiguous, but on the contrary wholly evidential of God. I therefore want to try to make clearer this presupposed concept of a religiously unambiguous situation.

There are, I suggest, two possible developments of our experience such that, if they occurred in conjunction with one another (whether in this life or in another life to come), they would assure us beyond rational doubt of the reality of God, as conceived in the Christian faith. These are, *first*, an experience of the fulfilment of God's purpose for ourselves, as this has been disclosed in the Christian revelation; in conjunction, *second*, with an experience of communion with God as he has revealed himself in the person of Christ.

The divine purpose for human life, as this is depicted in the New Testament documents, is the bringing of the human person, in society with his fellows, to enjoy a certain valuable quality of personal life, the content of which is given in the character of Christ – which quality of life (i.e. life in relationship with God, described in the Fourth Gospel as eternal life) is said to be the proper destiny of human nature and the source of man's final self-fulfilment and happiness. The verification situation with regard to such a fulfilment is asymmetrical. On the one hand, so long as the divine purpose remains unfulfilled, we cannot know that it never will be fulfilled in the future; hence no final falsification is possible of the claim that this fulfilment will occur – unless, of course, the prediction contains a specific time clause which, in Christian teaching, it does not. But on the other hand, if and when the divine purpose *is* fulfilled in our own experience, we must be able to recognise and rejoice in that fulfilment. For the fulfilment would not be for us the promised fulfilment without our own conscious participation in it.

It is important to note that one can say this much without being cognisant in advance of the concrete form which such fulfilment will take. The before-and-after situation is analogous to that of a small child looking forward to adult life and then, having grown to adulthood, looking back upon childhood. The child possesses and can use correctly in various contexts the concept of 'being grown-up', although he does not know, concretely, what it is like to be grown-up. But when he reaches adulthood he is nevertheless able to know that he has reached it; he is able to recognise the experience of living a grown-up life even though he did not know in advance just what to expect. For his understanding of adult maturity grows as he himself matures. Something similar may be supposed to happen in the case of the fulfilment of the divine purpose for human life. That fulfilment may be as far removed from our present condition as is mature adulthood from the mind of a little child; nevertheless, we possess already a comparatively vague notion of this final fulfilment, and as we move towards it our concept will itself become more adequate; and if and when we finally reach that fulfilment, the problem of recognising it will have disappeared in the process.

The other feature that must, I suggest, be present in a state of affairs that would verify theism, is that the fulfilment of God's purpose be apprehended *as* the fulfilment of God's purpose and not simply as a natural state of affairs. To this end it must be accompanied by an experience of communion with God as he has made himself known to men in Christ.

The specifically Christian clause, 'as he has made himself known to men in Christ', is essential, for it provides a solution to the problem of recognition in the awareness of God. Several writers have pointed out the logical difficulty involved in any claim to have encountered God.[14] How could one know that it was *God* whom one had encountered? God is described in Christian theology in terms of various absolute qualities, such as omnipotence, omnipresence, perfect goodness, infinite love, etc., which cannot as such be observed by us, as can their finite analogues, limited power, local presence, finite goodness, and human love. One can recognise that a being whom one 'encounters' has a given finite degree of power, but how does one recognise that he has *un*limited power? How does one observe that an encountered being is *omni*present? How does one perceive that his goodness and love, which one can perhaps see to exceed any human goodness and love, are actually infinite? Such qualities cannot be given in human experience. One might claim, then, to have encountered a Being whom one presumes, or trusts, or hopes to be God; but one cannot claim to have encountered a Being whom one recognised to be the infinite, almighty, eternal Creator.

This difficulty is met in Christianity by the doctrine of the incarnation – although this was not among the considerations which led to the formulation of that doctrine. The idea of incarnation provides answers to the two related questions: 'How do we know that God has certain absolute qualities which, by their very nature, transcend human experience?' and 'How can there be an eschatological verification of theism which is based upon a recognition of the presence of God in his Kingdom?'

In Christianity God is known as 'the God and Father of our Lord Jesus Christ'.[15] God is the Being about whom Jesus taught; the Being in relation to whom Jesus lived, and into a relationship with whom he brought his disciples; the Being whose *agape* toward men was seen on earth in the life of Jesus. In short, God is the transcendent Creator who has revealed himself in Christ. Now Jesus' teaching about the Father is a part of that self-disclosure, and it is from this teaching (together with that of the prophets who preceded him) that the Christian knowledge of God's transcendent being is derived. Only God himself knows his own infinite nature; and our human belief about that nature is based upon his self-revelation to men in Christ. As Karl Barth expresses it, 'Jesus Christ is the knowability of God.'[16] Our beliefs about God's infinite being are not capable of observational verification, being beyond the scope of human experience, but they are susceptible of indirect verification by the removal of rational doubt concerning the authority of Christ. An experience of the reign of the Son in the Kingdom of the Father would confirm that authority, and therewith, indirectly, the validity of Jesus' teaching concerning the character of God in his infinite transcendent nature.

The further question as to how an eschatological experience of the Kingdom of God could be known to be such has already been answered by implication. It is God's union with man in Christ that makes possible man's recognition of the fulfilment of God's purpose for man as being indeed the fulfilment of *God's* purpose for him. The presence of Christ in his Kingdom marks this as being beyond doubt the Kingdom of the God and Father of the Lord Jesus Christ.

It is true that even the experience of the realisation of the promised Kingdom of God, with Christ reigning as Lord of the New Aeon, would not constitute a logical certification of his claims, nor accordingly, of the reality of God. But this will not seem remarkable to any philosopher in the empiricist tradition, who knows that it is only a confusion to demand that a factual proposition be an analytic truth. A set of expectations based upon faith in the historic Jesus as the incarnation of God, and in his teaching as being divinely authoritative, could be so fully confirmed in *post mortem* experience as to leave no grounds for rational doubt as to the validity of that faith.

VI

There remains of course the problem (which falls to the New Testament scholar rather than to the philosopher) whether Christian tradition, and in particular the New Testament, provides a sufficiently authentic 'picture' of the mind and character of Christ to make such recognition possible. I cannot here attempt to enter into the vast field of biblical criticism, and shall confine myself to the logical point, which only emphasises the importance of the historical question, that a verification of theism made possible by the incarnation is dependent upon the Christian's having a genuine contact with the person of Christ, even though this is mediated through the life and tradition of the Church.

One further point remains to be considered. When we ask the question, '*To whom* is theism verified?' one is initially inclined to assume that the answer must be, 'To everyone.' We are inclined to assume that, as in my parable of the journey, the believer must be confirmed in his belief, and the unbeliever converted from his unbelief. But this assumption is neither demanded by the nature of verification nor by any means unequivocably supported by our Christian sources.

We have already noted that a verifiable prediction may be conditional. 'There is a table in the next room' entails conditional predictions of the form: if someone goes into the next room he will see, etc. But no one is compelled to go into the next room. Now it may be that the predictions concerning human experience which are entailed by the proposition that God exists are conditional predictions and that no one is compelled to fulfil those conditions. Indeed we stress in much of our theology that the manner of the divine self-disclosure to men is such that our human status as free and responsible beings is respected, and an awareness of God is never forced upon us. It may then be a condition of *post mortem* verification that we be already in some degree conscious of God by an uncompelled response to his modes of revelation in this world. It may be that such a voluntary consciousness of God is an essential element in the fulfilment of the divine purpose for human nature, so that the verification of theism which consists in an experience of the final fulfilment of that purpose can only be experienced by those who have already entered upon an awareness of God by the religious mode of apperception which we call faith.

If this be so, it has the consequence that only the theistic believer can find the vindication of his belief. This circumstance would not of course set any restriction upon who can become a believer, but it would involve that while theistic faith can be verified – found by one who holds it to be beyond rational doubt – yet it cannot be proved to the non-believer. Such an asymmetry would connect with that strand of New Testament teaching which speaks of a division of mankind even in the world to come.

Having noted this possibility I will only express my personal opinion that the logic of the New Testament as a whole, though admittedly not always its explicit content, leads to a belief in ultimate universal salvation. However, my concern here is not to seek to establish the religious facts, but rather to establish that there are such things as religious facts, and in particular that the existence or non-existence of the God of the New Testament is a matter of fact, and claims as such eventual experiential verification.

NOTES

1. This suggestion is closely related to Carnap's insistence that, in contrast to 'true', 'confirmed' is time-dependent. To say that a statement is confirmed, or verified, is to say that it has been confirmed at a particular time – and, I would add, by a particular person. See Rudolf Carnap, 'Truth and Confirmation', in Herbert Feigl and Wilfred Sellars, *Readings in Philosophical Analysis* (New York: Appleton-Century-Crofts, 1949) pp. 119f.

2. Antony Flew, 'Theology and Falsification', in Antony Flew and Alasdair MacIntyre (eds), *New Essays in Philosophical Theology* (London: SCM Press; New York: Macmillan, 1955). On the philosophical antecedents of this change from the notion of verification to that of falsification, see Karl R. Popper, *The Logic of Scientific Discovery* (London: Hutchinson, 1959).

3. Flew and MacIntyre, *New Essays in Philosophical Theology*, p. 126.

4. John Hick, *Faith and Knowledge* (Ithaca, NY: Cornell University Press; London: Oxford University Press, 1975) pp. 150–62.

5. Its clear recognition of this fact, with regard not only to Christianity but to any religion, is one of the valuable features of Ninian Smart's *Reasons and Faiths* (London: Routledge and Kegan Paul, 1958). He remarks, for example, that 'the claim that God exists can only be understood by reference to many, if not all, other propositions in the doctrinal scheme from which it is extrapolated' (p. 12).

6. Hick, *Faith and Knowledge*, pp. 150f.

7. C. I. Lewis, 'Experience and Meaning', *Philosophical Review*, 1934, repr. in Feigl and Sellars, *Readings in Philosophical Analysis*, p. 142.

8. Morris Schlick, 'Meaning and Verification', *Philosophical Review*, 1936, repr. in Feigl and Sellars, *Readings in Philosophical Analysis*, p. 160.
9. See for example, Antony Flew, 'Death', in Flew and MacIntyre, *New Essays in Philosophical Theology*; 'Can a Man Witness his own Funeral?', *Hibbert Journal*, 1956.
10. Gilbert Ryle, *The Concept of Mind* (London: Hutchinson, 1949), which contains an important exposition of the interpretation of 'mental' qualities as characteristics of behaviour.
11. 1 Corinthians 15.
12. On this possibility, see Anthony Quinton, 'Spaces and Times', *Philosophy*, xxxvii, no. 140 (Apr 1962).
13. As would seem to be assumed, for example, by Irenaeus (*Adversus Haereses*, ii. xxxiv. 1).
14. For example, R. W. Hepburn, *Christianity and Paradox* (London: Watts, 1958) pp. 56f.
15. 2 Corinthians 11:31.
16. Karl Barth, *Church Dogmatics* (Edinburgh: T. & T. Clark, 1957) ii, pt i, p. 150.

6

An Irenaean Theodicy

Can a world in which sadistic cruelty often has its way, in which selfish lovelessness is so rife, in which there are debilitating diseases, crippling accidents, bodily and mental decay, insanity, and all manner of natural disasters be regarded as the expression of infinite creative goodness? Certainly all this could never by itself lead anyone to believe in the existence of a limitlessly powerful God. And yet even in a world which contains these things innumerable men and women have believed and do believe in the reality of an infinite creative goodness, which they call God. The theodicy project starts at this point, with an already operating belief in God, embodied in human living, and attempts to show that this belief is not rendered irrational by the fact of evil. It attempts to explain how it is that the universe, assumed to be created and ultimately ruled by a limitlessly good and limitlessly powerful Being, is as it is, including all the pain and suffering and all the wickedness and folly that we find around us and within us. The theodicy project is thus an exercise in metaphysical construction, in the sense that it consists in the formation and criticism of large-scale hypotheses concerning the nature and process of the universe.

Since a theodicy both starts from and tests belief in the reality of God, it naturally takes different forms in relation to different concepts of God. In this paper I shall be discussing the project of a specifically Christian theodicy; I shall not be attempting the further and even more difficult work of comparative theodicy, leading in turn to the question of a global theodicy.

The two main demands upon a theodicy hypothesis are (1) that it be internally coherent, and (2) that it be consistent with the data both of the religious tradition on which it is based, and of the world, in respect both of the latter's general character as revealed by scientific enquiry and of the specific facts of moral and natural evil. These two criteria demand, respectively, possibility and plausibility.

Traditionally, Christian theology has centred upon the concept of God as both limitlessly powerful and limitlessly good and loving; and it is this concept of deity that gives rise to the problem of evil as a threat to theistic faith. The threat was definitively expressed in Stendhal's bombshell, 'The only excuse for God is that he does not exist!' The theodicy project is the attempt to offer a different view of the universe which is both possible and plausible and which does not ignite Stendhal's bombshell.

Christian thought has always included a certain range of variety, and in the area of theodicy it offers two broad types of approach. The Augustinian approach, representing until fairly recently the majority report of the Christian mind, hinges upon the idea of the Fall, which has in turn brought about the disharmony of nature. This type of theodicy is developed today as 'the free-will defence'. The Irenaean approach, representing in the past a minority report, hinges upon the creation of humankind through the evolutionary process as an immature creature living in a challenging and therefore person-making world. I shall indicate very briefly why I do not find the first type of theodicy satisfactory, and then spend the remainder of this paper in exploring the second type.

In recent years the philosophical discussion of the problem of evil has been dominated by the free-will defence. A major effort has been made by Alvin Plantinga and a number of other Christian philosophers to show that it is logically possible that a limitlessly powerful and limitlessly good God is responsible for the existence of this world. For all evil may ultimately be due to misuses of creaturely freedom. But it may nevertheless be better for God to have created free than unfree beings; and it is logically possible that any and all free beings whom God might create would, as a matter of contingent fact, misuse their freedom by falling into sin. In that case it would be logically impossible for God to have created a world containing free beings and yet not containing sin and the suffering which sin brings with it. Thus it is logically possible, despite the fact of evil, that the existing universe is the work of a limitlessly good creator.

These writers are in effect arguing that the traditional Augustinian type of theodicy, based upon the fall from grace of free finite creatures – first angels and then human beings – and a consequent going wrong of the physical world, is not logically impossible. I am in fact doubtful whether their argument is sound, and will return to the question later. But even if it should be sound, I suggest that their argument wins only a Pyrrhic victory, since the logical possibility that it would establish is one which, for very many people today, is fatally lacking in plausibility. For most educated inhabitants of the modern world regard the biblical story of Adam and Eve, and their temptation by the devil, as myth rather than as history; and they believe that so far from having been created finitely perfect and then falling, humanity evolved out of lower forms of life, emerging in a morally, spiritually, and culturally primitive state. Further, they reject as incredible the idea that earthquake and flood, disease, decay, and death are consequences either of a human fall, or of a prior fall of angelic beings who are now exerting an evil influence upon the earth. They see all this as part of a pre-scientific world view, along with the stories of the world having been created in six days and of the sun standing still for twenty-four hours at Joshua's command. One cannot, strictly speaking, disprove any of these ancient biblical myths and sagas, or refute their confident elaboration in the medieval Christian picture of the universe. But those of us for whom the resulting theodicy, even if logically possible, is radically implausible, must look elsewhere for light on the problem of evil.

I believe that we find the light that we need in the main alternative strand of Christian thinking, which goes back to impor-tant constructive suggestions by the early Hellenistic Fathers of the Church, particularly St Irenaeus (AD 120–202). Irenaeus himself did not develop a theodicy, but he did – together with other Greek-speaking Christian writers of that period, such as Clement of Alexandria – build a framework of thought within which a theodicy became possible which does not depend upon the idea of the Fall, and which is consonant with modern knowledge concern-ing the origins of the human race. This theodicy cannot, as such, be attributed to Irenaeus. We should rather speak of a type of theodicy, presented in varying ways by different subsequent thinkers (the greatest of whom has been Friedrich Schleiermacher), of which Irenaeus can properly be regarded as the patron saint.

The central theme out of which this Irenaean type of theodicy has arisen is the two-stage conception of the creation of human-kind, first in the 'image' and then in the 'likeness' of God. Re-expressing this in modern terms, the first stage was the gradual production of *Homo sapiens*, through the long evolutionary process, as intelligent ethical and religious animals. The human being is an animal, one of the varied forms of earthly life and continuous as such with the whole realm of animal existence. But the human being is uniquely intelligent, having evolved a large and immensely complex brain. Further, the human being is ethical – that is, a gregarious as well as an intelligent animal, able to realise and respond to the complex demands of social life. And the human being is a religious animal, with an innate tendency to experience the world in terms of the presence and activity of supernatural beings and powers. This then is early *Homo sapiens*, the intelligent social animal capable of awareness of the divine. But early *Homo sapiens* is not the Adam and Eve of Augustinian theology, living in perfect harmony with self, with nature, and with God. On the contrary, the life of such beings must have been a constant struggle against a hostile environment, in which they were capable of savage violence against their fellow human beings, particularly outside their own immediate group; and their concepts of the divine were primitive and often bloodthirsty. Thus existence 'in the image of God' was a potentiality for knowledge of and relationship with one's Maker rather than such knowledge and relationship as a fully realised state. In other words, people were created as spiritually and morally immature creatures, at the beginning of a long process of further growth and development, which constitutes the second stage of God's creative work. In this second stage, of which we are a part, the intelligent, ethical, and religious animal is being brought through his/her own free responses into what Irenaeus called the divine 'likeness'. The human animal is being created into a child of God. Irenaeus' own terminology (*eikon, homoiosis; imago, similitudo*) has no particular merit, based as it is on a misunderstanding of the Hebrew parallelism in Genesis 1:26; but his conception of a two-stage creation of the human, with perfection lying in the future rather than in the past, is of fundamental importance. The notion of the Fall was not basic to this picture, although it was to become basic to the great drama of salvation depicted by St Augustine and accepted within Western Christendom, including the churches stemming from the Reformation, until well into the nineteenth century. Irenaeus himself however could not, in the historical knowledge of his time, question the fact of the Fall; though he treated it as a relatively minor lapse, a youthful error, rather than as the infinite crime and cosmic disaster which has ruined the whole creation. But today we can acknowledge that there is no evidence at all of a period in the distant past when humankind was in the ideal state of a fully realised 'child of God'. We can accept that, so far as actual events in time are concerned, there never was a fall from an original righteousness and grace. If we want to continue to use the term Fall, because of its hallowed place in the Christian tradition, we must use it to refer to the immense gap between what we actually are and what in the divine intention is eventually to be. But we must not blur our awareness that the ideal state is not something already enjoyed and lost, but is a future and as yet unrealised goal. The reality is not a perfect creation which has gone tragically wrong, but a still continuing creative process whose completion lies in the eschaton.

Let us now try to formulate a contemporary version of the Irenaean type of theodicy, based on this suggestion of the initial creation of humankind, not as finitely perfect, but as immature creatures at the beginning of a long process of further growth and development. We may begin by asking why humans should have been created as imperfect and developing creatures rather than as the perfect beings whom God is presumably intending to create. The answer, I think, consists in two considerations which converge in their practical implications, one concerned with the human's relationship to God and the other with the relationship to other human beings. As to the first, we could have the picture of God creating finite beings, whether angels or persons, directly in his own presence, so that in being conscious of that which is other than one's self one is automatically conscious of God, the limitless divine reality and power, goodness and love, knowledge and wisdom, towering above one's self. In such a situation the disproportion between Creator and creatures would be so great that the latter would have no freedom in relation to God; they would indeed not exist as independent autonomous persons. For what freedom could finite beings have in an immediate consciousness of the presence of the one who has created them, who knows them through and through, who is limitlessly powerful as well as limitlessly loving and good, and who claims their total obedience? In order to be a person, exercising some measure of genuine freedom, the creature must be brought into existence, not in the immediate divine presence, but at a 'distance' from God. This 'distance' cannot of course be spatial; for God is omnipresent. It must be an epistemic distance, a distance in the cognitive dimension. And the Irenaean hypothesis is that this 'distance' consists, in the case of humans, in their existence within and as part of a world which functions as an autonomous system and from within which God is not overwhelmingly evident. It is a world, in Bonhoeffer's phrase, *etsi deus non daretur*, as if there were no God. Or rather, it is religiously ambiguous, capable both of being seen as a purely natural phenomenon and of being seen as God's creation and experienced as mediating his presence. In such a world one can exist as a person over against the Creator. One has space to exist as a finite being, a space created by the epistemic distance from God and protected by one's basic cognitive freedom, one's freedom to open or close oneself to the dawning awareness of God which is experienced naturally by a religious animal. This Irenaean picture corresponds, I suggest, to our actual human situation. Emerging within the evolutionary process as part of the continuum of animal life, in a universe which functions in accordance with its own laws and whose workings can be investigated and described without reference to a creator, the human being has a genuine, even awesome, freedom in relation to his or her Maker. The human being is free to acknowledge and worship God; and is free – particularly since the emergence of human individuality and the beginnings of critical consciousness during the first millennium BC – to doubt the reality of God.

Within such a situation there is the possibility of human beings coming freely to know and love their Maker. Indeed, if the end-state which God is seeking to bring about is one in which finite persons have come in their own freedom to know and love him, this requires creating them initially in a state which is not that of their already knowing and loving him. For it is logically impossible to create beings already in a state of having come into that state by their own free choices.

The other consideration, which converges with this in pointing to something like the human situation as we experience it, concerns our human moral nature. We can approach it by asking why humans should not have been created at this epistemic distance from God, and yet at the same time as morally perfect beings. That persons could have been created morally perfect and yet free, so that they would always in fact choose rightly, has been argued by such critics of the free-will defence in theodicy as Antony Flew and J. L. Mackie, and argued against by Alvin Plantinga and other upholders of that form of theodicy. On the specific issue defined in the debate between them, it appears to me that the criticism of the free-will defence stands. It appears to me that a perfectly good being, although formally free to sin, would in fact never do so. If we imagine such a being in a morally frictionless environment, involving no stresses or temptation, then we must assume that that person would exemplify the ethical equivalent of Newton's first law of motion, which states that a moving body will continue in uniform motion until interfered with by some outside force. By analogy, a perfectly good being would continue in the same moral course forever, there being nothing in the environment to throw him or her off it. But even if we suppose the morally perfect being to exist in an imperfect world, in which he or she is subject to temptations, it still follows that, in virtue of moral perfection, that being will always overcome those temptations – as in the case, according to orthodox Christian belief, of Jesus Christ. It is, to be sure, logically possible, as Plantinga and others argue, that a free being, simply as such, may at any time contingently decide to sin. However, a responsible free being does not act randomly, but on the basis of a moral nature. And a free being whose nature is wholly and unqualifiedly good will accordingly never in fact sin.

But if God could, without logical contradiction, have created humans as wholly good free beings, why did he not do so? Why was humanity not initially created in possession of all the virtues, instead of having to acquire them through the long hard struggle of life as we know it? The answer, I suggest, appeals to the principle that virtues which have been formed within the agent as a hard-won deposit of his own right decisions in situations of challenge and temptation, are intrinsically more valuable than virtues created within him ready made and without any effort on his own part. This principle expresses a basic value-judgement, which cannot be established by argument but which one can only present, in the hope that it will be as morally plausible, and indeed compelling, to others as to oneself. It is, to repeat, the judgement that a moral goodness which exists as the agent's initial given nature, without ever having been chosen by him or her in the face of temptations to the contrary, is intrinsically less valuable than a moral goodness which has been built up through the agent's own responsible choices through time in the face of alternative possibilities.

If, then, God's purpose was to create finite persons embodying the most valuable kind of moral goodness, he would have to create them, not as already perfect beings but rather as imperfect creatures who can then attain to the more valuable kind of goodness through their own free choices as in the course of their personal and social history new responses prompt new insights, opening up new moral possibilities, and providing a milieu in which the most valuable kind of moral nature can be developed.

We have thus far, then, the hypothesis that one is created at an epistemic distance from God in order to come freely to know and love the Maker; and that one is at the same time created as a morally immature and imperfect being in order to attain through freedom the most valuable quality of goodness. The end sought, according to this hypothesis, is the full realisation of the human potentialities in a unitary spiritual and moral perfection in the divine Kingdom. And the question we have to ask is whether humans as we know them, and the world as we know it, are compatible with this hypothesis.

Clearly we cannot expect to be able to deduce our actual world in its concrete character, and our actual human nature as part of it, from the general concept of spiritually and morally immature creatures developing ethically in an appropriate environment. No doubt there is an immense range of possible worlds, any one of which, if actualised, would exemplify this concept. All that we can hope to do is to show that our actual world is one of these. And when we look at our human situation as part of the evolving life of this planet we can, I think, see that it fits this specification. As animal organisms, integral to the whole ecology of life, we are programmed for survival. In pursuit of survival, primitives not only killed other animals for food but fought other human beings when their vital interests conflicted. The life of prehistoric persons must indeed have been a constant struggle to stay alive, prolonging an existence which was, in Hobbes' phrase, 'poor, nasty, brutish and short'. And in this basic animal self-regardingness humankind was, and is, morally imperfect. In saying this I am assuming that the essence of moral evil is selfishness, the sacrificing of others to one's own interests. It consists, in Kantian terminology, in treating others, not as ends in themselves, but as means to one's own ends. This is what the survival instinct demands. And yet we are also capable of love, of self-giving in a common cause, of a conscience which responds to others in their needs and dangers. And with the development of civilisation we see the growth of moral insight, the glimpsing and gradual assimilation of higher ideals, and tension between our animality and our ethical values. But that as a human being one has a lower as well as a higher nature, that one is an animal as well as a potential child of God, and that one's moral goodness is won from a struggle with one's own innate selfishness, is inevitable given one's continuity with the other forms of animal life. Further, the human animal is not responsible for having come into existence as an animal. The ultimate responsibility for humankind's existence, as a morally imperfect creature, can only rest with the Creator. As humans we do not, in our own degree of freedom and responsibility, choose our origin, but rather our destiny.

This then, in brief outline, is the answer of the Irenaean type of theodicy to the question of the origin of moral evil: the general fact of humankind's basic self-regarding animality is an aspect of creation as part of the realm of organic life; and this basic self-regardingness has been expressed over the centuries both in sins of individual selfishness and in the much more massive sins of corporate selfishness, institutionalised in slavery and exploitation and all the many and complex forms of social injustice.

But nevertheless our sinful nature in a sinful world is the matrix within which God is gradually creating children for himself out of human animals. For it is as men and women freely respond to the claim of God upon their lives, transmuting their animality into the structure of divine worship, that the creation of humanity is taking place. And in its concrete character this response consists in every form of moral goodness, from unselfish love in individual personal relationships to the dedicated and selfless striving to end exploitation and to create justice within and between societies.

But one cannot discuss moral evil without at the same time discussing the non-moral evil of pain and suffering. (I propose to mean by 'pain' physical pain, including the pains of hunger and thirst; and by 'suffering' the mental and emotional pain of loneliness, anxiety, remorse, lack of love, fear, grief, envy, etc.). For what constitutes moral evil as evil is the fact that it causes pain and suffering. It is impossible to conceive of an instance of moral evil, or sin, which is not productive of pain or suffering to anyone at any time. But in addition to moral evil there is another source of pain and suffering in the structure of the physical world, which produces storms, earthquakes, and floods and which afflicts the human body with diseases – cholera, epilepsy, cancer, malaria, arthritis, rickets, meningitis, etc. – as well as with broken bones and other outcomes of physical accident. It is true that a great deal both of pain and of suffering is humanly caused, not only by the inhumanity of man to man but also by the stresses of our individual and corporate life-styles, causing many disorders – not only lung cancer and cirrhosis of the liver but many cases of heart disease, stomach and other ulcers, strokes, etc. – as well as accidents. But there remain nevertheless, in the natural world itself, permanent causes of human pain and suffering. And we have to ask why an unlimitedly good and unlimitedly powerful God should have created so dangerous a world, both as regards its purely natural hazards of earthquake and flood, etc., and as regards the liability of the human body to so many ills, both psychosomatic and purely somatic.

The answer offered by the Irenaean type of theodicy follows from and is indeed integrally bound up with its account of the origin of moral evil. We have the hypothesis of humankind being brought into being within the evolutionary process as a spiritually and morally immature creature, and then growing and developing through the exercise of freedom in this religiously ambiguous world. We can now ask what sort of a world would constitute an appropriate environment for this second stage of creation. The development of human personality – moral, spiritual, and intellectual – is a product of challenge and response. It does not occur in a static situation demanding no exertion and no choices. So far as intellectual development is concerned, this is a well-established principle which underlies the whole modern educational process, from pre-school nurseries designed to provide a rich and stimulating environment, to all forms of higher education designed to challenge the intellect. At a basic level the essential part played in learning by the learner's own active response to environment was strikingly demonstrated by the Held and Hein experiment with kittens.[1] Of two litter-mate kittens in the same artificial environment one was free to exercise its own freedom and intelligence in exploring the environment, whilst the other was suspended in a kind of 'gondola' which moved whenever and wherever the free kitten moved. Thus the second kitten had a similar succession of visual experiences to the first, but did not exert itself or make any choices in obtaining them. And whereas the first kitten learned in the normal way to conduct itself safely within its environment, the second did not. With no interaction with a challenging environment there was no development in its behavioural patterns. And I think we can safely say that the intellectual development of humanity has been due to interaction with an objective environment functioning in accordance with its own laws, an environment which we have had actively to explore and to co-operate with in order to escape its perils and exploit its benefits. In a world devoid both of dangers to be avoided and rewards to be won we may assume that there would have been virtually no development of the human intellect and imagination, and hence of either the sciences or the arts, and hence of human civilisation or culture.

The fact of an objective world within which one has to learn to live, on penalty of pain or death, is also basic to the development of one's moral nature. For it is because the world is one in which men and women can suffer harm – by violence, disease, accident, starvation, etc. – that our actions affecting one another have moral significance. A morally wrong act is, basically, one which harms some part of the human community; whilst a morally right action is, on the contrary, one which prevents or neutralises harm or which preserves or increases human well-being. Now we can imagine a paradise in which no one can ever come to any harm. It could be a world which, instead of having its own fixed structure, would be plastic to human wishes. Or it could be a world with a fixed structure, and hence the possibility of damage and pain, but whose structure is suspended or adjusted by special divine action whenever necessary to avoid human pain. Thus, for example, in such a miraculously pain-free world one who falls accidentally off a high building would presumably float unharmed to the ground; bullets would become insubstantial when fired at a human body; poisons would cease to poison; water to drown, and so on. We can at least begin to image such a world. And a good deal of the older discussion of the problem of evil – for example in part xi of Hume's *Dialogues Concerning Natural Religion* – assumed that it must be the intention of a limitlessly good and powerful Creator to make for human creatures a pain-free environment; so that the very existence of pain is evidence against the existence of God. But such an assumption overlooks the fact that a world in which there can be no pain or suffering would also be one in which there can be no moral choices and hence no possibility of moral growth and development. For a situation in which no one can ever suffer injury or be liable to pain or suffering there would be no distinction between right and wrong action. No action would be morally wrong, because no action could have harmful consequences; and likewise no action would be morally right in contrast to wrong. Whatever the values of such a world, it clearly could not serve a purpose of the development of its inhabitants from self-regarding animality to self-giving love.

Thus the hypothesis of a divine purpose in which finite persons are created at an epistemic distance from God, in order that they may gradually become children of God through their own moral and spiritual choices, requires that their environment, instead of being a pain-free and stress-free paradise, be broadly the kind of world of which we find ourselves to be a part. It requires that it be such as to provoke the theological problem of evil. For it requires that it be an environment which offers challenges to be met, problems to be solved, dangers to be faced, and which accordingly involves real possibilities of hardship, disaster, failure, defeat, and misery as well as of delight and happiness, success, triumph and achievement. For it is by grappling with the real problems of a real environment, in which a person is one form of life among many, and which is not designed to minister exclusively to one's well-being, that one can develop in intelligence and in such qualities as courage and determination. And it is in the relationships of human beings with one another, in the context of this struggle to survive and flourish, that they can develop the higher values of mutual love and care, of self-sacrifice for others, and of commitment to a common good.

To summarise thus far:

1 The divine intention in relation to humankind, according to our hypothesis, is to create perfect finite personal beings in filial relationship with their Maker.
2 It is logically impossible for humans to be created already in this perfect state, because in its spiritual aspect it involves coming freely to an uncoerced consciousness of God from a situation of epistemic distance, and in its moral aspect, freely choosing the good in preference to evil.
3 Accordingly the human being was initially created through the evolutionary process, as a spiritually and morally immature creature, and as part of a world which is both religiously ambiguous and ethically demanding.
4 Thus that one is morally imperfect (i.e. that there is moral evil), and that the world is a challenging and even dangerous environment (i.e. that there is natural evil), are necessary aspects of the present stage of the process through which God is gradually creating perfected finite persons.

In terms of this hypothesis, as we have developed it thus far, then, both the basic moral evil in the human heart and the natural evils of the world are compatible with the existence of a Creator who is unlimited in both goodness and power. But is the hypothesis plausible as well as possible? The principal threat to its plausibility comes, I think, from the sheer amount and intensity of both moral and natural evil. One can accept the principle that in order to arrive at a freely chosen goodness one must start out in a state of moral immaturity and imperfection. But is it necessary that there should be the depths of demonic malice and cruelty which each generation has experienced, and which we have seen above all in recent history in the Nazi attempt to exterminate the Jewish population of Europe? Can any future fulfilment be worth such horrors? This was Dostoevsky's haunting question: 'Imagine that you are creating a fabric of human destiny with the object of making men happy in the end, giving them peace and rest at last, but that it was essential and inevitable to torture to death only one tiny creature – that baby beating its breast with its fist, for instance – and to found that edifice on its unavenged tears, would you consent to be the architect on those conditions?'[2]. The theistic answer is one which may be true but which takes so large a view that it baffles the imagination. Intellectually one may be able to see, but emotionally one cannot be expected to feel, its truth; and in that sense it cannot satisfy us. For the theistic answer is that if we take with full seriousness the value of human freedom and responsibility, as essential to the eventual creation of perfected children of God, then we cannot consistently want God to revoke that freedom when its wrong exercise becomes intolerable to us. From our vantage point within the historical process we may indeed cry out to God to revoke his gift of freedom, or to overrule it by some secret or open intervention. Such a cry must have come from millions caught in the Jewish Holocaust, or in the yet more recent laying waste of Korea and Vietnam, or from the victims of racism in many parts of the world. And the thought that humankind's moral freedom is indivisible, and can lead eventually to a consummation of limitless value which could never be attained without that freedom, and which is worth any finite suffering in the course of its creation, can be of no comfort to those who are now in the midst of that suffering. But whilst fully acknowledging this, I nevertheless want to insist that this eschatological answer may well be true. Expressed in religious language it tells us to trust in God even in the midst of deep suffering, for in the end we shall participate in his glorious Kingdom.

Again, we may grant that a world which is to be a person-making environment cannot be a pain-free paradise but must contain challenges and dangers, with real possibilities of many kinds of accident and disaster, and the pain and suffering which they bring. But need it contain the worst forms of disease and catastrophe? And need misfortune fall upon us with such heart-breaking indiscriminateness? Once again there are answers, which may well be true, and yet once again the truth in this area may offer little in the way of pastoral balm. Concerning the intensity of natural evil, the truth is probably that our judgements of intensity are relative. We might identify some form of natural evil as the worst that there is – say the agony than can be caused by death from cancer – and claim that a loving God would not have allowed this to exist. But in a world in which there was no cancer, something else would then rank as the worst form of natural evil. If we then eliminate this, something else; and so on. And the process would continue until the world was free of all natural evil. For whatever form of evil for the time being remained would be intolerable to the inhabitants of that world. But in removing all occasions of pain and suffering, and hence all challenge and all need for mutual care, we should have converted the world from a person-making into a static environment, which could not elicit moral growth. In short, having accepted that a person-making world must have its dangers and therefore also its tragedies, we must accept that whatever form these take will be intolerable to the inhabitants of that world. There could not be a person-making world devoid of what we call evil; and evils are never tolerable – except for the sake of greater goods which may come out of them.

But accepting that a person-making environment must contain causes of pain and suffering, and that no pain or suffering is going to be acceptable, one of the most daunting and even terrifying features of the world is that calamity strikes indiscriminately. There is no justice in the incidence of disease, accident, disaster and tragedy. The righteous as well as the unrighteous are struck down by illness and afflicted by misfortune. There is no security in goodness, but the good are as likely as the wicked to suffer 'the slings and arrows of outrageous fortune'. From the time of Job this fact has set a glaring question mark against the goodness of God. But let us suppose that things were otherwise. Let us suppose that misfortune came upon humankind, not haphazardly and therefore unjustly, but justly and therefore not haphazardly. Let us suppose that instead of coming without regard to moral considerations, it was proportioned to desert, so that the sinner was punished and the virtuous rewarded. Would such a dispensation serve a person-making purpose? Surely not. For it would be evident that wrong deeds bring disaster upon the agent whilst good deeds bring health and prosperity; and in such a world truly moral action, action done because it is right, would be impossible. The fact that natural evil is not morally directed, but is a hazard which comes by chance, is thus an intrinsic feature of a person-making world.

In other words, the very mystery of natural evil, the very fact that disasters afflict human beings in contingent, undirected and haphazard ways, is itself a necessary feature of a world that calls forth mutual aid and builds up mutual caring and love. Thus on the one hand it would be completely wrong to say that God sends misfortune upon individuals, so that their death, maiming, starvation or ruin is God's will for them. But on the other hand God has set us in a world containing unpredictable contingencies and dangers, in which unexpected and undeserved calamities may occur to anyone; because only in such a world can mutual caring and love be elicited. As an abstract philosophical hypothesis this may offer little comfort. But translated into religious language it tells us that God's good purpose enfolds the entire process of this world, with all its good and bad contingencies, and that even amidst tragic calamity and suffering we are still within the sphere of his love and are moving towards his Kingdom.

But there is one further all-important aspect of the Irenaean type of theodicy, without which all the foregoing would lose its plausibility. This is the eschatological aspect. Our hypothesis depicts persons as still in course of creation towards an end-state of perfected personal community in the divine Kingdom. This end-state is conceived of as one in which individual egoity has been transcended in communal unity before God. And in the present phase of that creative process the naturally self-centred human animal has the opportunity freely to respond to God's non-coercive self-disclosures, through the work of prophets and saints, through the resulting religious traditions, and through the individual's religious experience. Such response always has an ethical aspect; for the growing awareness of God is at the same time a growing awareness of the moral claim which God's presence makes upon the way in which we live.

But it is very evident that this person-making process, leading eventually to perfect human community, is not completed on this earth. It is not completed in the life of the individual – or at best only in the few who have attained to sanctification, or *moksha*, or *nirvāṇa* on this earth. Clearly the enormous majority of men and women die without having attained to this. As Erich Fromm has said, 'The tragedy in the life of most of us is that we die before we are fully born.'³ And therefore if we are ever to reach the full realisation of the potentialities of our human nature, this can only be in a continuation of our lives in another sphere of existence after bodily death. And it is equally evident that the perfect all-embracing human community, in which self-regarding concern has been transcended in mutual love, not only has not been realised in this world, but never can be, since hundreds of generations of human beings have already lived and died and accordingly could not be part of any ideal community established at some future moment of earthly history. Thus if the unity of humankind in God's presence is ever to be realised it will have to be in some sphere of existence other than our earth. In short, the fulfilment of the divine purpose, as it is postulated in the Irenaean type of theodicy, presupposes each person's survival, in some form, of bodily death and further living and growing towards that end-state. Without such an eschatological fulfilment, this theodicy would collapse.

A theodicy which presupposes and requires an eschatology will thereby be rendered implausible in the minds of many today. I nevertheless do not see how any coherent theodicy can avoid dependence upon an eschatology. Indeed I would go further and say that the belief in the reality of a limitlessly loving and powerful deity must incorporate some kind of eschatology according to which God holds in being the creatures whom he has made for fellowship with himself, beyond bodily death, and brings them into the eternal fellowship which he has intended for them. I have tried elsewhere to argue that such an eschatology is a necessary corollary of ethical monotheism; to argue for the realistic possibility of an after-life or lives, despite the philosophical and empirical arguments against this; and even to spell out some of the general features which human life after death may possibly have.⁴ Since all this is a very large task, which would far exceed the bounds of this paper, I shall not attempt to repeat it here but must refer the reader to my existing discussion of it. It is that extended discussion that constitutes my answer to the question whether an Irenaean theodicy, with its eschatology, may not be as implausible as an Augustinian theodicy, with its human or angelic Fall. (If it is, then the latter is doubly implausible; for it also involves an eschatology!)

There is however one particular aspect of eschatology which must receive some treatment here, however brief and inadequate. This is the issue of 'universal salvation' versus 'heaven and hell' (or perhaps annihilation instead of hell). If the justification of evil within the creative process lies in the limitless and eternal good of the end-state to which it leads, then the completeness of the justification must depend upon the completeness, or universality, of the salvation achieved. Only if it includes the entire human race can it justify the sins and sufferings of the entire human race throughout all history. But, having given human beings cognitive freedom, which in turn makes possible moral freedom, can the Creator bring it about that in the end all his human creatures freely turn to him in love and trust? The issue is a very difficult one; but I believe that it is in fact possible to reconcile a full affirmation of human freedom with a belief in the ultimate universal success of God's creative work. We have to accept that creaturely freedom always occurs within the limits of a basic nature that we did not ourselves choose; for this is entailed by the fact of having been created. If then a real though limited freedom does not preclude our being endowed with a certain nature, it does not preclude our being endowed with a basic Godward bias, so that, quoting from another side of St Augustine's thought, 'our hearts are restless until they find their rest in Thee'.[5] If this is so, it can be predicted that sooner or later, in our own time and in our own way, we shall all freely come to God; and universal salvation can be affirmed, not as a logical necessity but as the contingent but predictable outcome of the process of the universe, interpreted theistically. Once again, I have tried to present this argument more fully elsewhere, and to consider various objections to it.[6]

On this view the human, endowed with a real though limited freedom, is basically formed for relationship with God and destined ultimately to find the fulfilment of his or her nature in that relationship. This does not seem to me excessively paradoxical. On the contrary, given the theistic postulate, it seems to me to offer a very probable account of our human situation. If so, it is a situation in which we can rejoice; for it gives meaning to our temporal existence as the long process through which we are being created, by our own free responses to life's mixture of good and evil, into 'children of God' who 'inherit eternal life'.

NOTES

1. R. Held and A. Hein, 'Movement-Produced Stimulation in the Development of Visually Guided Behaviour', *Journal of Comparative and Physiological Psychology*, 56 (1963) 872–6.
2. Fyodor Dostoevsky, *The Brothers Karamazov*, tr. Constance Garnett (New York: Modern Library, n.d.) p. 254 (bk v, ch. 4).
3. Erich Fromm, 'Values, Psychology, and Human Existence', in A. H. Maslow (ed.), *New Knowledge of Human Values* (New York: Harper, 1959) p. 156.
4. John Hick, *Death and Eternal Life* (New York: Harper and Row; London: Collins, 1976).
5. *The Confessions of St Augustine*, tr. F. J. Sheed (New York: Sheed and Ward, 1942) p. 3 (bk I, ch. 1).
6. Hick, *Death and Eternal Life*, ch. 13.

7

Jesus and the World Religions

I

If we start from where we are, as Christians of our own day, we begin amidst the confusion and uncertainty which assail us when we try to speak about Jesus, the historical individual who lived in Galilee in the first third of the first century of the Christian era. For New Testament scholarship has shown how fragmentary and ambiguous are the data available to us as we try to look back across nineteen and a half centuries, and at the same time how large and how variable is the contribution of the imagination to our 'pictures' of Jesus. In one sense it is true to say that he has been worshipped by millions; and yet in another sense, in terms of subjective 'intentionality', a number of different beings, describable in partly similar and partly different ways, have been worshipped under the name of Jesus or under the title of Christ. Some have pictured him as a stern lawgiver and implacable judge, and others as a figure of inexhaustible gracious tenderness; some as a divine psychologist probing and healing the recesses of the individual spirit, and others as a prophet demanding social righteousness and seeking justice for the poor and the oppressed; some as a supernatural being, all-powerful and all-knowing, haloed in glorious light, and others as an authentically human figure living within the cultural framework of his time; and he has been pictured both as a pacifist and as a Zealot, as a figure of serene majesty and as a 'man for others' who suffered human agonies, sharing the pains and sorrows of our mortal lot. And each of these different 'pictures' can appeal to some element among the various strands of New Testament tradition. But in each case communal or individual imagination has projected its own ideal upon as much of the New Testament data as will sustain it, producing a Christ-figure who meets the spiritual needs of his devotees; while behind this gallery

106

of ideal portraits lies the largely unknown man of Nazareth. Clearly, Feuerbach's account of the idea of God as a projection of human ideals has a certain application here. Jesus was a real man who really lived in first-century Palestine; but the mental images of him upon which Christian devotion has been focused in different ages and in different parts of the Church are so widely various that they must in part reflect the variety of temperaments and ideals, and above all the varying spiritual needs, within the world of believers. Aspects of the traditions about Jesus have fused with men's hopes and desires to form these different 'pictures', so that like a great work of art the New Testament figure of Jesus has been able to become many things to many men.

To what extent is the exaltation in Christian faith of the man of Nazareth into the divine Christ, the only-begotten Son of God, Second Person of the Holy Trinity, a supreme example of this projection upon Jesus of ideals to answer our spiritual needs? At first sight the very possibility is alarming; for it questions the identification of the Galilean rabbi with the Christ-figure of developed Christian dogma. I shall argue, however, that the Nicene definition of God-the-Son-incarnate is only one way of conceptualising the lordship of Jesus, the way taken by the Graeco-Roman world of which we are the heirs, and that in the new age of world ecumenism which we are entering it is proper for Christians to become conscious of both the optional and the mythological character of this traditional language.

It may be helpful to observe the exaltation of a human teacher into a divine figure of universal power in another religious tradition which we can survey from the outside. The founder of Buddhism, Gautama, was a real historical individual who lived in north-east India from about 563 to about 483 BC. Born of a local princely family, he renounced his riches to seek spiritual truth. After finally attaining Enlightenment he travelled far and wide, teaching both individuals and groups. When he died at the age of about eighty he had founded a community of disciples, monks and nuns, which continues to this day and which has carried the Buddha's message throughout Asia, deeply influencing the lives of a considerable section of mankind. Gautama, the Buddha or Enlightened One, made no claim to be divine. He was a human being who had attained to *nirvāṇa* – complete transcendence of egoism, and oneness with eternal transpersonal Reality. But in some of the Mahāyāna Buddhism which began to develop at about the same time as Christianity the Buddha came to be revered as much more than an outstanding human individual who had lived and died some centuries earlier. In the distinctive Mahāyānist doctrine of the Three Bodies (*Trikāya*) of the Buddha, the earthly or incarnate body (*nirmānakāya*) is a human being who has become a Buddha and who teaches the way to others. Gautama was the most recent of these and the one in the period of whose spiritual influence the world still is; but there have been others before him and there will be yet others in the future. The *sambhogakāya*, sometimes translated as the Body of Bliss, is a transcendent or heavenly Buddha, a divine being to whom prayer is addressed. The earthly Buddhas are incarnations of the heavenly Buddhas, projections of their life into the stream of this world. But these transcendent Buddhas are ultimately all one in the Dharma Body (*dharmakāya*), which is Absolute Reality.

Thus Buddhology and Christology developed in comparable ways. The human Gautama came to be thought of as the incarnation of a transcendent, pre-existent Buddha as the human Jesus came to be thought of as the incarnation of the pre-existent Logos or divine Son. And in the Mahāyāna the transcendent Buddha is one with the Absolute as in Christianity the eternal Son is one with God the Father. Thus Gautama was the dharma (Truth) made flesh, as Jesus was the Word made flesh: indeed the Burmese translation of the New Testament treats Dharma as the equivalent of Logos, so that the opening sentence of St John's gospel reads (in Burmese) 'In the beginning was the Dharma . . .'.[1] However, I am not concerned here to explore more fully the very interesting analogies between Christian and Mahāyānist themes. The fact to which I am drawing attention is that in sections of Mahāyāna Buddhism – the situation differs again in Theravāda or southern Buddhism – the human Gautama has been exalted into an eternal figure of universal significance, one with his human brethren through the incarnate life lived two-and-a-half thousand years ago and one with Ultimate Reality in the *dharmakāya* or cosmic Buddha. This exaltation has presumably been powered by the hunger of the human spirit for a personal Saviour and has been supported intellectually by the sophisticated metaphysical doctrine of the Three Bodies. Mahāyāna Buddhists, of course, claim that this entire development was implicit in the work of the historical Gautama and that later thought has only brought out the fuller meaning of his teaching. Thus B. H. Streeter has aptly remarked that 'Mahāyāna stands to primitive Buddhism in a relation not unlike that of the gospel according to St John to that according to St Matthew.'[2]

In noting this Mahāyānist development of Buddhism one is not implying that the later interpretation of the human Gautama as cosmic Saviour and object of devotion is right or that it is wrong. But we are seeing at work a tendency of the religious mind which is also to be seen within the history of Christianity. The exaltation of the founder has of course taken characteristically different forms in the two religions. But in each case it led the developing tradition to speak of him in terms which he himself did not use, and to understand him by means of a complex of beliefs which was only gradually formed by later generations of his followers.

But, it will be said, there is at least one all-important difference between Jesus and Gautama which justifies the ascription of divine attributes to the one and not to the other – namely that Jesus rose from the dead. Does not his resurrection set him apart from all other men and show him to be God incarnate? Such an argument inevitably suggests itself; and yet it proves difficult to sustain. That there was some kind of experience of seeing Jesus after his death, an appearance or appearances which came to be known as his resurrection, seems virtually certain in view of the survival and growth of the tiny original Jesus movement. But we cannot ascertain today in what this resurrection-event consisted. The possibilities range from the resuscitation and transformation of Jesus' body to visions of the Lord in resplendent glory. But it must be doubted whether the resurrection-event – whatever its nature – was seen by Jesus' contemporaries as guaranteeing his divinity. For the raising of the dead to life, understood in the most literal sense, did not at that time and in those circles seem so utterly earth-shaking and well-nigh incredible as it does to the modern mind. This is evident from the numerous raisings of the dead referred to in the New Testament and the patristic writings. Jesus is said to have raised Lazarus (John 11:1–44), a widow's son (Luke 7:11–17), and Jairus' daughter (Mark 5:33–43 and Luke 8:49–56) and to have told John the Baptist's messengers to report that they had seen not only that the blind receive their sight and the lame walk but also that the dead are being raised up (Matthew 11:5); and Matthew records that at the time of Jesus' crucifixion 'the tombs also were opened, and many bodies of the saints who had fallen asleep were raised, and coming out of the tombs after his resurrection they went into the holy city and appeared to many' (Matthew 27:52–3). Again, the writer of the Epistle to the Hebrews claims as a sign of faith in olden times that 'Women received their dead by resurrection' (Hebrews 11:35; cf. 1 Kings 17:17–24). And Irenaeus, writing in the last quarter of the second century, refers to raisings of the dead both by the apostles and, frequently, within the later fellowship of the Church.[3] Thus the claim that Jesus had been literally raised from the dead did not automatically put him in a quite unique category. It indicated that he had a special place within God's providence; but this was not equivalent to seeing him as divine. For Jesus is not said to have risen by virtue of a divine nature which he himself possessed but to have been raised by God. Accordingly the first Christian preachers did not draw the conclusion that he was himself God but that he was a man chosen by God for a special role and declared by his resurrection to be Messiah and Lord (Acts 2:22 and 36).

From our point of view today it is less easy to accept stories of a physical resurrection, particularly when they refer to an event nearly twenty centuries ago and when the written evidence is in detail so conflicting and so hard to interpret. But nevertheless, if we imagine a physical resurrection taking place today it is still far from evident that we should necessarily regard it as a proof of divinity. George Caird has put the point well:

> Let us suppose that tomorrow you were confronted with irrefutable evidence that an acquaintance whom you had good reason to believe dead had been seen alive by reliable witnesses. You would certainly feel compelled to revise some of your ideas about science, but I doubt whether you would feel compelled to revise your ideas about God. I doubt whether you would conclude that your acquaintance was divine, or that a stamp of authenticity had been placed on all he ever said or did. . . .[4]

II

Returning, then, to the theme of the exaltation of a human being to divine status, the understanding of Jesus which eventually became orthodox Christian dogma sees him as God the Son incarnate, the Second Person of the Trinity living a human life. As such he was, in the words of the 'Nicene' creed, 'the only-begotten Son of God,

Begotten of the Father before all the ages, Light of Light, true God of true God, begotten not made, of one substance with the Father'. But this is as far from anything that the historical Jesus can reasonably be supposed to have thought or taught as is the doctrine of the Three Bodies from anything that the historical Gautama can reasonably be supposed to have thought or taught. If we accept, with the bulk of modern New Testament scholarship, that the Fourth Gospel is a product of profound theological meditation, expressing a Christian interpretation of Jesus which had formed fairly late in the first century, we cannot properly attribute its great Christological sayings – 'I and the Father are one', 'No one comes to the Father but by me', 'He who has seen me has seen the Father' – to Jesus himself. But we do nevertheless receive, mainly from the synoptic gospels, an impression of a real person with a real message, lying behind the often conflicting indications preserved in the traditions. These documents give us three sets of communal 'memories' of Jesus, variously influenced by the needs, interests and circumstances of the Christian circles within which they were produced. In offering my own impression I am of course doing what I have already suggested that everyone else does who depicts the Jesus whom he calls Lord: one finds amidst the New Testament evidences indications of one who answers one's own spiritual needs. I see the Nazarene, then, as intensely and overwhelmingly conscious of the reality of God. He was a man of God, living in the unseen presence of God, and addressing God as *abba*, father. His spirit was open to God and his life a continuous response to the divine love as both utterly gracious and utterly demanding. He was so powerfully God-conscious that his life vibrated, as it were, to the divine life; and as a result his hands could heal the sick, and the 'poor in spirit' were kindled to new life in his presence. If you or I had met him in first-century Palestine we would – we may hope – have felt deeply disturbed and challenged by his presence. We would have felt the absolute claim of God confronting us, summoning us to give ourselves wholly to him and to be born again as his children and as agents of his purposes on earth. To respond with our whole being might have involved danger, poverty, ridicule. And such is the interaction of body and mind that in deciding to give ourselves to God, in response to his claim mediated through Jesus, we might have found ourselves trembling or in tears or uttering the strange sounds that are called speaking with tongues.

But as well as challenge, we would also have been conscious, as the other side of the same coin, of a dynamic joy, a breakthrough into a new and better quality of existence, in harmony with the divine life and resting securely upon the divine reality. Thus in Jesus' presence, we should have felt that we were in the presence of God – not in the sense that the man Jesus literally *is* God, but in the sense that he was so totally conscious of God that we could catch something of that consciousness by spiritual contagion. At least this was what *might* happen. But there was also the possibility of turning away from this challenging presence, being unable or unwilling to recognise God's call as coming to us through a wholly unpretentious working-class young man, and so of closing ourselves to him and at the same time to God. Therefore to encounter Jesus, whether in the flesh or through the New Testament pictures of him, has always been liable to be a turning point in anyone's life, a crisis of salvation or judgement.

If this interpretation is at all on the right lines, Jesus cannot have failed to be aware that he was himself far more intensely conscious of God, and that he was far more faithfully obedient to God, than could be said of any contemporaries whom he had met or of whom he had heard. He must have been aware that whereas ordinary men and women had, most of the time, only a faint and second-hand sense of the divine presence, and while the Scribes and Pharisees were often using religion to support their own privileged position, he was himself directly and overwhelmingly conscious of the heavenly Father, so that he could speak about him with authority, could summon men and women to live as his children, could declare his judgement and his forgiveness, and could heal the sick by his power. Jesus must thus have been conscious of a unique position among his contemporaries, which he may have expressed by accepting the title of Messiah or, alternatively, by applying to himself the image of the heavenly Son of Man – two categories each connoting a human being called to be God's special servant and agent on earth.

Jesus' specially intimate awareness of God, his consequent spiritual authority and his efficacy as Lord and as giver of new life, required in his disciples an adequate language in which to speak about their master. He had to be thought of in a way that was commensurate with the total discipleship which he evoked. And so his Jewish followers hailed him as their Messiah, and this somewhat mysterious title developed in its significance within the mixed Jewish–Gentile Church ultimately to the point of deification.

But how did Jews come, with their Gentile fellow-Christians, to worship a human being, thus breaking their unitarian monotheism in a way which eventually required the sophisticated metaphysics of the Trinity? For whereas in the earliest Christian preaching, as we have echoes of it in Acts, Jesus was proclaimed as 'a man attested to you by God with mighty works and wonders and signs' (Acts 2:22), some thirty years later the gospel of Mark could open with the words 'The beginning of the gospel of Jesus Christ, the Son of God. . . .' And in John's gospel, written after another thirty or so years' development, this Christian language is attributed to Jesus himself and he is depicted as walking the earth as a consciously divine being.

Why and how did this deification take place? It is obvious, from the effects of his impact upon mankind, that Jesus was a figure of tremdendous spiritual power. Those who became his disciples were 'born again', living henceforth consciously in God's presence and gladly serving the divine purposes on earth; and their experience was transmitted scarcely diminished for several generations, Christian faith perhaps even being toughened in the fires of persecution. This vital and transforming stream of religious experience was focused on Jesus as Messiah and Lord. No doubt for the ordinary believer, living within the tightly knit Christian fellowship, it was at first sufficient to think and speak of him simply as the Lord. But before long pressures must have developed to use titles which would more explicitly present the challenge of Jesus' saving power, first within the Jewish community and then within the Gentile world of the Roman empire. And these could only be the highest titles available. Once men and women had been transformed by their encounter with Jesus, he was for them the religious centre of their existence, the object of their devotion and loyalty, the Lord in following whom they were both giving their lives to God and receiving their lives renewed from God. And so it was natural that they should express this lordship in the most exalted terms which their culture offered. Accordingly we find within the New Testament itself a variety of terms being tried out. Some of them failed to catch on: for example, Jesus' self-designation as the eschatological Son of Man who was to come on the clouds of heaven is not used outside the reports of his own teaching; and St Paul's distinctive designation of him as the second Adam, although it has persisted down to today, has never been

very widely or centrally used. St John's use of the idea of the Logos
has remained important, though mainly as a theologian's title. But
the central development is that which began with Jesus as the
Messiah of the Jews and culminated in the Nicene identification of
him as God the Son, Second Person of the Trinity, incarnate. It is
clear that ideas of divinity embodied in human life were widespread in the ancient world, so that there is nothing surprising in
the deification of Jesus in that cultural environment. Within
Judaism itself the notion of a man being called son of God already
had a long tradition behind it. The Messiah was to be an earthly
king of the line of David, and the ancient kings of David's line had
been adopted as son of God in being anointed to their office: the
words of Psalm 2:7, 'He said to me, "You are my son, today I have
begotten you"', were probably originally spoken at the coronation
ceremony. Another key text is Samuel 7:14, 'I will be his father, and
he shall be my son', again originally said of the earthly king. Thus
the exalted language which the early Church came to apply to
Jesus was already a part of the Jewish heritage. Of the splendid
poetry, for example, of the annunciation story, 'He will be great,
and will be called the Son of the Most High; and the Lord God will
give to him the throne of his father David, and he will reign over
the house of Jacob for ever; and of his kingdom there will be no
end' (Luke 1:32–3), R. H. Fuller says, 'There is nothing specifically
Christian about this passage, except for the context in which Luke
has inserted it, and it may well be a pre-Christian Jewish
fragment.'[5] Such language, so far from being newly created by the
impact of Jesus, was already present in the Jewish cultural tradition
and was readily applied to Jesus by those who saw him as the
Messiah.

How are we to understand this ancient language of divine
sonship? Was the king thought of as literally or as metaphorically
the son of God? The question is probably too sharply posed; for the
early cultures did not draw our modern distinction. But, in our
terms, the title seems to have been metaphorical and honorific. To
quote Mowinckel, 'The king stands in a closer relation to Yahweh
than anyone else. He is His "son" (Ps. 2:7). In mythological
language it is said that Yahweh has "begotten" him, or that he was
born of the dawn goddess on the holy mountain (Ps. 110:3).'[6] But
'in spite of all the mythological metaphors about the birth of a king,
we never find in Israel any expression of a "metaphysical"
conception of the king's divinity and his relation to Yahweh. It is

clear that the king is regarded as Yahweh's son by *adoption.*'[7] This, then, seems to have been one of the points of entry of the notion of divine sonship into the Hebrew tradition; and the belief that Jesus was of the royal line of David, and the application to him of the title of Messiah, revived around him the image of divine sonship. Hence the phrase, with which Mark begins his gospel, 'Jesus, Messiah, son of God'. And as Christian theology grew through the centuries it made the very significant transition from 'son of God' to 'God the Son', the Second Person of the Trinity. The transposition of the poetic image, son of God, into the trinitarian concept, God the Son, is already implicit in the Fourth Gospel and has ever since been authorised within the Church by a pre-critical acceptance of the Fourth Gospel reports of Jesus' teaching as historical For it is characteristic of this gospel that in it Jesus' message centres upon himself as Son of God in a unique sense which seems virtually equivalent to his being God incarnate. In this gospel Jesus is the subject of his own preaching; and the Church's theology has largely followed the Johannine rewriting of his teaching. It *is* a rewriting, however, for it is striking that in the earlier, synoptic gospels Jesus' teaching centres, not upon himself, but upon the Kingdom of God.

It seems likely that this deification of Jesus came about partly – perhaps mainly – as a result of the Christian experience of reconciliation with God. The new life into which Jesus had brought his disciples, and into which they had drawn others, was pervaded by a glorious sense of the divine forgiveness and love. The early Christian community lived and rejoiced in the knowledge of God's accepting grace. And it was axiomatic to them, as Jews influenced by a long tradition of priestly sacrifice, that 'without the shedding of blood there is no forgiveness of sins' (Hebrews 9:22). There was thus a natural transition in their minds from the experience of reconciliation with God as Jesus' disciples, to the thought of his death as an atoning sacrifice, and from this to the conclusion that in order for Jesus' death to have been a sufficient atonement for human sin he must himself have been divine.

Thus it was natural and intelligible both that Jesus, through whom men had found a decisive encounter with God and a new and better life, should come to be hailed as son of God, and that later this poetry should have hardened into prose and escalated from a metaphorical son of God to a metaphysical God the Son, of the same substance as the Father within the triune Godhead. This

was an effective way, within that cultural milieu, of expressing
Jesus' significance as the one through whom men had transfor-
mingly encountered God. They had experienced new life, new
power, new purpose. They were saved – brought out of the
darkness of worldly self-concern into the light of God's presence.
And because of the inherent conservatism of religion, the way in
which the significance of Jesus was expressed in the mythology
and philosophy of Europe in the first three centuries has remained
the normative Christian language which we inherit today. But we
should never forget that if the Christian Gospel had moved east,
into India, instead of west, into the Roman empire, Jesus' religious
significance would probably have been expressed by hailing him
within Hindu culture as a divine Avatar, and within the Mahāyāna
Buddhism which was then developing in India as a Bodhisattva,
one who has attained to oneness with Ultimate Reality but remains
in the human world out of compassion for mankind and to show
others the way of life. These would have been the appropriate
expressions, within those cultures, of the same spiritual reality.

III

In the past Christians have generally accepted the established
language about Jesus as part of their devotional practice without
raising the question of its logical character. They have not asked
what kind of language use one is engaging in when one says that
'Jesus was God the Son incarnate'. Is it a factual statement (a
combined statement, presumably, about empirical and metaphysical facts), or does it express a commitment, or make a value
judgement; and is its meaning literal, or metaphorical, or symbolic,
or mythological, or poetic . . . ? Such questions, although often
grappled with indirectly, have only been posed directly in the
recent period in which philosophical attention has been directed
systematically upon the uses of language, including religious
language; and as inhabitants of our own cultural world we
properly, and indeed inevitably, ask them.

We have to direct these questions particularly to the two-natures
Christology of Nicaea and Chalcedon, which eventually emerged
as the orthodox Christian doctrine. This is partly metaphysical and
partly empirical: empirical in asserting that Jesus was a human
being and metaphysical in asserting that he was God. Each of these

could be meant literally, or non-literally (i.e. symbolically, metaphorically, poetically or mythologically). But the Nicene formula was undoubtedly intended to be r̄ ʿᵘ₃tood literally. It asserts that Jesus was literally (not merely ɪₙetaphorically) divine and also literally (and not merely metaphorically) human. As divine he was not symbolically or poetically speaking God, or as-if God; he was, actually and literally, God – incarnate. And again, as human he was really, truly and literally a man.

The big question today concerning this doctrine is whether it has any non-metaphorical meaning. It is clearly literally meaningful to say that Jesus was a man, part of the genetic stream of human life; finite in intelligence, information and energy; and conditioned by a particular cultural and geographical milieu. But what does it mean to say that this man was the Second Person of the Holy Trinity? Prolonged efforts were made in the patristic period to give it a meaning, but they all proved unacceptable (i.e. heretical). To say with the Adoptionists that Jesus was a man adopted because of his special spiritual fitness into divine sonship, although (as we have seen) in agreement with the original Jewish notion of the king as adopted son of God, did not allow Jesus to be 'of the same substance as the Father'. Neither did the suggestion that Jesus was a man uniquely indwelt by the Holy Spirit or, in a modern version, the supreme instance of the 'paradox of grace'. Nor again was it thought sufficient to say that Jesus was a man completely responsive to God's will; for this did not acknowledge his divine status as pre-existent Logos and Second Person of the Trinity. Again, the suggestion (of Apollinaris) that in Jesus the eternal Logos took the place of the rational soul, whilst his 'animal soul' and body were human, affirmed Jesus' divinity at the cost of his humanity; for on this view his essential self was not human but divine. Against all these theories – which were well-meant attempts to give meaning to the God–man formula – orthodoxy insisted upon the two natures, human and divine, coinhering in the one historical Jesus Christ. But orthodoxy has never been able to give this idea any content. It remains a form of words without assignable meaning. For to say, without explanation, that the historical Jesus of Nazareth was also God is as paradoxical as to say that this circle drawn with a pencil on paper is also a square. Such a locution has to be given semantic content: and in the case of the language of incarnation every content thus far suggested has had to be repudiated. The Chalcedonian formula, in which the attempt rested, merely reiterated that Jesus was both God and man, but made no attempt to interpret the formula. It therefore seems reasonable to conclude that the real point and value of the incarnational doctrine is not indicative but expressive, not to assert a metaphysical fact but to express a valuation and evoke an attitude. The doctrine of the incarnation is not a theory which ought to be able to be spelled out but – in a term widely used throughout Christian history – a mystery. I suggest that its character is best expressed by saying that the idea of divine incarnation is a mythological idea. And I am using the term 'myth' in the following sense: a myth is a story which is told but which is not literally true, or an idea or image which is applied to someone or something but which does not literally apply, but which invites a particular attitude in its hearers. Thus the truth of a myth is a kind of practical truth consisting in the appropriateness of the attitude to its object. That Jesus was God the Son incarnate is not literally true, since it has no literal meaning, but it is an application to Jesus of a mythical concept whose function is analogous to that of the notion of divine sonship ascribed in the ancient world to a king. In the case of Jesus it gives definitive expression to his efficacy as saviour from sin and ignorance and as giver of new life; it offers a way of declaring his significance to the world; and it expresses a disciple's commitment to Jesus as his personal Lord. He is the one in following whom we have found ourselves in God's presence and have found God's meaning for our lives. He is our sufficient model of true humanity in a perfect relationship to God. And he is so far above us in the 'direction' of God that he stands between ourselves and the Ultimate as a mediator of salvation. And all this is summed up and given vivid concrete expression in the mythological language about Jesus as the Son of God 'who for us men and for our salvation came down from the heavens, and was made flesh of the Holy Spirit and the Virgin Mary, and became man, and was crucified for us under Pontius Pilate, and suffered and was buried, and rose again on the third day according to the Scriptures, and ascended into the heavens and sitteth on the right hand of the Father, and cometh again with glory to judge the living and the dead, of whose kingdom there shall be no end' (the 'Nicene' creed).

IV

For more than a thousand years the symbols of Jesus as Son of God, God the Son, God incarnate, Logos made flesh, served their purpose well. Within the life of the Church they have been for countless people effective expressions of devotion to Jesus as Lord. It did not matter very much that they had quickly come to be understood by the Christian mind not as symbols but as components in literal statements. This was probably inevitable, and was of a piece with the literal interpretation of the Bible in the same period. From a twentieth-century point of view this use of the Bible was always mistaken; but nevertheless it probably did comparatively little harm so long as it was not in conflict with growing human knowledge. However, beginning in the seventeenth and culminating in the nineteenth century such conflicts did develop, and the literalistic interpreters of the scriptures were led into the false position of denying first what astronomy and then what palaeontology and evolutionary biology were revealing. Today as we look back we see the inability of churchmen in the past to accept scientific knowledge as ultimately God-given, and their refusal to be prompted by it to a larger and more adequate understanding of the Bible, as deeply damaging to the Christian cause. Something rather similar, many of us are now beginning to realise, applies to the literalistic interpretation of the essentially poetic and symbolic language of our devotion to Jesus. For understood literally the Son of God, God the Son, God-incarnate language implies that God can be adequately known and responded to *only* through Jesus; and the whole religious life of mankind, beyond the stream of Judaic–Christian faith, is thus by implication excluded as lying outside the sphere of salvation. This implication did little positive harm so long as Christendom was a largely autonomous civilisation with only relatively marginal interaction with the rest of mankind. But with the clash between the Christian and Muslim worlds, and then on an ever-broadening front with European colonisation throughout the earth, the literal understanding of the mythological language of Christian discipleship has had a divisive effect upon the relations between that minority of human beings who live within the borders of the Christian tradition and that majority who live outside it and within other streams of religious life.

Transposed into the theological terms, the problem which has

come to the surface in the encounter of Christianity with the other
world religions is this: if Jesus was literally God incarnate, and if it
is by his death alone that man can be saved, and by their response
to him alone that they can appropriate that salvation, then the only
doorway to eternal life is Christian faith. It would follow from this
that the large majority of the human race so far have not been
saved. But is it credible that the loving God and Father of all men
has decreed that only those born within one particular thread of
human history shall be saved? Is not such an idea excessively
parochial, presenting God in effect as the tribal deity of the
predominantly Christian West? And so theologians have recently
been developing a mass of small print to the old theology,
providing that devout men of other faiths may be Christians
without knowing it, or may be anonymous Christians, or may
belong to the invisible Church, or may have implicit faith and
receive baptism by desire, and so on. These rather artificial theories
are all attempts to square an inadequate theology with the facts of
God's world. They are thoroughly well-intentioned and are to be
welcomed as such. But in the end they are an anachronistic
clinging to the husk of the old doctrine after its substance has
crumbled.

It seems clear that we are being called today to attain a global
religious vision which is aware of the unity of all mankind before
God and which at the same time makes sense of the diversity of
God's ways within the various streams of human life. On the one
hand, we must affirm God's equal love for all men and not only for
Christians and their Old Testament spiritual ancestors. And on the
other hand we must acknowledge that a single revelation to the
whole earth has never in the past been possible, given the facts of
geography and technology, and that the self-disclosure of the
divine, working through human freedom within the actual conditions of world history, was bound to take varying forms. We must
thus be willing to see God at work within the total religious life of
mankind, challenging men in their state of 'natural religion', with
all its crudities and cruelties, by the tremendous revelatory moments which lie at the basis of the great world faiths; and we must
come to see Christianity within this pluralistic setting. There is no
space here to develop a theology of religions along these lines,
taking account of the many problems which arise for such an
approach; but I have attempted to do this in *God and the Universe of
Faiths*[8] and can refer the reader to that attempt. I suggest that we

have in the end to say something like this: all salvation – that is, all creating of human animals into children of God – is the work of God. The different religions have their different names for God acting savingly towards mankind. Christianity has several overlapping names for this – the eternal Logos, the cosmic Christ, the Second Person of the Trinity, God the Son, the Spirit. If, selecting from our Christian language, we call God-acting-towards-mankind the Logos, then we must say that *all* salvation, within all religions, is the work of the Logos and that under their various images and symbols men in different cultures and faiths may encounter the Logos and find salvation. But what we cannot say is that all who are saved are saved solely and exclusively by Jesus of Nazareth. The life of Jesus was one point at which the Logos – that is, God-in-relation-to-man – has acted; and it is the only point that savingly concerns the Christian; but we are not called upon nor are we entitled to make the negative assertion that the Logos has not acted and is not acting anywhere else in human life. On the contrary, we should gladly acknowledge that Ultimate Reality has affected human consciousness for its liberation or 'salvation' in various ways within the Indian, the Semitic, the Chinese, the African . . . forms of life.

Finally, should *our* revelation of the Logos, namely in the life of Jesus, be made available to all mankind? Yes, of course; and so also should other particular revelations of the Logos at work in human life – in the Hebrew prophets, in the Buddha, in the Upanishads and the *Bhagavad Gita*, in the Qur'ān, and so on. The specifically Christian gift to the world is that men should come to know Jesus and take him into their religious life – not to displace but to deepen and enlarge the relationship with God to which they have already come within their own tradition. And we too, in turn, can be spiritually enriched by God's gifts mediated through other faiths. For we must not think of the religions as monolithic entities each with its own unchanging character. They are complex streams of human life, continuously changing, though in some periods so slowly that the change is barely perceptible and in other periods so fast that recognisable continuity is endangered. Thus Christianity seemed virtually static through the long medieval centuries but today seems to be in bewildering flux; and the oriental religions are now emerging from the tranquil flow of their own 'medieval' periods to enter the turbulent rapids of scientific, technological and cultural revolution. Further, the religions are now meeting one another in a new way as parts of the one world of our common humanity. They are for the first time encountering each other peacefully, as variations within the global human consciousness which is emerging through the increasingly complex network of modern communications. In this novel situation they will inevitably exert a growing influence upon one another, both by the attraction of elements which each finds to be good in the others and by a centripetal tendency to draw together in face of increasing secularisation throughout the world. We may therefore expect a cumulative sharing of religious insights and ideals, such as has already occurred in the influence of the Christian 'social gospel' within Hinduism and in the influence on the West of the Hindu and Buddhist traditions of spiritual meditation. This interpermeation of positive values has now, for all practical purposes, replaced the attempt at the mass conversion of the adherents of one world religion to another. In the case of Christianity the older missionary policy of the conversion of the world, proceeding largely along the highways opened up by Western arms and commerce, can now be seen to have failed; and any hope of renewing it has been ruled out by the ending of the era of Western political and religious imperialism. From now onwards the Christian mission in lands dominated by any of the other world religions must rest upon the positive attraction of the person and teaching of Jesus and of the life lived in discipleship to him, and not upon the power of an alien culture seeking to impose itself upon politically vulnerable or economically less developed peoples. Further, we have to present Jesus and the Christian life in a way compatible with our new recognition of the validity of the other great world faiths as being also, at their best, ways of salvation. We must therefore not insist upon Jesus being always portrayed within the interpretative framework built around him by centuries of Western thought. The Christian gift to the world is Jesus, the 'largely unknown man of Nazareth' whose impact has nevertheless created such powerful images in men's minds that he is for millions the way, the truth and the life. Within the varying cultures and changing circumstances of history he can still create fresh images and can become men's Lord and liberator in yet further ways. For in the different streams of human life a faith-response to Jesus can express itself in a wide variety of religious myths; and our own Western mythology of the incarnation of the Son of God must not be allowed to function as an iron mask from within which alone Jesus is allowed to speak to mankind. The Jesus who is for the world is not the property of the human organisation called the Christian Church, nor is he to be confined within its theoretical constructions.

We see in the life and thought of Gandhi, the father of modern India, a paradigm of the immense impact which Jesus and his teaching can have upon the adherents of another faith. Gandhi has been widely recognised as one of the great saints of the twentieth century; and he freely acknowledged the deep influence of Jesus upon him. A devoted life-time missionary in India, E. Stanley Jones, said of Gandhi that 'a little man, who fought a system in the framework of which I stand, has taught me more of the Spirit of Christ than perhaps any other man in East or West', and described him as 'more christianised than most Christians'.[9] The New Testament, Gandhi said, gave him 'comfort and boundless joy'.[10] Again, 'Though I cannot claim to be a Christian in the sectarian sense, the example of Jesus' suffering is a factor in the composition of my undying faith in non-violence which rules all my actions. . . . Jesus lived and died in vain if he did not teach us to regulate the whole of life by the eternal Law of Love.'[11] Nevertheless he remained a Hindu. He could never accept the orthodox Christian theology: 'It was more than I could believe,' he said, 'that Jesus was the only incarnate son of God and that only he who believed in him would have everlasting life. If God could have sons, all of us were His sons.'[12] Thus Gandhi was influenced by Jesus, not as he appears on the stained-glass window of the Nicene theology, but as he presents himself through the New Testament and above all in the Sermon on the Mount:

> What, then, does Jesus mean to me? To me, He was one of the greatest teachers humanity has ever had. To His believers, He was God's only begotten son. Could the fact that I do or do not accept this belief make Jesus have any more or less influence in my life? Is all the grandeur of His teaching and of His doctrine to be forbidden to me? I cannot believe so. To me it implies a spiritual birth. My interpretation, in other words, is that in Jesus' own life is the key to His nearness to God; that He expressed, as no other could, the spirit and will of God. It is in this sense that I see Him and recognise Him as the son of God.[13]

The further influence of Jesus, then, as we may hopefully foresee it, will be both inside and outside the Church. Within, the

traditional liturgical language will no doubt continue to be used,
Jesus being spoken of as the Son of God, God the Son, the Logos
incarnate, the God–man. But there will be a growing awareness of
the mythological character of this language, as the hyperbole of the
heart, most naturally at home in hymns and anthems and oratorios
and other artistic expressions of the poetry of devotion. Christianity will – we may hope – outgrow its theological fundamentalism,
its literal interpretation of the idea of incarnation, as it has largely
outgrown its biblical fundamentalism. As the stories (for example)
of the six-day creation of the world and the fall of Adam and Eve
after their temptation by the serpent in the Garden of Eden are
now seen as profound religious myths, illuminating our human
situation, so the story of the Son of God coming down from heaven
and being born as a human baby will be seen as a mythological
expression of the immense significance of our encounter with one
in whose presence we have found ourselves to be at the same time
in the presence of God. The outgrowing of biblical fundamentalism
was a slow and painful process which has unhappily left the
Church scarred and divided, and we are still living amidst the
tension between a liberal and a continuing fundamentalist Christianity. The Church has not yet found a way to unite the indispensable intellectual and moral insights of the one with the emotional
fervour and commitment of the other. Will the outgrowing of
theological fundamentalism be any easier and less divisive? If not,
the future influence of Jesus may well lie more outside the Church
than within it, as a 'man of universal destiny' whose teaching and
example will become the common property of the world, entering
variously into all its major religious and also secular traditions. I
can claim no prophetic insight into the ways in which God is going
to enter our human future. But all who believe in the reality of God
must believe that he will in his own ways be with mankind in the
centuries to come; and all who have been deeply impressed and
changed by the life and words of Jesus will confidently expect this
central figure of the gospels to continue to play his part in God's
dealings with us.

NOTES

1.	Trevor Ling, *A History of Religion East and West* (London: Macmillan,
	1968) p. 87.

2. B. H. Streeter, *The Buddha and the Christ* (London: Macmillan, 1932) p. 83.
3. Irenaeus, *Adversus Haereses*, ii. xxxi. 2.
4. G. B. Caird, 'The Christological Basis of Christian Hope', *The Christian Hope* (London: SPCK, 1970) p. 10.
5. R. H. Fuller, *The Foundations of New Testament Christology* (London: Fontana, 1969) p. 34.
6. S. Mowinckel, *He That Cometh*, tr. G. W. Anderson (Oxford: Basil Blackwell, 1959) p. 67.
7. Ibid., p. 78.
8. John Hick, *God and the Universe of Faiths* (London: Macmillan, 1973; New York: St Martin's Press, 1974; Fontana edn 1977).
9. E. Stanley Jones, *Mahatma Gandhi: An Interpretation* (London: Hodder and Stoughton, 1948) pp. 12 and 76.
10. M. K. Gandhi, *What Jesus Means to Me*, comp. R. K. Prabhu (Ahmedabad: Navajiran Publishing House, 1959) p. 4.
11. Quoted in S. K. George, *Gandhi's Challenge to Christianity* (Ahmedabad: Navajiran Publishing House, 1960) p. 7.
12. M. K. Gandhi, *An Autobiography: The Story of my Experiments with Truth* (1940; Boston, Mass.: Beacon Press, 1957) p. 136.
13. Gandhi, *What Jesus Means to Me*, pp. 9–10.

8

Eschatological Verification
Reconsidered

I

The world in which we find ourselves is religiously ambiguous. It is possible for different people (as also for the same person at different times) to experience it both religiously and non-religiously; and to hold beliefs which arise from and feed into each of these ways of experiencing. A religious person may report that in moments of prayer he or she is conscious of existing in the unseen presence of God, and is aware – sometimes at least – that his/her whole life and the entire history of the world is taking place within the ambience of the divine purpose. But on the other hand the majority of people in our modern world do not participate in that form of experience and are instead conscious of their own and others' lives as purely natural phenomena, so that their own experience leads them at least implicitly to reject the idea of a transcendent divine presence and purpose. If they are philosophically minded, they may well think that the believer's talk is the expression of what Richard Hare has called a *blik*, a way of feeling and thinking about the world which expresses itself in pseudo-assertions, pseudo because they are neither verifiable nor falsifiable and are therefore factually empty.[1] The religious person speaks of God as a living reality in whose presence we are, and of a divine purpose which gives ultimate meaning to our lives. But is not the world the same whether or not we suppose it to exist in God's presence; and is not the course of history the same whether or not we describe it as fulfilling God's purposes? Is not the religious description thus merely a gratuitous embellishment, a logical fifth wheel, an optional language-game which may assuage some psychological need of the speaker but which involves no claims of substance concerning the objective nature or structure of the universe? Must not the central religious use of language then be accounted a non-cognitive use, whose function is not to assert alleged facts but to express a speaker's, or a community of speakers', emotions within the framework of a factually content-less *blik*, 'slant' or 'onlook'?

The logical positivists of the 1920s and 1930s expressed this by saying that since such sentences as 'God loves mankind' are neither analytically true nor empirically verifiable they must be cognitively meaningless. They asked how God-talk could be verified; and most of the responses which they received from the theological world amounted to a repudiation of the question rather than an answer to it. Later, Antony Flew in the 'Theology and Falsification' debate asked whether such sentences as 'God loves mankind' are falsifiable – that is, such that if they are false they could ever be discovered to be so.[2] What conceivable state of affairs, he asked, would show that there is no loving God? He was given two kinds of answer. One was the non-cognitivist response, embodied in Hare's concept of the *blik* and in R. B. Braithwaite's account of religious belief as a disguised expression of intention to live according to a certain ethical pattern.[3] Such answers share the assumption that religious beliefs are cognitively empty. The other response was the cognitivist answer formulated in different ways by Basil Mitchell[4] and Ian Crombie.[5] These both point implicitly or explicitly, as it seems to me, to some notion of eschatological verification for their further development; and it is this notion that I want to discuss here.

The broad idea is that the theistic conception of the universe, and of what is going on in human life, *is* capable of experiential verification, although according to Christianity the verifying situation lies in the final fulfilment of God's purpose for us beyond this present life. Perhaps I may be allowed to repeat here a parable in which I have previously embodied this general idea, before going on to its more precise elaboration.

Two people are travelling together along a road. One of them believes that it leads to a Celestial City, the other that it leads nowhere; but since it is the only road there is, both must travel it. Neither has been this way before, and therefore neither is able to say what they will find around each next corner. During their journey they meet both with moments of refreshment and delight, and with moments of hardship and danger. All the time one of them thinks of her journey as a pilgrimage to the Celestial City, and interprets the pleasant parts as encouragements, and the

obstacles as trials of her purpose and lessons in endurance,
prepared by the sovereign of that city and designed to make of her
a worthy citizen of the place when at last she arrives there. The
other, however, believes none of this and sees their journey as an
unavoidable and aimless ramble. Since he has no choice in the
matter, he enjoys the good and endures the bad. But for him there
is no Celestial City to be reached, no all-encompassing purpose
ordaining their journey; only the road itself and the luck of the
road in good weather and in bad.

During the course of the journey the issue between them is not
an experimental one. They entertain different expectations not
about the coming details of the road, but about its ultimate
destination. And yet when they do turn the last corner it will be
apparent that one of them has been right all the time and the other
wrong. Thus although the issue between them has not been
experimental it has nevertheless from the start been a real issue.
They have not merely felt differently about the road; for one was
feeling appropriately and the other inappropriately in relation to
the actual state of affairs. Their opposed interpretations of the road
constituted genuinely rival assertions, though assertions whose
assertion-status has the peculiar characteristic of being guaranteed
retrospectively by a future crux.[6]

There has been a good deal of discussion of this notion since it
was first explicitly formulated in my *Faith and Knowledge* (1st edn) in
1957, and in an article, 'Theology and Verification', in 1960; and I
want on this second time round to take account of this discussion.[7]
I shall try to profit from those criticisms and suggestions which
seem to me to be wholly or partly valid by restating the theory in a
more acceptable way. For, whilst the basic conception seems to me
to be sound, and indeed unavoidable, yet various clarifications,
modifications and developments can I think usefully be made.
Accordingly the present paper supplements rather than supplants
the earlier one.

II

First a look back to the older discussions of verification. The
attempts by the logical positivists to achieve a fully satisfactory
verifiability criterion of factual meaningfulness never succeeded,
and the quest for this elusive formula petered out at least a

generation ago. But this does not mean that the insight or intuition which motivated the quest was illusory. On the contrary, the central core of the positivist contention seems undeniable. For it is simply the basic empiricist position that to exist, or to be the case, is to make a difference. That is to say, to assert that *x* exists is to assert an in-principle-observable difference between the actual universe and a possible universe which differs from it only in that the latter does not include *x*. That there is such a difference constitutes '*x* exists' a factual statement; and to observe those features of the universe which differentiate it from a possible *x*-less universe is to verify '*x* exists'. And, likewise, to assert *p* is to assert an in-principle-observable difference between the actual universe and a possible universe which differs from it only in that in the latter it is true that not-*p*. That there is such a difference constitutes *p* a factual statement; and to observe the features of the universe which differentiate it from a possible universe in which not-*p* is to verify *p*. Accordingly to say that *x* exists or that *p* is the case, but to deny that the existence of *x* or the truth of *p* makes any such in-principle-experienceable difference, would be to speak in a way that is pointless or meaningless. This, I would suggest, is the basic and non-controversial principle for which the logical positivists were contending. They contended for it within the framework of their own faith that established theories in the physical sciences are normative for all knowledge; and accordingly they assumed that the experienceable difference made by the truth of *p* must always be a difference of the kind that is registered in sense data.[8] Such a restrictive assumption was merely an *a priori* dogma. But, discounting this dogma, it is a perfectly good question to ask one who asserts that God exists, or that a divine purpose is being fulfilled in human life, what in-principle-experiencable difference it makes *whether* God exists or *whether* a divine purpose is being fulfilled in human life. We should therefore not allow ourselves to be tempted by Alvin Plantinga's short way with Flew's falsifiability challenge:

> In the light of ... the fact that it seems impossible to state the verifiability criterion, the question becomes acute: how *are* we to understand Flew's challenge? What exactly is he requiring of theological statements? Is he chiding the theist for ignoring some version of the verifiability criterion? If so, which version? Until these questions are answered it is impossible to determine whether his challenge is legitimate or even what the challenge *is*.

If the notion of verifiability cannot so much as be explained, if we cannot so much as say what it is for a statement to be empirically verifiable, then we scarcely need worry about whether religious statements are or are not verifiable.[9]

Again, George Mavrodes, emphasising that no satisfactory verification criterion has yet been formulated, concludes that the attempt to point to possible situations which would confirm the truth of theism is misconceived.[10] These refusals to face the verifiability/ falsifiability challenge strike me as examples of an unhelpful philosophical pedantry. For one does not have to have achieved a definitive formulation of a verifiability or falsifiability criterion to see that a supposedly declarative statement is pointless if it fails to claim that the facts of the universe are in some respect thus and not otherwise; and also that it is important for the theologian to be able to show that the central propositions with which he is concerned are *not* empty or pointless. Herbert Feigl's modest suggestion of 'confirmability-in-principle' as 'at least a *necessary* condition of factual meaningfulness', is surely entirely acceptable; and as Feigl himself pointed out, with particular reference to theology, it excludes only 'doctrines which are immune against tests of even the most indirect sort'.[11] I do not think that the theologian need be afraid of this basic principle of logical empiricism. Nor, incidentally, should he be afraid of the idea of 'testing' his beliefs: for testing, in this context, is not the sin of 'putting God to the test' but the true piety which waits patiently for the Lord to vindicate his faithful on the last day.

III

The idea of 'making an experienceable difference' covers the scale from complete and conclusive verifiability down through the various degrees of confirmability. At the top of this scale is the situation in which rational doubt as to the truth of p is entirely excluded; or (making explicit the role of the observer) in which doubt is entirely excluded from a rational observer's mind. Let us call this the point of cognitive conclusiveness. The nature of the doubt-excluding situation will of course differ according to the content of the proposition in question. That situation may be a simple or a complex state of affairs, depending upon the extent to which the difference made by the truth of p is specifically or variably defined, and the extent to which this difference is localised, or diffused in space or time or both. If the difference is sufficiently specific and local it will be capable of being observed in a single act of perception, which will then conclusively verify p. Let us call the characteristic of being capable of being verified by a single observation simple (as distinguished from complex) verifiability. For example, the difference made by there being a table in the next room can be registered by a single visual observation (perhaps supported by touching) so that 'There is a table in the next room' is close to exhibiting maximally simple verifiability. If on the other hand the difference made by the truth of p is variable in nature and/or diffused in extent, p may have to be confirmed by many cumulative observations. For example, 'John Smith is an honest man' cannot be verified by a single observation, for the experienceable difference made by his being an honest man is spread out over time and is also variable in the forms that it can take. The same is true of the theory of evolution, or indeed any large-scale scientific hypothesis. Let us describe these as having complex verifiability. In such cases there may be increasing confirmation until the point of cognitive conclusiveness is reached. This is the point at which rational doubt as to the truth of p has been entirely excluded and at which the concepts of confirmation and verification coincide.

This distinction between simple and complex verifiability enables us to avoid a wrong approach to the question of the verification of theistic statements. We should not ask, what single observation would verify them, but what development of our experience would progressively confirm them to the point at which there is no longer any room for rational doubt? For the existence of God is not a localised and therefore finite fact, comparable in this respect with the existence of a table in the next room, which can be verified by going into the next room and seeing and touching the table; and falsified by finding that there is no table there. The reality of God cannot be verified, analogously, by going to heaven and simply observing him there. For God is not one object or person among others in the heavenly world. As I pointed out in the 1960 article,

God is described in Christian theology in terms of various absolute qualities, such as omnipotence, omnipresence, perfect goodness, infinite love, which cannot as such be observed by us, as can their finite analogues, limited power, local presence, finite goodness, and human love. One can recognise that a being whom one 'encounters' has a given finite degree of power, but how does one recognise that he has *un*limited power? How does one observe that an encountered being is *omni*potent? How does one perceive that his goodness and love, which one can perhaps see to exceed any human goodness and love, are actually infinite? Such qualities cannot be given in human experience.[12]

I would therefore suggest that the proposition whose eschatological verification we should consider is not 'God exists'; for this treats divine existence as an isolable and bounded fact. What we are seeking to verify is the truth of the theistic interpretation of the process of the universe, and this *verificandum* is embodied in a more complex proposition such as 'The theistic account of the character of the universe, and of what is taking place in its history, is true.' This proposition does not of course, and is not designed to, by-pass the question of the existence of God; for God must be referred to in giving an account of the meaning of 'theistic' in this context. God will appear in this account as the supreme being who controls the process of the universe and who is bringing it to the end which God intends. But the infinite nature of God's attributes – the infinity of God's power, knowledge, love, and so on – are not involved in this account. When the theist speaks, for example, of the power by which God rules the course of the universe, he or she believes, and is assuming, the infinity of that power, but this infinity is not in fact exercised in relation to the finite realm which is the field of human cognition. The degree of divine power exercised in relation to the universe as it is experienced and to be experienced by human beings is a power sufficient to fulfil God's purposes for the creation; but it is not, strictly speaking, infinite power. And the same principle applies to the other divine attributes. The Deity is believed by Christians to be infinite; and we must inquire presently concerning the grounds of this belief. But God's alleged impingement upon the creation, raising the question whether its character as a divinely ruled process might be capable of confirmation or verification, is necessarily a finite impingement: power exerted non-destructively upon a finite object must itself be finite.

Thus an eschatological situation which is to verify the truth of the theistic account of the universe and of what is taking place in it will not have the impossible task of verifying the infinite nature of God's attributes, but the more limited task of confirming to the full that the history of the universe has led to an end-state in which the postulated divine purpose for humanity can be seen to be fulfilled. The assertion that is to be verified is thus an assertion about what is going on in human existence and its environment. The theistic claim is that what is going on is the gradual creation of perfected finite persons who are eventually to live in unimpeded communion with God. The religious ambivalence of the present world, including its characteristic mixture of good and evil, sets us at an epistemic distance from God which leaves room for further confirmation, whilst at the same time making possible a free response of faith to God. But – it is claimed – as we approach perfection we will become increasingly open to and conscious of God in environments in which the ambiguities of this life will have been left behind and in which the divine goodness and love will be increasingly evident. Thus the movement towards the end-state involves a gradual transformation of the individual in the course of that person's transition – no doubt through various intermediate environments – to the final unambiguous situation which is traditionally symbolised as heaven. This situation will be religiously unambiguous in the following sense: in the present world men and women believe in the reality of God on the basis of a religious experience which is a (putative) consciousness of living in the divine presence. Some aspects of the world manifestly cohere with and thus support this belief whilst others do not. All that is good, beautiful, creative and uplifting in the world process agrees with and thus far confirms the belief in a good and loving Creator, whilst pain and suffering, wickedness and ugliness are dissonant circumstances which thus far disconfirm that belief. I have argued elsewhere that it is rational for the religious person now, in this life, experiencing the world process with its mixture of good and evil as taking place in the presence and according to the purpose of God, to believe with full subjective certainty in the reality of God.[13] But this does not mean that his or her faith, rational though it is, is not capable of further and fuller confirmation as the creative process increasingly unfolds towards its completion in the eschatological state.[14] In that state one's God-consciousness will be at a maximum. One will be continuously aware of living in the divine presence; and that awareness will no longer be in tension with the circumstances of sin and suffering, ugliness and deprivation, which at present leave room for rational doubt. We are contemplating an experience of progressive sanctification (not, incidentally, embodied in the original parable of the journey) accompanied by an increasingly powerful and pervasive sense of existing in the presence of an invisible transcendent power who knows us, who loves us, and who can be seen to be drawing us towards a perfection in which we are to dwell in joyous communion with that transcendent reality. I suggest that this would constitute mounting and increasingly massive confirmation of theistic faith; and that the completion of the process in the endless life of the 'Kingdom of God' would constitute a situation of cognitive conclusiveness in which there would be no room for rational doubt concerning the truth of the religious understanding of human existence, or concerning the reality of the divine being, awareness of whom is the central characteristic of the eschatological situation.

It will be of interest to some at least that the last book of the Bible contains a picture of the eschaton which largely accords with this hypothesis. The life of heaven is to be the life of a community inhabiting a city. God is not a visible object there, but nevertheless will be intimately present to the community of the redeemed; for 'Behold, the dwelling of God is with men. He will dwell with them, and they shall be his people' (Revelation 21:3). The new heaven and earth are to be free from evil; for God 'will wipe away every tear from their eyes, and death shall be no more, neither shall there be mourning nor crying nor pain any more' (v. 4). Men and women will be so totally conscious of God that there will be no need of a temple. They will be living all the time in the temple of the divine presence: for the city's 'temple is the Lord God Almighty and the Lamb' (v. 22).

IV

But, it may perhaps be objected, in this eschatological situation God will still be no more available to human observation, or God's existence verified, than now. Human beings will still be expected to believe in a God whom they cannot see. How then can theistic belief be said to have been verified? The answer is, I think, implicit in what has already been proposed. The redeemed (whom I assume ultimately to include everyone – though this is of course a theological rather than a philosophical opinion) will have experienced in this world, or will have come to experience at some stage between this world and the final heavenly state, what they take to be an awareness of existing in the presence of God and of being freely led within the divine providence towards the fulfilment of their human potentialities in the community of humanity perfected. In experiencing their life in this way, and in believing in accordance with their experience, they believe in the reality of God and in the process of the universe as God's creative work. And this belief is progressively confirmed and then verified in the experience of moving towards and then participating in the eschatological situation of a perfected human community in which the consciousness of God's presence is universally shared.

But, let us now ask, might not a group of hard-boiled atheists arrive in the eschatological world and persist in holding to a naturalistic interpretation of all that is going on? And does not this possibility show that what I have been calling eschatological verification should really be called eschatological faith? There are two replies to be made to this suggestion. First, there is indeed a sense in which all cognition, involving as it does an element of interpretation, can be said to involve faith. The idea of verification trades upon the difference between interpretation in circumstances which leave room for rational doubt as to the truth of the interpretation, and interpretation in circumstances which leave no such room. And the notion of heaven is that of a situation which excludes rational doubt concerning the truth of the theistic interpretation. But heavenly cognition, like earthly cognition, will still involve the element of interpretation which I for one wish to identify with faith. However, second, the picture of a squad of atheists arriving in heaven is precluded by the hypothesis that we reach the eschatological world by fulfilling the God-given potentialities of our nature, including the potentiality for full God-consciousness. There can therefore be no atheists in heaven. If the theological opinion is correct that all people without exception will eventually attain to full God-consciousness, then the reason why there are no atheists in heaven will be that in the end there are no atheists: every former atheist will in the course of his or her personal history in the realms between this and the heavenly world have become a theist. If on the other hand this universalist opinion is mistaken, then the reason why there are no atheists in heaven will be that so long as one remains an atheist one is not in heaven; for heaven is the final state of perfect communion between God and God's creatures.

But, granting that all the citizens of heaven will be continuously conscious of existing in God's presence, can we not nevertheless still ask whether they may not be in a state of delusion? They may have what they take to be a vivid awareness of the divine presence; and it may be entirely reasonable for them, on the basis of this experience, to believe unquestioningly in the reality of God and to go on for ever experiencing in this way and being utterly convinced of God's reality. But may they not nevertheless be being eternally hallucinated? Is not this still a logical possibility; and must we not therefore conclude that the question of God's existence will still not have been definitively settled?

Here we encounter the old and much discussed notion of unappeasable scepticism. For perpetual scepticism in relation to an eternally coherent theistic experience of heaven would raise the same issues as perpetual scepticism in relation to the reality of our present physical environment and of other persons. Although the question is highly debatable, I accept solipsism as a logical possibility. It seems to me logically possible that the world in which I am living, and the other people with whom I suppose myself to be jointly inhabiting it, exist only as modifications of my own consciousness, and that I am the only consciousness there is. In that case my continued coherent experience of an external environment and of other people existing independently of myself fail to constitute contrary evidence, since the 'evidence' itself exists only in my own mind. But, together with many philosophers today, whilst acknowledging the logical possibility of such unappeasable scepticism I simply reject it as insane. And I would suggest that it would be at least equally insane to invoke this kind of scepticism in relation to an endlessly continued experience of heaven.

But what about the infinite divine attributes, consideration of which was postponed earlier in the discussion? I have acknowledged that even in an eschatological life lived in unimpeded consciousness of God's presence we cannot expect to experience the infinity of the divine being. This is not to say that we shall experience the presence of a finite deity, but that we shall experience the presence of a deity who indefinitely exceeds ourselves, but whose infinity can nevertheless not be given within the confines of human experience. That God is infinite, and has the divine properties in an infinite mode, is a conclusion of natural theology. I think there are good arguments in natural theology for this conclusion, though it would be too large an extension of the discussion to examine them here. The point at the moment is that the reality of God, defined as infinite, is not verifiable within human experience, although the reality of an indefinitely great God, whom we may believe on the basis of philosophical reasoning to be infinite, is in principle confirmable to the point of cognitive conclusiveness.

There is however also available to us the answer offered in my 1960 article, namely that the infinity of God is a revealed truth, believed on the authority of a teacher, namely Christ, whose veracity will be confirmed in the eschatological situation:

> Our beliefs about God's infinite being are not capable of observational verification, being beyond the scope of human experience, but they are susceptible of indirect verification by the removal of rational doubt concerning the authority of Christ. An experience of the reign of the Son in the Kingdom of the Father would confirm that authority, and therewith, indirectly, the validity of Jesus' teaching concerning the character of God in his infinite transcendent nature.[15]

However I now see two difficulties in this response. One arises from a concern not to restrict the discussion within exclusively Christian boundaries. No longer thinking of Jesus as the one and only revelation of God, I do not want to treat his teaching as our sole source of knowledge of God's nature. But another related difficulty is that it is far from clear that Jesus did in fact teach that God is infinite. He lived in close and intimate awareness of God, dwelling consciously in the heavenly Father's unseen presence and giving himself wholly to serve the divine purposes on earth; but we do not seem to have any evidence that he had occasion to raise the question of God's infinity. In general, the experience of God as a personal presence to whom one speaks in prayer is an experience in the finite mode; and, if the thought of God as infinite is associated with it, this has been imported from some other source – probably the natural theology embodied in one's religious tradition.

One can perhaps best express this theologically by saying that God as infinite transcends existence: God *is* but does not exist. But God as related to the world – in Pascal's phrase 'the God of

Abraham, of Isaac and of Jacob' in distinction from the God of the philosophers – does exist.

V

The question has been raised whether the experiences which are supposed to verify theism are theistic or non-theistic experiences.[16] On the one hand, it is said, if the supposedly verifying experiences are non-theistic ones – such as hearing a voice – they can never verify a religious belief; for no number of non-theological facts can add up to a theological fact. But if on the other hand the verifying experiences are religious experiences – such as hearing *God's* voice – then the argument runs in a circle; for we still need a further verification that the voice is indeed God's voice. Any proffered verification of this will consist either in a non-theistic experience (which, being non-theistic, can never do the job) or in a theistic experience – which will again require a further verification of *its* theistic character; and then the same question will arise about that experience, and so on *ad infinitum*.

But rather than worry about how to get out of this predicament we can avoid getting into it. We should begin, I would suggest, where the present essay began: with the fact that some people experience the events of their lives and of the world theistically – that is, in terms of the concept of God.[17] All conscious experience of our environment is in terms of the concepts by which we apprehend (or of course misapprehend) objects and situations as having this or that character or meaning. In other words, all experiencing is, as I have argued elsewhere,[18] experiencing-as. The (theistically) religious mind experiences life as being lived in the unseen presence of God and within the sphere of an on-going divine purpose. That some people have experienced and that some do experience in this way is an historical fact: the Bible is largely an anthology of first-hand reports of this mode of experiencing-as, and there are contemporary believers who experience in essentially the same way. The question, then, is whether the theistic conviction which, as I have said above, arises from and feeds into this way of experiencing, will be confirmed by the individual's further, including *post mortem*, experiences; and whether it will be confirmed to the point of cognitive conclusiveness which we call verification. The eschatological religions, at least, claim that this will in fact happen; and I have been arguing that this claim gives factual-assertion status to their systems of beliefs.

It should be added that in principle such verification could occur in *this* world also. The world could conceivably change into a 'heaven on earth' in which perfect human beings live in a full God-consciousness unimpeded by any jarring circumstances. But although there have been strands of teaching predicting something like this, both in messianic Judaism and in millenarian Christianity, yet the larger tradition of the theistic religions is the one which the notion of eschatological verification brings to bear upon the logic of religious language. It should perhaps be stressed again that 'eschatological verification' is not a desperate *ad hoc* device invented to meet a sceptical challenge but draws out that aspect of the traditional theistic system of belief which establishes that system as a complex factual assertion.

Some have seen it as a fatal flaw in the theory of eschatological verification that it rests upon belief in continued human existence after death. For this belief seems to them a fantastic fairy-tale, not to be taken seriously. Here I can only say that the Christian understanding of the universe includes belief in life after death as an indispensable component and that if that belief could be proved to be false Christian theism (though not every kind of theism) would thereby be falsified. For the 'life everlasting' is in my view one of the essential claims by which Christian theism stands or falls; and that there are such cruxes is of course the nub of the theistic response to the verification/falsification challenge.

It is in relation to this idea of human survival of death that the verifiability/falsifiability asymmetry noted in my 1960 article arises. That is to say, the prediction that I shall, after my bodily death, be conscious, continue to undergo new experiences, and have memories of my death and of my life before and after it, is a prediction which will be conclusively verified in my own experience if it is true but which will not be falsified in my own experience if it is false. However it does not follow from this that theism is necessarily unfalsifiable-if-false. This depends upon the actual nature of the universe, given that theism is false. If materialist naturalism is true and human beings perish totally at death, then theism would not be falsifiable – unless, again, it could be *proved* that we perish totally at death, in which case this proof would at the same time serve to falsify theism. But, as another possibility, the facts of the universe could be such that theism will

eventually be definitively seen to be false – as has been argued by
Gregory Kavka in terms of the obverse of the kind of *post mortem*
situation which would verify theism, namely a universe unending-
ly dominated by an evil power.[19] There is, then, the following
partial asymmetry between the verifiability and the falsifiability of
Christian theism. If Christian theism is true, its truth will be
confirmed within future human experience to the point of cognitive conclusiveness; but if it is false its falsity may or may not be
conclusively established in future human experience, depending
upon the actual non-theistic character of the universe.

POSTSCRIPT

What is the relation between religious pluralism and this concept
of eschatological verification?

I have presented the idea here in theistic, and indeed Christian,
terms. But it could also be stated in Jewish, in Muslim or in theistic
Hindu terms. Again, it could be presented in non-theistic terms,
depicting the end state as conceived in advaitic Hindu or in the
various schools of Buddhist thought. From the point of view of the
theory of the humanly conditioned *personae* and *impersonae* of the
Real outlined in Chapter 10, and of the eschatological theory
outlined in Chapter 9, it seems likely that the different expectations
cherished within the different traditions will ultimately turn out to
be partly correct and partly incorrect. It could be that in a
mind-dependent *bardo* phase immediately after death (see below,
pp. 157–8) these expectations will be fulfilled in the experience of
believers – Christians, Hindus, Muslims, and so on each encountering what their different traditions have taught them to
anticipate. But as they advance beyond that phase and the process
of ego-transcendence continues, their pictures of the universe, and
their expectations concerning its future development, will themselves develop, becoming gradually more adequate to the reality.
And within the long span of this development it may well be that
the final state will prove to be beyond the horizon of our present
powers of imagination.

Thus the long-term development of the universe and of human
existence as part of it may be other than any of our earthly religious
traditions anticipate. From this more comprehensive point of view
the question is not whether the truth of a Christian, or a Muslim, or

a Hindu, or a Buddhist interpretation is ultimately verifiable within human experience but whether the truth of a religious as opposed to a naturalistic interpretation of the universe is ultimately capable of being verified. The answer is 'Yes.' For, if there is a further development of human experience, beyond this present life, which is incompatible with a naturalistic understanding of the universe but which develops and enlarges our various religious understandings of it, this will constitute verification of the religious side of the religious/naturalistic opposition.

And so the principle of eschatological verification is highly relevant to the question of the basically factual character of religious understandings of the universe, and to the ultimate resolution of the debate between religious and naturalist (including atheistic) believers. It is probably not, however, directly relevant to the assessment of the conflicting truth-claims of the various traditions.

NOTES

1. Richard M. Hare, 'Theology and Falsification', in Antony Flew and Alasdair MacIntyre (eds), *New Essays in Philosophical Theology* (London: SCM Press; New York: Macmillan, 1955). Repr. in numerous places.
2. Antony Flew, 'Theology and Falsification', ibid.
3. R. B. Braithwaite, *An Empiricist's View of the Nature of Religious Belief* (Cambridge and New York: Cambridge University Press, 1955). Repr. in numerous places.
4. Basil Mitchell, 'Theology and Falsification', in Flew and MacIntyre, *New Essays in Philosophical Theology*. Cf. Mitchell's *The Justification of Religious Belief* (London: Macmillan; New York: Seabury Press, 1973) ch. 1.
5. Ian Crombie, 'Theology and Falsification', in Flew and MacIntyre, *New Essays in Philosophical Theology*.
6. John Hick, 'Theology and Verification', repr. as Ch. 5 above, pp. 74–5.
7. W. Bean, 'Eschatological Verification: Fortress or Fairyland?', *Methodos*, XVI, no. 62 (1964); William T. Blackstone, *The Problem of Religious Knowledge* (Englewood Cliffs, NJ: Prentice-Hall, 1963) ch. 7; Carl-Reinhold Brakenheilm, *How Philosophy Shapes Theories of Religion: An Analysis of Contemporary Philosophies of Religion with Special Regard to the Thought of John Wilson, John Hick and D. Z. Phillips* (Lund: Gleerup, 1975) ch. 3; William H. Brenner, 'Faith and Experience: A Critical Study of John Hick's Contribution to the Philosophy of Religion' (unpublished doctoral dissertation, University of Virginia, 1970) ch. 4; James I. Campbell, *The Language of Religion* (New York: Bruce,

1971) ch. 4; Edward Cell, *Language, Existence and God* (New York: Abingdon Press, 1971) ch. 8; Stephen T. Davis, 'Theology, Verification, and Falsification', *International Journal for Philosophy of Religion*, VI, no. 1 (1975); Peter Donovan, *Religious Language* (London: Sheldon Press, 1976) ch. 7; D. R. Duff-Forbes, 'Theology and Falsification Again', *Australasian Journal of Theology*, XXXIX (1961); Rem B. Edwards, *Religion and Reason* (New York: Harcourt Brace Jovanovich, 1972) ch. 14; Gregory S. Kavka, 'Eschatological Falsification', *Religious Studies*, XII, no. 2 (1976); Kenneth H. Klein, *Positivism and Christianity: A Study of Theism and Verifiability* (The Hague: Martinus Nijhoff, 1974) ch. 4; George I. Mavrodes, 'God and Verification', *Canadian Journal of Theology*, XIX (1964); James Alfred Martin, *The New Dialogue between Philosophy and Theology* (New York: Seabury Press; London: A. & C. Black, 1966) ch. 3; Basil Mitchell, *The Justification of Religious Belief* (London: Macmillan; New York: Seabury Press, 1973) ch. 1; Kai Nielsen, 'Eschatological Verification', *Canadian Journal of Theology*, IX (1963), repr. in Malcolm L. Diamond and Thomas V. Litzenburg (eds), *The Logic of God: Theology and Verification* (Indianapolis: Bobbs-Merrill, 1975); Kai Nielsen, *Contemporary Critiques of Religion* (London: Macmillan; New York: Herder and Herder, 1971) ch. 4; Terence Penelhum, *Problems of Religious Knowledge* (London: Macmillan; New York: Herder and Herder, 1971) ch. 4, and *Religion and Rationality* (New York: Random House, 1971) ch. 11; H. H. Price, *Belief* (London: George Allen and Unwin; New York: Humanities Press, 1969) ser. II, lecture 10; Paul F. Schmidt, *Religious Knowledge* (Glencoe, NY: The Free Press, 1961) ch. 4; Michael Tooley, 'John Hick and the Concept of Eschatological Verification', *Religious Studies*, XII, no. 2 (1976); Keith E. Yandell, *Basic Issues in the Philosophy of Religion* (Boston, Mass.: Allyn and Bacon, 1971) ch. 6.

8.   In his article 'John Hick and the Concept of Eschatological Verification' (*Religious Studies*, XII), Michael Tooley speaks of 'the verifiability principle' as though there were a single such criterion available to be applied to theology. He seems to be taking his stand somewhere back in the 1930s. From this position he argues that the existence of persons, both human and divine, as 'experientially transcendent entities' is in principle unverifiable and therefore that the theory of eschatological verification fails. He claims that, 'given the verifiability principle, there is a very plausible argument which demonstrates that no factual meaning can be assigned to talk about experientially transcendent entities' (p. 198), whether human or divine. I would agree that a conception of verification which is so restrictive as to exclude statements about human persons will also exclude statements about God. However Tooley has himself elsewhere argued, surely rightly, that such a concept of verification is untenable ('Theological Statements and the Question of an Empiricist Criterion of Cognitive Significance', in Diamond and Litzenburg, *The Logic of God*). It is because I also take this view that in both my 1960 article and in the present essay I have defined verifiability more broadly, in terms of removal of grounds for rational doubt.

9.   Alvin Plantinga, *God and Other Minds* (Ithaca, NY: Cornell University

Press, 1967) p. 168.

10. George Mavrodes, 'God and Verification', *Canadian Journal of Theology*, x (1964) repr. in Diamond and Litzenburg, *The Logic of God*.

11. Herbert Feigl, 'Some Major Issues and Developments in the Philosophy of Science of Logical Empiricism', *Minnesota Studies in the Philosophy of Science*, I (Minneapolis: University of Minnesota Press, 1956) 15.

12. Hick, 'Theology and Verification', Ch. 5 above, p. 83.

13. John Hick, *Faith and Knowledge*, 2nd edn (Ithaca, NY: Cornell University Press, 1966; London: Macmillan, 1967) ch. 9, and *Arguments for the Existence of God* (London: Macmillan, 1970; New York: Herder and Herder, 1971) ch. 7.

14. Michael Tooley says, 'If Hick is claiming both that religious people now have experiences which provide them with knowledge, or at least warranted belief, about the existence of God, and that theological statements can be shown to be verifiable, and hence factually significant, only by appealing to the possibility of certain experiences after death, his overall position would seem to be inconsistent' (*Religious Studies*, XII, no. 2, p. 182). But surely there is no inconsistency here. There is a present belief, based on present religious experience, in the reality of God; and there is the philosophical question whether, under a reasonable verifiability criterion, this is a genuinely factual belief; to which the answer is that it is part of a system or organism of beliefs which includes verifiable eschatological expectations. These expectations ensure that what seems to the believer to be an affirmation of existence is not, in reality, merely a factually contentless *blik*.

15. Hick, 'Theology and Verification', Ch. 5 above, p. 84.

16. Kai Nielsen based his main critique of the theory of eschatological verification on the premise that the verification of a religious belief must be in non-religious terms ('Eschatological Verification', *Canadian Journal of Theology*, IX), and Michael Tooley in his recent article likewise assumes that 'the description of the experiences that verify any statement should ultimately be couched in purely observational terms' (*Religious Studies*, XII, no. 2, p. 189), by which in this case he means 'purely nontheological terms' (p. 190). This seems to me fundamentally mistaken. The verification of a factual statement must be in terms of *experience*; but not only is human experience not confined to the registering of bare sense data, but it is even doubtful whether it ever takes this form. Here Tooley is again taking us back to the 1930s.

17. Michael Tooley asks, 'could a person understand what experiences Hick has in mind here [referring to the eschatological situation] if he did not understand theological language? If not, reference to these purportedly verifying experiences will not explain the meaning of theological statements to one who does not already understand them' (ibid., p. 188). However I have not suggested that the eschatological situation will explain the meaning of theological statements to one who does not already understand them. I begin from the fact that there is already, in this present life, a putative

awareness of God, expressed in religious statements which the religious believer understands. (This is not of course to say that anyone ever wholly understands God.) These statements are part of a unitary body of beliefs which include eschatological beliefs, and it is these latter that give factual-assertion status to the system as a whole.

18. John Hick, 'Religious Faith as Experiencing-as', repr. as Ch. 3 above.
19. Kavka, 'Eschatological Falsification', *Religious Studies*, xii, no. 2.

9

Present and Future Life

It is a curious feature of the present time that a boom in secular interest in the idea of a life after death seems to be matched by a recession in high-level theological interest in that possibility. There is today a wave of popular non-religious concern about death and about a *post mortem* existence, expressed in parapsychology, occultism, thanatology, and talk of mediumship, reincarnation, out-of-the-body experiences and the reports of those who have been revived after having been clinically dead. And yet at the same time some of the best Christian thinking today is inclined to de-emphasise the idea of the life to come, even to the point of virtually abandoning it as an element in the Christian message. It is true that there is much talk of the future (sometimes with a Capital F), and of Christian hope and of the radically eschatological character of the Gospel. For example, Jürgen Moltmann has said that 'From first to last, and not merely in the epilogue, Christianity is eschatology, is hope, forward looking and forward moving. . . .'[1] But when we read on we find that the hope of which he speaks is, in so far as it has any content, a this-worldly hope and that 'the life everlasting' has been reduced to a penumbra of mythic imagery. Again, Wolfhart Pannenberg has said that 'eschatology is no longer a marginal problem of theology, which one could leave to the last chapter of dogmatics, but the basis upon which everything in Christian tradition is built';[2] and he has spoken of God in eschatological terms as 'the absolute future'. However we find that the life beyond death of which he speaks is not really a future life at all but our past life seen again in a new light. To summarise in this way the eschatologies of these two distinguished thinkers does not of course do justice to their thought, but merely serves as a reminder of one aspect of it. I have discussed this aspect more fully elsewhere.[3] My point at the moment is simply that the current vogue of high eschatological language does not centre upon or even necessarily entail the idea of a life beyond death. And, whilst Christian thought is today very various, so that no characterisation

145

will apply right across the board, yet it can I think be said that among many of our more thoughtful theological contemporaries there is a feeling that talk of an after-life is not only too improbable factually, but also too morally and religiously dubious, to consti- tute a proper branch of Christian belief.

My purpose in this lecture is to oppose this view – highly though I respect those who hold it.

Let me then proceed immediately to take up the two main considerations which, if I hear them aright, have led many theolo- gians today to de-emphasise that element of the Christian tradition referred to in the creed as 'the life everlasting'. One is that the doctrine is unbelievable to the modern mind; and the other, that it rests upon a kind of self-concern from which true religion should have freed us. I think that some are particularly moved by one of these considerations, some by the other, and others again by both.

Let us confront first the widespread view that belief in a *post mortem* life is no longer a rational possibility for the inhabitants of our science-oriented twentieth-century thought-world. Here the human being is prevailingly seen as an animal that has evolved a large and marvellously complex brain in virtue of which it has not only survived and multiplied but has created an inner environ- ment of ideas expressed in a rich outer fabric of cultural forms. Consciousness, which is the 'space' of this inner world, is held to be a reflexive functioning of the brain, so that the entire mental life, conscious and unconscious, either consists in or is an epiphe- nomenal reflection of a patterned process of cerebral events. There is in fact no important difference, from the point of view of the question of the continuation of personal life after bodily death between the older epiphenomenalism and the more recent mind– brain identity theory. According to the latter, electro-chemical accounts of neural events and psychological accounts of mental events are alternative descriptions of the same thing, which is the functioning of the brain. And, according to the older variation, conscious experience is a secondary by-product of a cerebral history, so that mental events are produced by brain events but never *vice versa*. Accordingly, mental episodes such as thinking and willing cannot cause their corresponding brain occurrences but simply reflect existing brain activity. On either view the unique stream of images and feelings and of intellectual and volitional activities constituting a personal self-consciousness must inevit- ably terminate as the brain ceases to function. Hence, any notion of the conscious personality persisting after the death of the physical organism can only be a fantasy. Such fantasies are generated, presumably, by the complexity of cortical connections which the brain has developed beyond the requirement of immediate biological needs, a surplus capacity whose play gives rise to humanity's religions, art, literature, philosophy – and also, presumably, science.

So far as its implications for eschatology are concerned, this naturalistic view of the human being has been accepted by a number of our leading theologians today. Let me cite briefly two representative figures, one from Europe and the other from the United States. Wolfhart Pannenberg says that modern anthropology 'removes the basis for the idea of immortality of the soul';[4] and again, that the 'concept of the undying continuation of the soul while the body perishes has become untenable today'.[5] And Gordon Kaufman says that

> Men of other ages and cultures, subscribing to different psychologies, could develop doctrines of the 'immortality of the soul' according to which man's true essence is divine and survives bodily death; to modern psychology and medicine, man appears as a psychosomatic unity whose spiritual life is inseparably bound to its physical base. The end of the body, therefore, is the end of the man. . . .[6]

And I think you will agree that these statements can be matched from the writings of a number of other theologians on both sides of the Atlantic.

This unqualified rejection by some of our foremost Christian thinkers of the dualist view of the human person as ontologically other than the functioning of one's physical brain is, I believe, at best very premature and at worst a disastrous mistake. Let me remind you of some of the main unresolved points of doubt and debate concerning mind–brain identity. The first is that it is a theory which tends to be taken for granted within a general naturalistic horizon of thought, but not a conclusion established by any of the special sciences, and certainly not by brain research. Indeed it has been rejected in favour of mind–brain dualism by some of the leaders in this field. Second, the mind–brain identity theory involves deep philosophical problems, which are also shared by epiphenomenalism. One of these is the paradox that if the mind is either identical with or a reflection of the physical functioning of the brain, whilst this is itself an integral part of the system of nature, then believing, judging, proving, inferring, and so on are, or are reflections of, causally determined physical events. To claim that this is the status of your own beliefs and reasonings (including of course your belief about the nature of mental activity) is to present them as having the significance only of causally necessitated physical events. Thus belief in the truth of the mind–brain identity or of the epiphenomenalist theory is a belief which categorises itself as either identical with or as the reflection of a causally determined physical process. But, having concluded that one's conclusions represent the causally deter- mined state of a particular portion of matter, one has undermined one's preference for the state of one's own lump of grey matter rather than for that of another lump of grey matter which has come to a different conclusion. Third, some of the evidence of para- psychology – particularly the evidence for interactions, not medi- ated by physical signals, between one stream of consciousness and another – is extremely hard to fit into the mind–brain identity or epiphenomenalist theories.

I am not going to develop these three points here. I mention them simply as a reminder that, regardless of any theological implications, the naturalistic view of mind as either identical with or as wholly dependent upon and determined by brain is debatable and debated, alike as scientific hypothesis and as philosophical theory. But from a theological point of view there is also the problem that the idea of God is already the idea of disembodied consciousness. All schools of Christian thought are agreed that, whatever more we may mean by 'God', we at least mean unlimited personal consciousness and, further, that the divine consciousness is neither produced by, dependent upon, nor identical with a physical brain. A theologian who postulates a divine conscious- ness without physical basis has thus already moved irrevocably beyond the naturalistic horizon; and for such a one to declare impossible a non-material human mind after affirming the non- material divine mind is to strain out a gnat after swallowing a camel!

But the view of the human being as an indissoluble psycho- physical unity is generally applied by these theologians specifically against the idea of the immortality of the soul, in distinction from the alternative idea of the resurrection of the body, which they see as more acceptable. And it is true that if you adopt the view of the human creature as a purely bodily being, but reject much of the wider naturalistic world-view of which this is today a part, you can then switch from 'Hellenic immortality' to 'Hebraic resurrection' without depriving your theology of its eschatological fulfilment. However, this move will not admit you into the cultural world from which a belief in the mind's survival of bodily death would have excluded you. For within that cultural world resurrection is as fantastic as immortality. Leaving aside the totally unbelievable notion of the coming forth of corpses from their graves, a realistic conception of resurrection would have to postulate the divine re-creation of psycho-physical beings in another world or worlds. More about this later. But note at the moment that it lies as far outside our contemporary naturalistic horizon as does the mind's survival of the death of the body. It is true that resurrection in this sense is not in fact ruled out by any established conclusions in any of the special sciences, any more than is the survival of consciousness after bodily death; but it *is* ruled out by the assumptions and habits of judgement operating within a science-based culture. And therefore, if one has abandoned the idea of the survival of the mind because of its rejection by this culture, it would be consistent to reject the idea of resurrection also for the same reason.

Let me now take stock and then move on. I have pointed out that there is a long-standing debate amongst scientists and philosophers about the status of mental life. This debate is at present open and could go either way; or it could indeed prove to be a perpetual debate, never destined to be definitively settled within either science or philosophy. In this situation it seems to me odd that many theologians should so readily adopt a monistic theory, whether in the form of epiphenomenalism or of mind–brain identity. For their own starting-point as theologians is the existence of divine mind prior to and independent of matter. I do not say that these two positions are totally irreconcilable; for there could in principle be non-embodied divine mind but no non-embodied creaturely minds. But I nevertheless wonder why theologians should be so quick to opt for a mind–brain identity or an epiphenomenalist theory which is not only unproved but which also generates profound philosophical and theological problems. If their concern is to avoid contradicting contemporary secular assumptions, I fear that they have set themselves an impossible task. For when, having renounced the mind's survival of bodily death, they go on to speak of resurrection and of a divine re-creation of the psycho-physical person, they transgress the limits set by our science-oriented culture quite as flagrantly as if they had asserted the immortality of the soul.

But now let us turn to a more profound consideration which has led many theologians today, and indeed often the same ones, to de-emphasise the Christian doctrine of the life to come. This is the thought that the doctrine is morally or spiritually harmful. It has of course always been regarded by Marxists as the opium of the people, a drug which reconciles the downtrodden masses to their unjust lot by filling their imaginations with a heavenly paradise to come. And there certainly have been periods in the history of many societies in which the idea of a future life has been exploited as an instrument of social control. I should guess that those days are now over, even in the most backward countries; and certainly they are long since over so far as the United States and Europe are concerned. But the idea which influences a number of contemporary theologians centres upon the individual rather than the community. It is that the concern for personal immortality (whether by the resurrection of the body or the immortality· of the soul) is a selfish and thus a basically irreligious concern. It is a concern for the perpetuation of the little ego. The beloved 'I' wants to live for ever; it cannot bear the thought that the universe should some day go on without it. And there is indeed something profoundly unbecoming in the spectacle of the average grubby little human ego demanding to be immortalised. I am sure that those who emphasise this, and who accordingly have qualms about the widespread desire for personal immortality, are thus far right. But I do not think that they are right in going on to conclude that the doctrine of a future life is mistaken. Rather, I would suggest, their insight is in harmony with the deeper teaching of the great world religions – in the context of which, however, it is not inimical to the idea of a life or lives to come but on the contrary requires this. Let me then remind you of three great themes which are common, in different forms, to the major religious traditions.

The first is that of the immense potentialities of the human spirit. From a naturalistic or humanist standpoint one can speculate about the further evolutionary possibilities of the human species. Future forms of *Homo sapiens*, thousands or millions of years hence, may be more intelligent, more morally mature, and more successful in organising their social life than humanity today. But, if there are in fact to be such developments, we today cannot know of them or participate in them. We can at best be related to such people of the future as means to an end. But the great world religions, without being concerned to assert or deny the possibility of such developments, affirm the value of the present individual not merely as a means to a further end but as already an end. They say to each human being: *you* are a child of God, made in the divine image and loved by God, and you can begin now to experience the new life in conscious relationship to God; or *you* are a potential Buddha, and can attain the liberation which is *nirvāṇa*; or *you* are in the depths of your being one with Brahman and can become *jivanmukti*, a liberated soul whilst still on this earth. Thus the message of the religions is not only for men and women of the remote future but for each living man and woman now. Further, the immense potentialities of human existence, which give the religious message the quality of a gospel, are not restricted (except in some extreme double-predestinarian dogmas) to any section or period of humanity but are affirmed of *all* human beings. And when we look at the lives of the saints and hear of the experiences of the mystics of the different traditions we see revealed aspects of the human potential which have yet to be realised in ourselves. In Christianity we sometimes express this by saying that we see in the life of Jesus the perfection of the human nature that he shared with us. And salvation, or liberation, or entry into eternal life, means fulfilling this potentiality in relationship with the divine Reality known as infinite love, or known as *Satchitananda* (infinite being–consciousness–happiness), or known as the eternal cosmic Buddha. This, then, is the first of the religious themes to which I want to draw attention: the message, addressed to every individual, of the illimitably better possibility to which every human creature is heir.

Moving now to a second theme, the great world faiths also teach that the realising of the deeper human potential is a matter not of perpetuating but rather of transcending our present self-enclosed individual existence. The little ego is challenged to self-renunciation and the overcoming of egoity in the larger corporate life of perfected humanity. Thus in Jesus' teaching we are called to love others as much as we love ourselves, to give and forgive without limit, not to retaliate but to live a life of other-regarding love. One who responds fully to this call has ceased to be a self-seeking ego and has become a channel of the divine grace and

love. And in the later Christian tradition the mystics were to speak
of the way of 'self-naughting' and even sometimes of the eventual
absorption of the creature within the divine life. The other semitic
faiths, Judaism and Islam, call in the one case for a life of complete
obedience to the divine Torah, and in the other for a total
submission of the human ego to the will of Allah. The great Eastern
religions of Hinduism and Buddhism both teach that separate
egoity is ultimately false, although it can sustain its false existence
through innumerable psycho-physical lives until at last the point is
reached of readiness to lose oneself in the infinite being–
consciousness–happiness of Brahman, or in the infinite mystery of
nirvāṇa. Thus in each case, though in very different ways, it is
taught by the great religions that the 'grubby little human ego' is a
fallen and sin-bound creature, alienated from its true ground and
destiny; or that it is a self-positing illusion within *māyā* or within
the pain-ridden process of *samsara*. And in each case it is taught
that the present grasping ego must learn to renounce itself, and to
give up its claim on existence, in order to enter into the life that is
eternal.

There are of course many important differences among the
conceptions of the eschaton developed by the different religions.
In Hinduism there is both the advaitist conception of total reab-
sorption of spirits, now divided by innumerable false ego-
boundaries, back into the one spirit or atman, which is identical
with the ultimate reality of Brahman; and there is also the
visistādvaitist conception of some kind of continuous strands of
creaturely identity within the infinite divine life. Buddhism likewise embraces a range of understandings of *nirvāṇa* from sheer
non-existence to participation in the eternal but indescribable Void
or Absolute. In Christianity there is both the picture of the
perfected saints dwelling as separate individuals in the Heavenly
City or Kingdom, and the more mystical anticipation of absorption
in the beatific vision of God. Such a range of pictures is in no way
surprising, since conceptions of humanity's ultimate state can only
be pointers to something totally beyond our present experience.
However, these different conceptions can I think be seen to be
convergent; and one way of indicating the convergence is offered
by the modern understanding of personality as essentially self-
transcending and interpersonal. From this point of view the
fulfilment of human personality cannot consist in the perfection of
isolated units, but on the contrary in their transcending of their

ego-boundaries in a perfect community of mutual love. Christian thought possesses in the Trinitarian concept of God as three-in-one and one-in-three an illuminating model for such personal multiplicity in unity. Perhaps in the eschaton human existence will be many-in-one and one-in-many in the life of corporate humanity. But whether or not this model is appropriate there is, surely, general agreement that it is not our present little ego, held together by greedy self-concern, that is to be part of the eternal outcome of the temporal process, but rather that which we can eventually become; and that which we can eventually become lies far beyond individual egoity.

And then a third theme in the teachings of the great world religions is that, whilst the ultimate goal is a state in which individual ego-boundaries have been transcended, yet to attain to this the present conscious ego must voluntarily relinquish its own self-centred existence; and the function of religion is to carry men and women through this momentous choice. It is in the sinful 'fallen' creature, or the false ego, which now exists that the conscious exercise of freedom is taking place; and it is therefore to this present imperfect self that the claims and promises of the gospel are addressed. For, whilst the greater life that is available to us is always apprehended as a prevenient reality or as a gift of divine grace, it nevertheless has to be received by men and women as they actually are or as they will actually become in the course of their further living. The greater life, if it is to come about, has to be accepted by the 'grubby little egos' of human beings immersed in the multifarious pressures of history. The great choice is normally made through innumerable small choices. And the unique set of human interactions in time, which we call history, is the sphere within which these vital choices are made. Accordingly, the kind of belief in a life after death which I shall now argue is required by a religious understanding of life is one which postulates a further history, a *post mortem* history, in which the work of attaining to self-transcendence is continued to its completion.

In developing this argument let us move from the very general statements that have to be made when we are speaking of the religions of the world collectively, to the more specific statements that we can make in the context of a particular religion, namely Christianity. And indeed since Christianity is itself so diverse I shall be using as my theological framework one particular strand. This is the tradition of reflection which goes back through much contemporary and recent thinking to the great figure of Schleier-macher in the nineteenth century, and ultimately back to the Hellenistic Fathers, particularly Irenaeus, in the second century. According to this type of theology, human existence as we know it is a phase in the cosmic process which is God's gradual creation of 'children of God' – that is, finite personal life lived consciously and joyfully within the infinite divine life. Irenaeus, and others of the Hellenistic Fathers, thought in terms of a two-stage creation of the human being. The first stage – putting it in modern terms – was the production through the evolution of the universe and the evolution of life on this earth (and perhaps on many other planets of many other stars as well) of finite moral and spiritual conscious-ness. But the human creature thus made as intelligent ethical animal, with a potentiality for relationship with God, is only the raw material for the second phase of the creative process, which is the bringing of men and women, through their own free personal responses, to perfect humanity in relation to God. In Irenaeus's terminology, drawn from Genesis 1:26, humanity has been made in the image of God and is now being drawn into the finite likeness of God. The terminology itself is artificial; but Irenaeus's basic theological hypothesis remains extremely fruitful – namely, an immense creative process, in the first phase of which the human being is not the ideal pre-fallen paradisal Adam and Eve of the Augustinian theology, but is to be thought of as an immature, child-like creature who is only at the beginning of a long further process of development.

Now if our present life is being lived within this second phase, in which intelligent animals are gradually being transformed into children of God, we can very properly ask whether the process is confined to our earthly life or continues beyond it.

It is, I think, obvious and non-controversial that such a trans-formation, if it is indeed taking place, is not normally completed in the present life. Most human beings are still extremely imperfect as moral and spiritual persons by the time they die. Even when they die at the end of a long and humanly successful life they are still far short of the complete realisation of the human potential; and of course the majority of all those who have been born throughout human history until now have in fact died in infancy or before reaching maturity, or have not lived 'humanly successful' lives. The question then is whether our ultimate perfection, which is so obviously not attained in this life, is to be accomplished in a flash at each individual's death or whether it requires further living beyond death.

The very serious drawback of any notion of instantaneous perfecting at the moment of death is that it would render pointless the slow and difficult process of personal growth through our own free reactions within the contingencies of human history. For if that large part of our perfecting which does not occur in this life is able to be accomplished instantaneously by divine fiat, without our needing freely to go through the intermediate stages, it seems to follow that God could have created humanity initially as the perfect beings whom God wished to have. The traditional way of escape from this conclusion provided by the Augustinian theology is of course the doctrine that God did create perfect creatures – the angels – in an ideal state, but that some of them wilfully rebelled. But it has long been evident that this speculation is incoherent; for perfect creatures in a perfect environment, although free to fall, would never in fact do so. Either, then, the experience of living and learning within a challenging environment is necessary to the creation of free personal beings who are to be 'children of God' – in which case it would seem that the creative process must continue beyond death until it is completed; or else that kind of experience and exercise of free will is not necessary because God can equally well create perfect children 'ready made' – in which case there is no point or justification to the long story of human existence, with all the deep pain and suffering that it involves.

Surely this second alternative rules itself out by the way in which it would render our present struggling human existence pointless. We must then proceed on the basis that life as we know it is part of a long person-making process which is not completed in this present life and which we can only presume to continue beyond it. This presumption is confirmed by the insight of the Eastern religions that spiritual 'liberation' requires far more than one life for its achievement. They accordingly teach the reincarnation of the soul in life after life until ego-hood is finally transcended. In the West most of us have not accepted this doctrine of earthly reincarnation or rebirth; and, whilst the subject is much too large to be discussed properly here, I think that we have respectable reasons (which I have tried to discuss elsewhere[7]) for our cautious and on the whole negative response. But nevertheless the perception that one life is not enough is surely sound. I would therefore suggest that if we accept (1) the witness of the great world religions that human existence as we now know it is 'fallen', wrapped in illusion, full of suffering; and (2) that nevertheless a far, far better state is possible, a state of perfection, fulfilment, as child of God; and (3) that this state cannot be simply imposed upon us but has to be freely entered into through innumerable choices of self-transcendence; and (4) that this process is not normally completed in the present life – then we should also accept the unanimous witness of the great religious traditions to a further life or lives beyond death.

Accordingly, in addition to eschatology, concerned with the ultimate and eternal state to which the religions point, there is also what we may call pareschatology, concerned with what takes place between this present life and that final state. The pareschaton is the time in which the individual changes from a still self-centred state at the end of this life, to one of the transcendence of egoity within the unity of perfected humanity living in an ideal relationship to God. The main form of pareschatology in Christian thought is of course the Catholic doctrine of purgatory. Unfortunately this has traditionally been combined with the dogma that the soul's relationship to God is settled in the moment of death, so that there can thereafter be no further vital free choices or personal growth and development. Thus purgatory as traditionally conceived is not a continued life of moral responses to other people within a common environment through which the self can continue to grow towards its perfection. It has been conceived, rather, as the process through which the soul, already definitively 'saved' in the moment of death, endures the remaining painful consequences of its earthly sins and is thus made fit to enter the Heavenly Kingdom. But this is essentially a juridical conception, concerned with the judgement of the person at a particular moment, regardless of his or her individual circumstances and development. I suggest that such a scheme of divine judgement is not a morally coherent possibility. It would be manifestly unfair to judge men and women and allot them eternal happiness or loss of happiness on the basis of their performance in this life and/or their state at the moment of death. For people are born, through no virtue of fault of their own, in circumstances of very different moral and spiritual advantage. There are immense variations of genetic make-up, and at least as great variations in the moral character of the environments into which people are born. Consider the contrast between, on the one hand, a child born to good, loving and moderately affluent parents and brought up in an atmosphere of religious faith within a settled and stable society, and, on the other hand, an orphan deprived of all parental affection and guidance, living in the teeming slums of an overcrowded and vice-ridden city in which he or she is subjected to a variety of vicious influences, is part of a sub-culture in which crime is a way of life and dies a violent death at the age of seventeen. To judge them both on the moral quality of their lives would be patently unjust. Again, the state in which someone is at the moment of death would provide only a very haphazard criterion since death may come unexpectedly at any time. It is thus surely very difficult to conceive of the divine Being distributing human beings to eternal happiness or unhappiness (or, on a milder view of divine rejection, simply ceasing to hold them in existence) on the basis of their performance in this brief and chancy life. Rather than such a harsh juridical approach, does it not seem more appropriate to think in terms of the actual nature and quality of human existence as it changes through time, and to postulate a divine purpose of drawing men and women towards the realisation of their God-given potentialities? Since any such purpose is obviously not fulfilled in the present life it would seem that it must continue beyond this life. But in that case the pareschaton will not be the spiritually static purgatory of Catholic tradition, but is more likely to be a further temporal process in which further moral and spiritual growth is possible.

If I am challenged to say more about what this might mean, I can only offer one or two very tentative first steps of speculation, guided partly by the evidence of religious and other experience and partly by what seem to me to be rational likelihoods.

I am assuming then that when the physical organism dies the conscious personality continues to exist. And I speculate that in the first phase of its *post mortem* existence it is not embodied, and accordingly receives no new sensory input, but experiences a kind of dream environment built out of the materials of memory by the moulding power of conscious and repressed desires developed in the course of its earthly life. This will be a period of self-revelation and self-judgement, a kind of psychoanalytic experience in which we become aware of our own character so largely hidden from us in this life, and perhaps as a result form new and different hopes and aspirations. This conception of the first phase of existence after death is based on the Tantric Mahāyāna document the *Bardo Thödol* or *Tibetan Book of the Dead*. For what it is worth – and it is I think very hard to decide what, if anything, it is worth – the reports, received through Western mediums, purporting to reflect the experiences of persons who have recently died, agree generally with the *Bardo Thödol*. For it is explicit in this ancient document that the *bardo* experience is a projection of the individual's own imagination, so that its form depends upon that person's operative beliefs and expectations. The *Bardo Thödol* describes the *post mortem* experiences which would be undergone by a devout Tibetan Buddhist. But a member of our post-Christian Western secular society might well, in default of any strong religious imagery, create his or her *bardo* world out of memories of earth, so that such a next world would be very like the present world; and this is in fact generally what is indicated by the minds which express themselves in the mediumistic trance.

Then I speculate that after this *bardo* phase, which lasts for a longer or shorter time according to the needs of the individual, there is another period of embodiment, which Christians anticipate as the resurrection. This is a bodily existence lived in interaction with other people in a common environment. The resurrection environment, including the bodies which are part of it, is physical though probably not part of the physical universe of which our present bodies are part. Thus we may well have to postulate a plurality of universes or spatial systems. There are of course formidable philosophical problems about personal identity from embodiment in one space to re-embodiment in another space. I have tried to confront these problems elsewhere,[8] but the questions involved are too intricate to be tackled adequately in the closing stages of this lecture. I would only suggest to anyone who takes the idea of resurrection or re-embodiment seriously enough to consider how it might be spelled out, that no realistic alternative has yet been offered to the idea of a further psycho-physical existence which is probably located in another space.

If we are allowed to speculate this far we have a hypothetical basis on which to speculate yet a little further. The reason for postulating a life after death, within the theological framework adopted here, is that it is entailed by the possibility of human beings exercising their freedom in response to the challenges and opportunities of history so as to be able to attain eventually to the point of self-transcending life in a universal perfected humanity. Accordingly, the form of *post mortem* existence that we postulate must be one in which further moral and spiritual choices are possible. This means, I think, that it must be a real life in a real world with its own concrete character and history, and with its own exigencies and crises and perils within which decisions and risks, successes and failures, achievements and disasters can occur. All this points to the hypothesis that the individual's next life will, like the present life, be a bounded span with its own beginning and end. In other words I am suggesting that it will be another mortal existence. For it is our mortality that gives to our present life its shape and meaning. It is because of the boundaries of birth and death that time is precious, that right and wrong actions have their momentous character within the irreversible flow of events, and that life can have the kind of meaning that presupposes aims and purposes. It is indeed very hard to see how a finite and imperfect human person could undergo further development except within a temporal horizon such as death provides.

The next question that arises is whether we should postulate only one such further bounded life or more than one. We have to consider this in relation to the creation of an eschatological situation in which the innumerable human individuals have reached a self-transcending relationship to one another, constituting a new humanity which is many-in-one and one-in-many. It is evident that this is very far from being achieved in the present life; and it therefore seems more realistic to think of its coming about at the end of a number of lives than to see this happening at the end of only one more. We are thus led – very tentatively – to postulate a series of lives, presumably in a corresponding series of worlds, through which finite persons can gradually progress towards the completion of the divine purpose for them.

To those whose religious thinking is conducted entirely within the borders of the Christian tradition, such speculations will almost inevitably seem wild and baseless. For if one's experience is confined to one's own familiar conceptual village the life of other villages will seem merely alien and bizarre. But those who are aware of the wider religious life of humankind will recognise that the present speculation is a variation on the very ancient and widespread conception of a multiplicity of lives – except that, where Buddhism and Hinduism, as the principal channels of this tradition, teach a horizontal process of reincarnation along the plane of earthly history, I have been outlining what might be called a vertical, or perhaps better a diagonal, series of many lives in many worlds, moving nearer to the divine heart of reality. And I speculate that, as human beings reach their final self-transcending perfection, the life in which this occurs becomes their last embodiment and they pass from it into *nirvāṇa* or heaven or eternal life, beyond separate egoity in space and time.

You have perhaps noticed that I have spoken much of the soul's progress but very little of its regress. I nevertheless assume that at every stage regress is possible as well as progress and that the total journey of the self from human animal to child of God is no smooth and automatic ascent but a hard and adventurous journey with many ups and downs and stops and starts. I do however also assume eventual 'universal salvation'. This assumption provokes large problems, particularly concerning the relation between an ultimate predestination to salvation and the genuine human freedom which I have also stressed. But this is another large topic which I have discussed at length elsewhere.[9]

Finally, a very brief word about method. It will be evident that the speculations which I have outlined unite some of the basic features of the eschatologies and pareschatologies of both West and East. And it does seem to me to be an appropriate and fruitful method today to assume that the teachings of the world religions express different human perceptions of and responses to the same divine Reality, so that a fuller conception of that reality, and likewise of human destiny in relation to it, is to be expected from religious study on a global scale than from study restricted to a single tradition.

NOTES

1. Jürgen Moltmann, *Theology of Hope* (London: SCM Press, 1967) p. 16.
2. Wolfhart Pannenberg, 'Can Christianity Do Without an Eschatology?', in G. B. Caird *et al.* (eds), *The Christian Hope* (London: SPCK, 1970) p. 31.
3. John Hick, *Death and Eternal Life* (London: Collins; New York: Harper and Row, 1976; new edn London: Macmillan, 1985) ch. 11.
4. Wolfhart Pannenberg, *What is Man?* (Philadelphia: Fortress Press, 1970) p. 48.
5. Wolfhart Pannenberg, *Jesus – God and Man* (London: SCM Press, 1968) p. 87.
6. Gordon D. Kaufman, *Systematic Theology* (New York: Charles Scribner's Sons, 1968) p. 464.
7. Hick, *Death and Eternal Life*, ch. 19.
8. Ibid., ch. 15.
9. Ibid., ch. 13.

10

A Philosophy of Religious Pluralism

Wilfred Cantwell Smith in his work on the concepts of religion and of religions has been responsible, more than any other one individual, for the change which has taken place within a single generation in the way in which many of us perceive the religious life of mankind.

Seen through pre-Cantwell Smith eyes there are a number of vast, long-lived historical entities or organisms known as Christianity, Hinduism, Islam, Buddhism, and so on. Each has an inner skeletal framework of beliefs, giving shape to a distinctive form of religious life, wrapped in a thick institutional skin which divides it from other religions and from the secular world within which they exist. Thus Buddhism, Islam, Christianity, and the rest, are seen as contraposed socio-religious entities which are the bearers of distinctive creeds; and every religious individual is a member of one or other of these mutually exclusive groups.

This way of seeing the religious life of humanity, as organised in a number of communities based upon rival sets of religious beliefs, leads to the posing of questions about religion in a certain way. For the beliefs which a religion professes are beliefs about God, or the Ultimate, and as such they define a way of human salvation or liberation and are accordingly a matter of spiritual life and death. Looking at the religions of the world, then, in the plural we are presented with competing claims to possess the saving truth. For each community believes that its own gospel is true and that other gospels are false in so far as they differ from it. Each believes that the way of salvation to which it witnesses is the authentic way, the only sure path to eternal blessedness. And so the proper question in face of this plurality of claims is, which is the true religion?

In practice, those who are concerned to raise this question are normally fully convinced that theirs is the true religion; so that for them the task is to show the spiritual superiority of their own creed and the consequent moral superiority of the community which embodies it. A great deal of the mutual criticism of religions, and of the derogatory assessment of one by another, has been in fulfilment of this task.

This view of mankind's religious life as divided into great contraposed entities, each claiming to be the true religion, is not however the only possible way of seeing the religious situation. Cantwell Smith has offered an alternative vision.

He shows first that the presently dominant conceptuality has a history that can be traced back to the European Renaissance. It was then that the different streams of religious life began to be reified in Western thought as solid structures called Christianity, Judaism, and so forth. And having reified their own faith in this way Westerners have then exported the notion of 'a religion' to the rest of the world, causing others to think of themselves as belonging to the Hindu, or the Confucian, or the Buddhist religion, and so on, over against others. But an alternative perception can divide the scene differently. It sees something of vital religious significance taking different forms all over the world within the contexts of the different historical traditions. This 'something of vital religious significance' Cantwell Smith calls faith. I would agree with some of his critics that this is not the ideal word for it; for 'faith' is a term that is more at home in the Semitic than in the Indian family of traditions and which has, as his own historical researches have shown, become badly over-intellectualised. But I take it that he uses the term to refer to the spiritual state, or existential condition, constituted by a person's present response to the ultimate divine Reality. This ranges from the negative response of a self-enclosed consciousness which is blind to the divine presence, whether beyond us or in the depths of our own being, to a positive openness to the Divine which gradually transforms us and which is called salvation or liberation or enlightenment. This transformation is essentially the same within the different religious contexts within which it occurs: I would define it formally as the transformation of human existence from self-centredness to Reality-centredness. This is the event or process of vital significance which one can see to be occurring in individuals all over the world, taking different forms within the contexts of the different perceptions of the Ultimate made available by the various religious traditions.

These cumulative traditions themselves are the other thing that one sees with the aid of the new conceptuality suggested by

Cantwell Smith. They are distinguishable strands of human history in each of which a multitude of religious and cultural elements interact to form a distinctive pattern, constituting, say, the Hindu, Buddhist, Confucian, Jewish, Christian or Muslim tradition. These traditions are not static entities but living movements; and they are not tightly homogeneous but have each become in the course of time internally highly various. Thus there are large differences between, for example, Buddhism in the time of Gautama and Buddhism after the development of the Mahāyāna and its expansion northwards into China; or between the Christian movement in Roman Palestine and that in medieval Europe. And there are large differences today between, say, Zen and Amida Buddhism in Japan, or between Southern Baptist and Northern Episcopalian Christianity in the United States. Indeed, since we cannot always avoid using the substantives, we might do well to speak of Buddhisms, Christianities, and so on, in the plural. A usage consonant with Cantwell Smith's analysis has however already become widespread, and many of us now often prefer to speak not of Christianity but of the Christian tradition, the Hindu tradition, and so on, when referring to these historically identifiable strands of history.

These cumulative traditions are composed of a rich complex of inner and outer elements cohering in a distinctive living pattern which includes structures of belief, life-styles, scriptures and their interpretations, liturgies, cultic celebrations, myths, music, poetry, architecture, literature, remembered history and its heroes. Thus the traditions constitute religious cultures, each with its own unique history and ethos. And each such tradition creates human beings in its own image. For we are not human in general, participating in an eternal Platonic essence of humanity. We are human in one or other of the various concrete ways of being human which constitute the cultures of the earth. There is a Chinese way of being human, an African way, an Arab way, a European way, or ways, and so on. These are not fixed moulds but living organisms which develop and interact over the centuries, so that the patterns of human life change, usually very slowly but sometimes with startling rapidity. But we are all formed in a hundred ways of which we are not normally aware by the culture into which we were born, by which we are fed, and with which we interact.

Let us then enter, with Cantwell Smith, into the experiment of thinking, on the one hand, of 'faith', or human response to the divine, which in its positive and negative forms is salvation and non-salvation and, on the other hand, of the cumulative religious traditions within which this occurs; and let us ask what the relation is between these two realities – on the one hand salvation/ liberation and on the other the cumulative traditions.

In various different forms this question has been much discussed within the Christian world, particularly during the last hundred and fifty years or so, as Christians have become increasingly conscious of the continuing reality of the other great religious traditions. For this period has seen renaissances within the Hindu and Buddhist worlds – to an important extent, it would seem, in reaction to eighteenth- and nineteenth-century Christian imperialism – and a resurgence of Islam is currently taking place. These developments have precipitated intense debate among Christian thinkers in which many different options have been and are being canvassed. Both because of the fullness of this discussion within Christianity, and because I am myself a Christian and am concerned with the problem from a Christian point of view, I propose to describe the main options in Christian terms. They are three in number.

The first, which we may call 'exclusivism', relates salvation/ liberation exclusively to one particular tradition, so that it is an article of faith that salvation is restricted to this one group, the rest of mankind being either left out of account or explicitly excluded from the sphere of salvation. The most emphatic and influential expression of such a faith occurred in the Catholic dogma *Extra ecclesiam nulla salus* (outside the Church, no salvation) and the corresponding assumption of the nineteenth-century Protestant missionary movement: outside Christianity, no salvation. In these developments Christian thought went beyond a mere overlooking of non-Christian humanity – which might perhaps simply be attributed to restricted vision – to a positive doctrine of the unsaved status of that wider human majority. Exclusiveness of this strong kind was supported by a juridical conception of salvation. If salvation consists in a change of status in the eyes of God from the guilt of participation in Adam's original sin to a forgiveness made possible by Christ's sacrifice on the cross, the appropriation of which is conditional upon a personal response of faith in Christ, this salvation can very naturally be seen as restricted to the Christian faith community. If on the other hand salvation is understood as the actual transformation of human life from self-centredness to Reality-centredness, this is not necessarily restricted within the boundaries of any one historical tradition. One cannot know *a priori* where or to what extent it occurs; one can only look at the living of human life in its endlessly varied circumstances and try to discern the signs of this transformation. Except in those whom we call saints, in whom the transformation is sufficiently advanced to be publicly evident, such discernment is often extremely difficult; for salvation/liberation, understood in this way, is to be found in many stages and degrees in the varying qualities of true humanity, often realised more in some areas of life than in others, and with advances and regressions, efforts and lapses in all the respects in which human beings develop and change through the experience of life in time. There may of course – as the Hindu and Buddhist traditions generally teach – be a final moment of enlightenment in which the transformation is completed and Reality-centredness definitively supersedes the last remnants of self-centredness. But, even if this should be a universal pattern, the journey leading towards that final moment must be long and slow; and progress on the journey can to some extent be humanly discerned as the process of salvation gradually taking place. This understanding of salvation/liberation as the actual transformation of human beings is more easily open than is the juridical understanding of it to the possibility that the salvific process may be taking place not only within one tradition but within a number of traditions.

Christian exclusivism has now largely faded out from the 'mainline' churches, but is still powerful in many of the 'marginal' fundamentalistic sects; and it should be added that the 'margins' of Christianity are probably more extensive today than ever before.

However, we may now turn to a second Christian answer to our question, which can be labelled 'inclusivism'. This can be expressed in terms either of a juridical or of a transformation-of-human-existence conception of salvation. In the former terms it is the view that God's forgiveness and acceptance of humanity have been made possible by Christ's death, but that the benefits of this sacrifice are not confined to those who respond to it with an explicit act of faith. The juridical transaction of Christ's atonement covered *all* human sin, so that all human beings are now open to God's mercy, even though they may never have heard of Jesus Christ and why he died on the cross of Calvary. I take it that it is this form of inclusivism that the present Pope was endorsing in his first encyclical when he said that 'man – ever man without any exception whatever – has been redeemed by Christ, and because with man – with each man without any exception whatever – Christ is in a way united, even when man is unaware of it'.[1] This statement could however also be an expression of the other form of Christian inclusivism, which accepts the understanding of salvation as the gradual transformation of human life and sees this as taking place not only within Christian history but also within the contexts of all the other great world traditions. It regards this however, wherever it happens, as the work of Christ – the universal divine Logos, the Second Person of the divine Trinity, who became incarnate in Jesus of Nazareth. Thus we can speak of 'the unknown Christ of Hinduism' and of the other traditions, and indeed the unknown Christ within all creative transformations of individuals and societies. And, if we ask how this differs from simply saying that within all these different streams of human life there is a creative and re-creative response to the divine Reality, the answer of this kind of Christian inclusivism is that Christians are those, uniquely, who are able to identify the source of salvation because they have encountered that source as personally incarnate in Jesus Christ.

Both forms of inclusivism do however involve certain inner strains and certain awkward implications.[2] How are they to be combined with the traditional *Extra ecclesiam* dogma? The best known attempt is that of Karl Rahner, with his concept of the 'anonymous Christian'. Those who do not have an explicit Christian faith but who nevertheless seek, consciously or unconsciously, to do God's will can be regarded as, so to speak, honorary Christians – and this even though they do not so regard themselves and even though they may insist that they are not Christians but Muslims, Jews, Hindus, or whatever. Rahner's is a brave attempt to attain an inclusivist position which is in principle universal but which does not thereby renounce the old exclusivist dogma. But the question is whether in this new context the old dogma has not been so emptied of content as no longer to be worth affirming. When salvation is acknowledged to be taking place without any connection with the Christian Church or Gospel, in people who are living on the basis of quite other faiths, is it not a somewhat empty gesture to insist upon affixing a Christian label to them? Further, having thus labelled them, why persist in the aim of

gathering all humankind into the Christian Church? Once it is
accepted that salvation does not depend upon this, the conversion
of the people of the other great world faiths to Christianity hardly
seems the best way of spending one's energies.

The third possible answer to the question of the relation between
salvation/liberation and the cumulative religious traditions can best
be called pluralism. As a Christian position this can be seen as an
acceptance of the further conclusion to which inclusivism points. If
we accept that salvation/liberation is taking place within all the
great religious traditions, why not frankly acknowledge that there
is a plurality of saving human responses to the ultimate divine
Reality? Pluralism, then, is the view that the transformation of
human existence from self-centredness to Reality-centredness is
taking place in different ways within the contexts of all the great
religious traditions. There is not merely one way but a plurality of
ways of salvation or liberation. In Christian theological terms, there
is a plurality of divine revelations, making possible a plurality of
forms of saving human response.

What however makes it difficult for Christians to move from
inclusivism to pluralism, holding the majority of Christian theologians today in the inclusivist position despite its evident logical
instability, is of course the traditional doctrine of the incarnation,
together with its protective envelope, the doctrine of the Trinity.
For in its orthodox form, as classically expressed at the Councils of
Nicaea and Chalcedon, the incarnational doctrine claims that Jesus
was God incarnate, the Second Person of the Triune God living a
human life. It is integral to this faith that there has been (and will
be) no other divine incarnation. This makes Christianity unique in
that it, alone among the religions of the world, was founded by
God in person. Such a uniqueness would seem to demand Christian exclusivism – for must God not want all human beings to enter
the way of salvation which he has provided for them? However,
since such exclusivism seems so unrealistic in the light of our
knowledge of the wider religious life of mankind, many theologians have moved to some form of inclusivism, but now feel
unable to go further and follow the argument to its conclusion in
the frank acceptance of pluralism. The break with traditional
missionary attitudes and long-established ecclesiastical and liturgical language would, for many, be so great as to be prohibitive.

There is however the possibility of an acceptable Christian route
to religious pluralism in work which has already been done, and

which is being done, in the field of Christology with motivations quite other than to facilitate pluralism, and on grounds which are internal to the intellectual development of Christianity. For there is a decisive watershed between what might be called all-or-nothing Christologies and degree Christologies. The all-or-nothing principle is classically expressed in the Chalcedonian Definition, according to which Christ is 'to be acknowledged in Two Natures', 'Consubstantial with the Father according to his Deity, Consubstantial with us according to his Humanity'. Substance is an all-or-nothing notion, in that A either is or is not composed of the same substance, either has or does not have the same essential nature, as B. Using this all-or-nothing conceptuality Chalcedon attributed to Christ two complete natures, one divine and the other human, being in his divine nature of one substance with God the Father. Degree Christologies, on the other hand, apply the term 'incarnation' to the activity of God's Spirit or of God's grace in human lives, so that the divine will is done on earth. This kind of reinterpretation has been represented in recent years by, for example, the 'paradox of grace' Christology of Donald Baillie (in *God was in Christ*, 1948) and the 'inspiration Christology' of Geoffrey Lampe (in *God as Spirit*, 1977). In so far as a human being is open and responsive to God, so that God is able to act in and through that individual, we can speak of the embodiment in human life of God's redemptive activity. And in Jesus this 'paradox of grace' – the paradox expressed by St Paul when he wrote 'it was not I, but the grace of God which is in me' (I Corinthians 15:10) – or the inspiration of God's Spirit, occurred to a startling extent. The paradox, or the inspiration, are not however confined to the life of Jesus; they are found, in varying degrees, in all free human response to God. Christologies of the same broad family occur in the work of Norman Pittenger (*The Word Incarnate*, 1957), John Knox (*The Humanity and Divinity of Christ*, 1967), and earlier in John Baillie (*The Place of Jesus Christ in Modern Christianity*, 1929), and more recently in the authors of *The Myth of God Incarnate* (1977).

These modern degree Christologies were not in fact for the most part developed in order to facilitate a Christian acceptance of religious pluralism. They were developed as alternatives to the old substance Christology, in which so many difficulties, both historical and philosophical, had become apparent. They claim to be compatible with the teachings of Jesus and of the very early Church, and to avoid the intractable problem, generated by a substance Christology, of the relation between Jesus' two natures. But, as an unintended consequence, degree Christologies open up the possibility of seeing God's activity in Jesus as being of the same kind as God's activity in other great human mediators of the divine. The traditional Christian claim to the unique superiority of Christ and of the Christian tradition is not of course precluded by a degree Christology; for it may be argued (as it was, for example, by both Baillie and Lampe) that Christ was the *supreme* instance of the paradox of grace or of the inspiration of the Spirit, so that Christianity is still assumed to be the *best* context of salvation/ liberation. But, whereas, starting from the substance Christology, the unique superiority of Christ and the Christian Church are guaranteed *a priori*, starting from a degree Christology they have to be established by historical evidence. Whether this can in fact be done is, clearly, an open question. It would indeed be an uphill task today to establish that we know enough about the inner and outer life of the historical Jesus, and of the other founders of great religious traditions, to be able to make any such claim; and perhaps an even more uphill task to establish from the morally ambiguous histories of each of the great traditions, complex mixtures of good and evil as each has been, that one's own tradition stands out as manifestly superior to all others.

I think, then, that a path exists along which Christians can, if they feel so drawn, move to an acceptance of religious pluralism. Stated philosophically such a pluralism is the view that the great world faiths embody different perceptions and conceptions of, and correspondingly different responses to, the Real or the Ultimate from within the major variant cultural ways of being human; and that within each of them the transformation of human existence from self-centredness to Reality-centredness is manifestly taking place – and taking place, so far as human observation can tell, to much the same extent. Thus the great religious traditions are to be regarded as alternative soteriological 'spaces' within which, or 'ways' along which, men and women can find salvation/liberation/ enlightenment/fulfilment.

But how can such a view be arrived at? Are we not proposing a picture reminiscent of the ancient allegory of the blind men and the elephant, in which each runs his hands over a different part of the animal, and identifies it differently, a leg as a tree, the trunk as a snake, the tail as a rope, and so on? Clearly, in the story the situation is being described from the point of view of someone who can observe both elephant and blind men. But where is the vantage-point from which one can observe both the divine Reality and the different limited human standpoints from which that Reality is being variously perceived? The advocate of the pluralist understanding cannot pretend to any such cosmic vision. How then does he profess to know that the situation is indeed as he depicts it? The answer is that he does not profess to *know* this, if by knowledge we mean infallible cognition. Nor indeed can anyone else properly claim to have knowledge, in this sense, of either the exclusivist or the inclusivist picture. All of them are, strictly speaking, hypotheses. The pluralist hypothesis is arrived at inductively. One starts from the fact that many human beings experience life in relation to a limitlessly greater transcendent Reality – whether the direction of transcendence be beyond our present existence or within its hidden depths. In theory such religious experience is capable of a purely naturalistic analysis which does not involve reference to any reality other than the human and the natural. But to participate by faith in one of the actual streams of religious experience – in my case, the Christian stream – is to participate in it as an experience of transcendent Reality. I think that there is in fact a good argument for the rationality of trusting one's own religious experience, together with that of the larger tradition within which it occurs, so as both to believe and to live on the basis of it; but I cannot develop that argument here.[3] Treating one's own form of religious experience, then, as veridical – as an experience (however dim, like 'seeing through a glass, darkly') of transcendent divine Reality – one then has to take account of the fact that there are other great streams of religious experience which take different forms, are shaped by different conceptualities, and embodied in different institutions, art forms, and life-styles. In other words, besides one's own religion, sustained by its distinctive form of religious experience, there are also other religions, through each of which flows the life blood of a different form of religious experience. What account is one to give of this plurality?

At this point the three answers that we discussed above become available again: exclusivism, inclusivism and pluralism. The exclusivist answer is that only one's own form of religious experience is an authentic contact with the Transcendent, other forms being delusory: the naturalistic interpretation applies to those other forms, but not to ours. This is a logically possible position; but clearly it is painfully vulnerable to the charge of being entirely arbitrary. It thus serves the cause of general scepticism, as David Hume noted with regard to claims that the miracles of one's own religion are genuine whilst those of others are spurious.[4]

Moving to the inclusivist answer, this would suggest that religious experience in general does indeed constitute a contact with the Transcendent, but that this contact occurs in its purest and most salvifically effective form within one's own tradition, other forms having value to the varying extents to which they approximate to ours. This is a more viable position than the previous one, and less damaging to the claim that religion is not a human projection but a genuine human response to transcendent Reality. There is however a range of facts which do not fit easily into the inclusivist theory, namely the changed and elevated lives, moving from self-centredness towards Reality-centredness, within the other great religious traditions. Presumably there must be a strong correlation between the authenticity of the forms of religious experience and their spiritual and moral fruits. It would then follow from the inclusivist position that there should be a far higher incidence and quality of saintliness in one tradition – namely, that in which contact with the Transcendent occurs in 'its purest and most salvifically effective form' – than in the others. But this does not seem to be the case. There is of course no reliable census of saints! Nor indeed is the concept of a saint by any means clear and unproblematic; very different profiles of saintliness have operated at different times and in different places. But if we look for the transcendence of egoism and a recentring in God or in the transcendent Real, then I venture the proposition that, so far as human observation and historical memory can tell, this occurs to about the same extent within each of the great world traditions.

If this is so, it prompts us to go beyond inclusivism to a pluralism which recognises a variety of human religious contexts within which salvation/liberation takes place.

But such a pluralistic hypothesis raises many questions. What is this divine Reality to which all the great traditions are said to be oriented? Can we really equate the personal Yahweh with the non-personal Brahman, Shiva with the Tao, the Holy Trinity with the Buddhist *Trikāya*, and all with one another? Indeed, do not the Eastern and Western faiths deal incommensurably with different problems?

As these questions indicate, we need a pluralistic theory which enables us to recognise and be fascinated by the manifold differ-

ences between the religious traditions, with their different concep-
tualisations, their different modes of religious experience, and their
different forms of individual and social response to the divine. I
should like in these final pages to suggest the ground plan of such
a theory – a theory which is, I venture to think, fully compatible
with the central themes of Cantwell Smith's thought.

Each of the great religious traditions affirms that in addition to
the social and natural world of our ordinary human experience
there is a limitlessly greater and higher Reality beyond or within
us, in relation to which or to whom is our highest good. The
ultimately real and the ultimately valuable are one, and to give
oneself freely and totally to this One is our final salvation/
liberation/enlightenment/fulfilment. Further, each tradition is conscious that the divine Reality exceeds the reach of our earthly
speech and thought. It cannot be encompassed in human concepts. It is infinite, eternal, limitlessly rich beyond the scope of our
finite conceiving or experiencing. Let us then both avoid the
particular names used within the particular traditions and yet use a
term which is consonant with the faith of each of them – Ultimate
Reality, or the Real.

Let us next adopt a distinction that is to be found in different
forms and with different emphases within each of the great
traditions, the distinction between the Real *an sich* (in him/her/
itself) and the Real as humanly experienced and thought. In
Christian terms this is the distinction between God in God's
infinite and eternal self-existent being, 'prior' to and independent
of creation, and God as related to and known by us as creator,
redeemer and sanctifier. In Hindu thought it is the distinction
between *nirguna* Brahman, the Ultimate in itself, beyond all human
categories, and *saguna* Brahman, the Ultimate as known to finite
consciousness as a personal deity, Iśvara. In Taoist thought, 'The
Tao that can be expressed is not the eternal Tao' (*Tao-Te Ching*, 1).
There are also analogous distinctions in Jewish and Muslim
mystical thought in which the Real *an sich* is called *en Soph* and *al
Haqq*. In Mahāyāna Buddhism there is the distinction between the
dharmakāya, the eternal cosmic Buddha-nature, which is also the
infinite Void (*śūnyatā*), and on the other hand the realm of
heavenly Buddha figures (*sambhogakāya*) and their incarnations in
the earthly Buddhas (*nirmāṇakāya*. This varied family of distinctions suggests the perhaps daring thought that the Real *an sich* is
one but is nevertheless capable of being humanly experienced in a

variety of ways. This thought lies at the heart of the pluralistic hypothesis which I am suggesting.

The next point of which we need to take account is the creative part that thought, and the range of concepts in terms of which it functions, plays in the formation of conscious experience. It was above all Immanuel Kant who brought this realisation into the stream of modern reflection, and it has since been confirmed and amplified by innumerable studies, not only in general epistemology but also in cognitive psychology, in the sociology of knowledge, and in the philosophy of science. The central fact, of which the epistemology of religion also has to take account, is that our environment is not reflected in our consciousness in a simple and straightforward way, just as it is, independently of our perceiving it. At the physical level, out of the immense richness of structure and detail around us, only that minute selection that is relevant to our biological survival and flourishing affects our senses; and these inputs are interpreted in the mind/brain to produce our conscious experience of the familiar world in which we live. Its character as an environment within which we can learn to behave appropriately can be called its *meaning* for us. This all-important dimension of meaning, which begins at the physical level as the habitability of the material world, continues at the personal, or social, level of awareness as the moral significance of the situations of our life, and at the religious level as a consciousness of the ultimate meaning of each situation and of our situation as a whole in relation to the divine Reality. This latter consciousness is not however a general consciousness of the divine, but always takes specific forms; and, as in the case of the awareness of the physical and of the ethical meaning of our environment, such consciousness has an essential dispositional aspect. To experience in this way rather than in that involves being in a state of readiness to behave in a particular range of ways, namely that which is appropriate to our environment having the particular character that we perceive (or of course misperceive) it to have. Thus to be aware of the divine as 'the God and Father of our Lord Jesus Christ', in so far as this is the operative awareness which determines our dispositional state, is to live in the kind of way described by Jesus in his religious and moral teaching – in trust towards God and in love towards our neighbours.

How are these various specific forms of religious awareness formed? Our hypothesis is that they are formed by the presence of the divine Reality, this presence coming to consciousness in terms of the different sets of religious concepts and structures of religious meaning that operate within the different religious traditions of the world. If we look at the range of actual human religious experience and ask ourselves what basic concepts and what concrete images have operated in its genesis, I would suggest that we arrive at something like the following answer. There are, first, the two basic religious concepts which between them dominate the entire range of the forms of religious experience. One is the concept of Deity, or God, i.e. the Real as personal; and the other is the concept of the Absolute, i.e. the Real as non-personal. (The term 'Absolute' is by no means ideal for the purpose, but is perhaps the nearest that we have.) We do not however, in actual religious experience, encounter either Deity in general or the Absolute in general, but always in specific forms. In Kantian language, each general concept is schematised, or made concrete. In Kant's own analysis of sense-experience the schematisation of the basic categories is in terms of time; but religious experience occurs at a much higher level of meaning, presupposing and going beyond physical meaning and involving much more complex and variable modes of dispositional response. Schematisation or concretisation here is in terms of 'filled' human time, or history, as diversified into the different cultures and civilisations of the earth. For there are different concrete ways of being human and of participating in human history, and within these different ways the presence of the divine Reality is experienced in characteristically different ways.

To take the concept of God first, this becomes concrete as the range of specific deities to which the history of religion bears witness. Thus the Real as personal is known in the Christian tradition as God the Father; in Judaism as Adonai; in Islam as Allah, the Qur'ānic Revealer; in the Indian traditions as Shiva, or Vishnu, or Paramātmā, and under the many other lesser images of deity which in different regions of India concretise different aspects of the divine nature. This range of personal deities who are the foci of worship within the theistic traditions constitutes the range of the divine *personae* in relation to mankind. Each *persona*, in his or her historical concreteness, lives within the corporate experience of a particular faith-community. Thus the Yahweh *persona* exists and has developed in interaction with the Jewish people. He is a part of their history, and they are a part of his; and he cannot be extracted from this historical context. Shiva, on the other hand, is a quite different divine *persona*, existing in the experience of hundreds of millions of people in the Shaivite stream of Indian religious life. These two *personae*, Yahweh and Shiva, live within different worlds of faith, partly creating and partly created by the features of different human cultures, being responded to in different patterns of life, and being integral to different strands of historical experience. Within each of these worlds of faith great numbers of people find the ultimate meaning of their existence, and are carried through the crises of life and death; and within this process many are, in varying degrees, challenged and empowered to move forward on the way of salvation/liberation from self-centredness to Reality-centredness. From the pluralist point of view Yahweh and Shiva are not rival gods, or rival claimants to be the one and only God, but rather two different concrete historical *personae* in terms of which the ultimate divine Reality is present and responded to by different large historical communities within different strands of the human story.

This conception of divine *personae*, constituting (in Kantian language) different divine phenomena in terms of which the one divine noumenon is humanly experienced, enables us to acknowledge the degree of truth within the various projection theories of religion from Feuerbach through Freud to the present day. An element of human projection colours our mental images of God, accounting for their anthropomorphic features – for example, as male or female. But human projection does not – on this view – bring God into existence; rather it affects the ways in which the independently existing divine Reality is experienced.

Does this epistemological pattern of the schematisation of a basic religious concept into a range of particular correlates of religious experience apply also to the non-theistic traditions? I suggest that it does. Here the general concept, the Absolute, is schematised in actual religious experience to form the range of divine *impersonae* – Brahman, the Dharma, the Tao, *nirvāṇa*, *śūnyāta*, and so on – which are experienced within the Eastern traditions. The structure of these *impersonae* is however importantly different from that of the *personae*. A divine *persona* is concrete, implicitly finite, sometimes visualisable and even capable of being pictured. A divine *impersona*, on the other hand, is not a 'thing' in contrast to a person. It is the infinite being–consciousness–bliss (*saccidānanda*) of Brahman; or the beginningless and endless process of cosmic change (*pratītya samutpāda*) of Buddhist teaching; or again the ineffable 'further shore' of *nirvāṇa*, or the eternal Buddha-nature (*dharmakāya*); or the ultimate Emptiness (*śūnyāta*) which is also the fullness or suchness of the world; or the eternal principle of the Tao. It is thus not so much an entity as a field of spiritual force, or the ultimate reality of everything, that which gives final meaning and joy. These non-personal conceptions of the Ultimate inform modes of consciousness varying from the advaitic experience of becoming one with the Infinite, to the Zen experience of finding a total reality in the present concrete moment of existence in the ordinary world. And according to the pluralistic hypothesis these different modes of experience constitute different experiences of the Real as non- or trans-personal. As in the case of the divine *personae*, they are formed by different religious conceptualities which have developed in interaction with different spiritual disciplines and methods of mediatation. The evidence that a range of *impersonae* of the one Ultimate Reality are involved in the non-theistic forms of religious experience, rather than the direct unmediated awareness of Reality itself, consists precisely in the differences between the experiences reported within the different traditions. How is it that a 'direct experience' of the Real can take such different forms? One could of course at this point revert to the exclusivism or the inclusivism whose limitations we have already noted. But the pluralist answer will be that even the most advanced form of mystical experience, as an experience undergone by an embodied consciousness whose mind/brain has been conditioned by a particular religious tradition, must be affected by the conceptual framework and spiritual training provided by that tradition, and accordingly takes these different forms. In other words the Real is experienced not *an sich*, but in terms of the various non-personal images or concepts that have been generated at the interface between the Real and different patterns of human consciousness.

These many different perceptions of the Real, both theistic and non-theistic, can only establish themselves as authentic by their soteriological efficacy. The great world traditions have in fact all proved to be realms within which or routes along which people are enabled to advance in the transition from self-centredness to Reality-centredness. And, since they reveal the Real in such different lights, we must conclude that they are independently valid. Accordingly, by attending to other traditions than one's own one may become aware of other aspects or dimensions of the Real, and of other possibilities of response to the Real, which had not been made effectively available by one's own tradition. Thus a mutual mission of the sharing of experiences and insights can proceed through the growing network of inter-faith dialogue and the interactions of the faith-communities. Such mutual mission does not aim at conversion – although occasionally individual conversions, in all directions, will continue to occur – but at mutual enrichment and at co-operation in face of the urgent problems of human survival in a just and sustainable world society.

There are many topics which I have not had space to take up in this chapter. I have spoken of 'the great world traditions'; but what about the other smaller ones, including the many new religious movements which are springing up around us today? And what about the great secular faiths of Marxism and Maoism and humanism? Again, I have spoken of salvation/liberation as the transformation of human existence from self-centredness to Reality-centredness; but what about the social and political dimensions of this transformation? These are among the many important questions which any complete philosophy of religious pluralism must answer. But I hope that in this paper I may have said enough to indicate the possible fruitfulness of this general standpoint, a standpoint to which Wilfred Cantwell Smith's work has contributed so centrally and so notably.

NOTES

1. *Redemptor hominis*, tr. Vatican Polyglot Press (London: Catholic Truth Society, 1979) para. 14.
2. For a further discussion of these strains, see John Hick, *Problems of Religious Pluralism* (London: Macmillan; New York: St Martin's Press, 1985) pp. 52–3.
3. See Michael Goulder and John Hick, *Why Believe in God?* (London: SCM Press, 1983).
4. David Hume, *An Enquiry Concerning Human Understanding*, x. ii. 95.

11
On Grading Religions

The idea of grading religions and placing them in an order of merit is to some repugnant, as involving a pretence to a divine perspective, whilst to others it seems entirely natural and proper, at least to the extent of their confidently assessing their own religion more highly than all others. We shall have to consider precisely what it is that might be graded, and in what respects and by what criteria. But, if we think for a moment of the entire range of religious phenomena, no one is going to maintain that they are all on the same level of value or validity. Indeed the most significant religious figures, the founders and reformers of great traditions, have invariably been deeply critical of some of the religious ideas and practices around them. Thus Gautama rejected the idea of the eternal atman or soul, which was integral to the religious thought of India in his time; the great Hebrew prophets criticised mere outward observances and sacrifices, proclaiming that what the Lord requires is to 'let justice roll down like waters, and righteousness like an ever-flowing stream' (Amos 5:24); Jesus, in the same tradition, attacked the formalism and insincerity of some of the religious leaders of his own time who 'tithe mint and rue and every herb, and neglect justice and the love of God' (Luke 11:42); Muhammad rejected the polytheism of his contemporary Arabian society; Guru Nanak in India and Martin Luther in Europe attacked much in the accumulated traditions into which they were born; and so on. Thus some kind of assessing of religious phenomena seems to be a corollary of deep religious seriousness and openness to the divine.

And we lesser mortals, who follow in the footsteps of these great spirits, can see that within our own tradition, even without attempting comparison with others, different aspects have to be regarded as higher or lower, better or worse, even divine and demonic. It will be sufficient for the moment to make the point as a Christian looking at his own tradition. Christianity, as the strand of history which began with the life of Jesus, is immensely varied.

178

The beliefs held by Christians have ranged from the sublime to the ridiculous – from, for example the belief that God loves us human creatures as an ideal father loves his children, to the belief that, to quote the 1960 Chicago Congress on World Mission, 'in the years since the war, more than one billion souls have passed into eternity and more than half of these went to the torment of hell fire without even hearing of Jesus Christ, who he was, or why he died on the cross of Calvary'.[1] Again, Christian practice has ranged from the saintly to the demonic – from, for example, the marvellous self-giving compassionate love of St Francis of Assisi or Mother Teresa of Calcutta, to the hatred expressed in the Christian persecutions of the Jews through some fifteen centuries. Thus it is obvious to a Christian, even without looking beyond the borders of the Christian tradition, that religion is not necessarily or always good and that some kind of assessment of religious phenomena is in principle in order. And the examples that I have given could readily be paralleled by an adherent of any other of the great world faiths looking at his or her own strand of religious history. Each tradition has to distinguish between higher and lower within its own life. Is there not then at least a *prima facie* case, not only for grading within a given tradition, but also for grading traditions, according to the adequacy of their conceptions of the divine and the value of the forms of life which flow from those conceptions?

In response to this question I am going to restrict my discussion to four of the world's major religious movements, two of Semitic and two of Indian origin: Christianity and Islam, Hinduism and Buddhism. This selection will, I hope, be narrow enough to prevent the discussion from being completely unmanageable and yet wide enough to allow for comparison within each group and between the two groups. It does, however, mean leaving out of account immense ranges of the religious life of humanity, including primitive, or primal, religion; the ancient religions of Asia and the Mediterranean world which were in place when the great world faiths emerged; much of the religious life of China; and all of the new religious movements originating in the nineteenth and twentieth centuries, including those that are springing up around us today. It also means leaving aside the whole vast and immensely important phenomenon of modern secularism, both in its humanist and in its Marxist forms. A complete discussion would of course have to include all these other areas. But the central issues will I think confront us sufficiently, and indeed inescapably, through the four traditions that I have selected.

Let us begin by noting the broad common pattern in virtue of which it makes sense to attempt a comparative study of religions. For unless they had something in common it would be impossible to compare them, still less to grade them on a common scale. They do however in fact, I suggest, exhibit a common structure, which is soteriological in the broad sense that it offers a transition from a radically unsatisfactory state to a limitlessly better one. They each speak in their different ways of the wrong or distorted or deluded character of present human existence in its ordinary unchanged condition. It is a 'fallen' life, lived in alienation from God, or it is caught in the illusion of *māyā*, or it is pervaded throughout by *dukkha*. But they also proclaim, as the basis of their gospel, that the Ultimate, the Real, the True, with which our present existence is out of joint, is good, or gracious, or is to be sought or responded to: the ultimately real is also the ultimately valuable. It is a limitlessly loving or merciful God; or it is the infinite being–consciousness–bliss of Brahman; or the ineffable 'further shore' of *nirvāna*; or *śūnyāta*, in whose emptiness of ego the world of time and change is found again as fullness of 'wondrous being'. And, completing the soteriological structure, they each offer their own way to the Real – through faith in response to divine grace; or through total submission to God; or through the spiritual discipline and maturing which leads to *moksha* or to Enlightenment. In each case, salvation/liberation consists in a new and limitlessly better quality of existence which comes about in the transition from self-centredness to Reality-centredness.

This soteriological structure is embodied in two kinds of religious phenomena, cognitive and practical. The cognitive core of a religious tradition consists, as to its content, in a (putative) experience of the Real and, as to its form, in a basic vision of reality. The form and the content, however, belong inextricably together. Thus Vedantic saints experience their oneness with the eternal Self; and the basic vision informing this experience sees reality as the eternal Brahman, within which are our many illusorily distinct selves. Gautama experienced a total transcendence of ego in the moment of *nirvāna*; the informing vision being of a beginningless and endless process of interdependent change in which consciousnesses trapped in a false ego-identity, with all its sorrows and anxieties, can find liberation in the egolessness of *nirvāna*. Jesus experienced a filial relationship with God as his heavenly Father;

and the informing vision sees reality as consisting in the all-loving and all claiming personal Creator and the creation. Muhammad experienced the overwhelming call of Allah to proclaim the divine message on earth; and his informing vision was, again, of God the absolute Creator and Lord, omnipotent and yet merciful, and the creation. Around these basic visions of reality subsequent generations constructed intellectual systems – theologies and religious philosophies – which interpret the meaning of the vision in terms of the concepts and styles of thinking available within their own cultural situations.

The other aspect of religious existence consists in the ways of life, both individual and communal, ritual and ethical, which flow from these different conceptions of the universe. The way of life, in so far as it is actually realised, is appropriate to the vision of reality. If one believes that God is gracious and merciful, one may thereby be released from self-centred anxiety and enabled to imitate the divine love and compassion. If one believes that one is, in one's deepest being, identical with the infinite and eternal Brahman, one will seek to negate the present false ego and its distorting vision in order to attain that which both transcends and underlies it. If one believes that Ultimate Reality is the Buddha-nature, and that the aim of living is to become a Buddha, one will seek to enter into the egoless openness and infinite compassion of the Buddha. And so with other pictures of reality; each, when deeply accepted, renders appropriate a style of life, a way of being human, which is also a way to the ultimate end of the Kingdom of God, heaven, eternal life, *nirvāṇa*, Buddhahood, *moksha*. . . .

By what criteria, then, may we assess and grade these different visions of reality and their associated ways of life?

If we ask how most people in fact do this, the answer is fairly clear. How does the ordinary, not highly learned or reflective, Christian or Muslim, Buddhist or Hindu, assess the relative merits of the visions of reality presented by his/her own and other traditions? One normally simply assumes, as a manifest fact, that one's own familiar tradition represents 'the truth, the whole truth, and nothing but the truth', and assesses other traditions in accordance with their similarities with and differences from it. Such a procedure is indeed almost inevitable. One has been spiritually formed by a certain tradition, with its gospel or dharma, its revelation or teaching, its founder or book, its creeds and myths, its supporting community and spiritual discipline; and all this

constitutes the religious air that one breathes, the religious suste-
nance by which one lives, the inspiration of one's peak experiences. As Ernst Troeltsch said, writing from a Christian standpoint,
'We cannot live without a religion, yet the only religion that we can
endure is Christianity, for Christianity has grown up with us and
has become part of our very being'.[2] And parallel statements could
be made from a Muslim, a Buddhist, or a Hindu point of view. And
so naturally one makes one's own tradition the touchstone by
which to judge others. For, in all our judging, assessing, accepting
and rejecting, we can only start from where we are, using such
degree of truth as we have (or believe that we have) as our
stepping-stone to further truth. And so one begins by looking at
the other religious traditions of the world through the appraising
eyes of one's own tradition.

But there is an obvious consideration which should prevent one
from stopping at this point. Let me put it from my own point of
view as a Christian. Traditionally, Christianity has rejected or
subordinated other traditions because of its own claim to an
unique and final revelation. But suppose that I, who am a Christian, had instead been born to devout Buddhist parents in a
Buddhist culture. In one sense, of course, this is an impossible
supposition. It is meaningless to say, 'If I (who am an Englishman)
had instead been born a Thai, or a Burmese, or a Sri Lankan or a
Japanese', for that person would not then be the present *me*. The
point has to be put differently. When *someone* is born to Buddhist
parents in a Buddhist culture, that person is very likely to be a
Buddhist, and to be related to the Real in ways made possible by
Buddhist understanding and practice. He or she will think of the
Real as the Dharma or as the Buddha or as *nirvāṇa* or as *śūnyāta* (for
there are wide variations within the Buddhist world), and find his
or her own way to reality inwardly in meditation and outwardly on
the Noble Eightfold Path. And, having been formed within the
Buddhist tradition, with its own modes of understanding and its
own forms of spirituality, he will experience Buddhism as 'the
way, the truth, and the life' and see other forms of religious
existence as better or worse according as they approximate to the
Dharma. Again, when someone is born to devout Muslim parents
within an Islamic society, that person is very likely to be a Muslim
and to form his or her relationship to the transcendent through the
ideas and spirituality of Islam. Such a person will think of the Real
as Allah the all-merciful, and will see the way of salvation as

submission to the divine will as revealed in the Qur'ān, a submission which has been aptly characterised as 'giving the world back to God'. Internalising this vision as his or her own vision of reality, and participating in its incarnation in human life, the same person will naturally see Islam as 'the way, the truth and the life' and will judge other reported revelations by the standard set in the holy Qur'ān. And so also when someone is born to devout Hindu parents in India; or indeed within any other powerful tradition. In all these cases, in which one's spiritual being and outlook are effectively formed by a particular stream of religious life, one naturally perceives it from within as 'the way, the truth, and the life' and judges alternatives in its light. And so we have the familiar world-wide situation of people being formed by a particular vision, which functions as the standard by which they judge all others.

There is a complication to be added to this picture in the fact of conversion from one tradition to another. However, as between the great world faiths these are marginal. For example, after the century or so of intense Christian missionary activity in India prior to independence and partition in 1947, the Christian population of the entire sub-continent is about 2.4 per cent.[3] Although numbering millions, and being influential out of proportion to their number, the Christian percentage remains marginal to the vast teeming of life of India, Pakistan and Bangladesh. And if one could add together all the adherents and fellow-travellers of the Indian-inspired movements in the Christian West – Theosophy, Divine Light, Self-Realisation, Hare Krishna, Transcendental Meditation, and so on[4] – and also all the Western adherents of Islam – European Muslims, Black Muslims, and the like – the total, although considerable, would still be similarly marginal. The broad fact is that the great missionary faiths – Buddhism, Christianity and Islam – successfully propagated themselves in their early periods of expansion, and still do so among the peoples of the 'primal' religions, but have met with only marginal success in areas that were already within the orbit of another of the great developed world faiths. Thus, whilst conversions occur and will presumably always occur, they do not significantly affect the broad picture of the massive transmission of each tradition from generation to generation in ways which makes it authoritative to those formed within it.

We are left, then, with the conclusion that in the great majority of cases – I should guess well over 95 per cent – the tradition within which a religious person finds his or her relationship to the Real depends to a very great extent upon where and when that person is born. For normally, in the world as a whole, the faith that a person accepts is the only faith that has been effectively made available to him or her. We can refer to this manifest dependence of spiritual allegiance upon the circumstances of birth and up-bringing as the genetic and environmental relativity of religious perception and commitment. And it is an extraordinary, and to some a disturbing, thought that one's basic religious vision, which has come to seem so obviously right and true, has been largely selected by factors entirely beyond one's control – by the accidents of birth. It is not that one cannot move from one stream of religious life to another, but that this is a rare occurrence, usually presup-posing privileged educational opportunities; so that the great majority of human beings live throughout their lives within the tradition by which they were formed. In view of this situation, can one be unquestioningly confident that the religion which one happens to have inherited by birth is indeed normative and that all others are properly to be graded by their likeness or unlikeness to it? Certainly, it is possible that one particular religious tradition is uniquely normative, and that I happen to have had the good fortune to be born into it. And indeed, psychologically, it is very difficult not to assume precisely this. And yet the possibility must persistently recur to any intelligent person, who has taken note of the broad genetic and environmental relativity of the forms of religious commitment, that to assess the traditions of the world by the measure of one's own tradition may merely be to be behaving, predictably, in accordance with the conditioning of one's up-bringing.

These considerations do not logically oblige anyone to look for other criteria for assessing religious phenomena than simply their congruence or lack of congruence with the features of one's own tradition. But they do I think make it difficult to be happy with what might be called genetic confessionalism as a deliberate view. And so the search for criteria becomes one in which any reflective religious person can properly take part. The project is further supported by the thought that the kind of criteria that we are seeking must have been operating, at least to some extent, in the first phase of those religious traditions which have a founder and which began as a departure from an existing situation. For we cannot attribute the original positive response to Gautama, or to

Jesus, or to Muhammad to the conditioning of Buddhist or
Christian or Muslim upbringing. The general religious back-
grounds of ancient India and the ancient Middle East respectively
were of course importantly relevant. But human discriminative
capacities must also have been at work, operating in accordance
with at least implicit criteria, in the initial response to these great
religious figures; and the question is whether we can uncover
these criteria. Presumably essentially the same principles have
operated in subsequent generations in each person's assessment of
the tradition to which he or she adheres as belief-worthy, revelatory, plausible, rightly claiming allegiance. For a Christian, or a
Buddhist, or a Muslim, or a Hindu has somehow concluded that
their inherited tradition represents 'the way, the truth, and the life'
– either absolutely or at least so far as that particular individual is
concerned. And this concluding must have involved implicit
principles of judgement, principles which we now want to try to
discern.

If we ask the very basic question why a religious vision of the
universe should ever be plausible to human beings, we can only
appeal to the evident fact that we are religious animals, with a basic
tendency to think of and to experience the world in terms of a more
ultimate reality than that of our ordinary everyday consciousness.
And if we next ask why a variety of religious conceptions and
visions have become plausible within different streams of human
life, we have I think to draw upon the fact that the main cultures of
the world have been sufficiently different to constitute different
ways of being human – including the Chinese, the Indian, the
African, the Semitic and the Graeco-Semitic ways. These different
ways of being human have involved different ways of being
religious. One should not exaggerate the differences; for it is
noteworthy that, as each major tradition has developed, it has
become internally pluralistic and has produced within itself all the
main forms of religious existence. Thus, the religious life of India
includes both monistic and theistic strands; and religious thought
in the West includes much more than a simple monotheism. But
still there are manifest differences between the Semitic and the
Indian ways of being religious, and between either of these and,
say, the Chinese or the African ways.

We know all too little about the factors which have gone to shape
the ancient cultures of the earth; but we do know something about
the origins of the major religious traditions which have formed

within them. These modes of awareness of, and ways of living in
relation to, the Divine or the Real come about through human
mediators – outstanding individuals who have been extraordinari-
ly open and responsive to the higher reality. The primary
mediators are the founders of religious traditions, whilst secondary
mediators continue and develop these traditions. Those whom we
can identify as the great primary mediators – Gautama, Confucius,
Moses, Jesus, Muhammad – have initiated streams of religious life
that have lasted for many centuries and that have drawn into
themselves hundreds of millions of people. (There are also lesser
founders of new traditions or sub-traditions, such as Guru Nanak,
Joseph Smith, Mary Baker Eddy, Bah-a'ullah, Annie Besant, Kim-
bangu, Mokichi Okada, and many others, whose movements
presuppose and arise out of one or other of the existing traditions.)
The primary mediators are personally present or remembered, as
in the cases of Guatama, Confucius, Jesus and Muhammad, or are
concealed as the anonymous authors of, for example, the Vedas,
the Upanishads or the Pentateuch; and in these cases secondary
mediators inevitably assume a proportionately more important role
in the developing tradition.

Now when human beings respond to a religious figure, so that
that person becomes, through their response, a *mediator* of the
divine, what criteria are operating? One, surely is a moral criterion.
Although detailed moral codes often differ widely from society to
society, and meta-ethical theories are highly various and often
incompatible, there does seem to be a universal capacity to
distinguish (though always within the framework of certain
assumptions) between benefiting and harming, and a tendency to
bestow moral praise upon actions which benefit and blame upon
those which harm others. Basically, the notion of a morally bad
action is that of an action which is believed in some respect to harm
some community or person; and the notion of a morally praisewor-
thy action is that of one which in some way either wards off harm
to or promotes the welfare of the community or one or more of its
members. Given this basic consensus, the varying beliefs and
assumptions within which it operates produce the differences
between the specific moral codes of different societies. (For example, the cannibal's belief that in eating the flesh of a dead enemy
one is thereby taking into oneself certain of that person's qualities,
clearly affects estimates of the kinds of actions that produce a
benefit.) There are also importantly different assumptions concern-

ing the diameter of the circle of human beings who properly count when assessing benefit and harm. An absolute egoist would attach moral significance only to what affects him or her; members of a primitive tribe commonly counted only fellow members; a nation state normally attributes greater value to its own citizens than to foreigners; whilst for the modern liberal moral outlook all human beings count, and count equally, as those who may be benefited or harmed by human actions.

Now when we encounter, whether directly or indirectly, one who claims or is claimed to be a mediator of the divine or of religious truth, we take note of the supposed mediator's moral character, and would be unable to accept that person as genuine if he or she seemed to us morally questionable. Let us take Jesus as an example. Here the mediator and the message form a whole, and it is to this whole that the Christian responds. The teaching is accepted partly because the mediator is accepted, and the mediator is accepted partly because the message is. It is the coherence of the two – a body of teaching about God, and about how men and women should live as God's children, together with a life lived in history on the basis of that teaching – that is so impressive. No one aspect of the teaching was in fact strictly new or peculiar to Jesus; but the living of that teaching in a historical personality has made a profound impression, haunting the moral imagination of millions ever since. But if Jesus had taught hatred, selfishness, greed, and the amassing of wealth by exploiting others, he would never have been regarded as a true 'son of God', revealing the divine to mankind. His teaching went far beyond the accepted morality of his hearers, but it went further in, so to speak, the same direction, rather than calling for a reversal in which evil was now to be called good and good evil. His followers would not have been able to recognise as having authority a body of teaching that sheerly contradicted their own present moral insight. And again the moral teaching, however sublime, would not have gripped them as it did if it had not been incarnated in Jesus' own life. If Jesus had not lived in accordance with his own teaching, but had been seen by those who began to follow him to be selfish, cynical, deceitful, and unscrupulous, then the Jesus movement would never have developed as it did into the great world faith which we know as Christianity. The same is, I believe, true of each of the other great mediators of the divine to mankind. And so we can I think confidently identify the operation of an ethical criterion in the recognition of a mediator of the Divine or the Real.

A second element in our acceptance of someone as such a mediator is that he – for so far the major mediators have all been men – opens up a new, exciting and commanding vision of reality in terms of which people feel called to live. It may be theistic, so that as they begin to experience life in terms of it they become aware of living in God's gracious presence and under God's limitless claim. Or it may be a non-theistic vision; and as it becomes their own they feel called to transcend the empirical ego which obscures their true nature. The mediator is possessed by his own vision of reality, and experiences in terms of it; and in setting it before others he finds that he is launching a new spiritual movement. His vision must of course be capable of being plausible to his hearers; and this has always required a sufficient continuity between the new message and the basic assumptions of the culture in which both mediator and hearers participate. Thus Confucius was unmistakably Chinese, Gautama unmistakably Indian, Jesus and Muhammad unmistakably of the Semitic religious world; and we cannot realistically imagine, say Christianity having begun in fifth-century-BC India and Buddhism in first-century-AD Palestine, or Islam as having originated in fifth-century-BC China and Confucianism in sixth-century-AD Arabia. Each presupposes a religio-cultural situation within which the mediator's message had a basic intelligibility and plausibility. Thus religious founders have to be children of their own time as well as, and indeed as a prerequisite of being, the creators of new traditions. But, given this condition, it is a major element in the emergence of a great mediator that he perceives and presents to suffering humanity a new vision of reality in which the divine is real and is at hand and in which there is therefore hope for a limitlessly better existence.

The third element in the power of the mediator to win acceptance for his message is an extension of the second, namely that the new vision of reality be able so to possess our minds and hearts as to exhibit a transforming power in our lives. For such a vision is not, to those who see through its lens, a mere theory or hypothesis; it is a fresh way of experiencing, into which they are swept up and by which they are carried forward into a new life. Thus Gautama was so powerfully conscious, in his Enlightenment, of the way of liberation from the misery of self-centredness to the ego-free state of *nirvāṇa*, and so fully manifested this liberated state in his life and his teachings, that his influence has led many others to follow the same path. His mediation of the Real was authenticated by a transformation in the consciousness and behaviour of those who responded to his message. Again, Jesus, through the power of his own intense awareness of the present reality and demanding love of the Heavenly Father, drew others into that same awareness. And living in the assurance of God's love they were set free from self-concern to love one another; seeing the world as God's world (even though still in process of being rescued from the power of the devil) they could live confidently and without anxiety for the future. Again, Muhammad was so overwhelmingly aware of the power of divine self-revelation, setting forth the true pattern of life and claiming our absolute obedience, that his call to give the world back to God in free submission exploded in people's minds and spread within a century across nearly half the globe.

We have, then, three factors which can be discerned in the founding of religious traditions. First, the life of the mediator of the Divine or the Real was such that the ordinary moral sense of humanity could recognise him to be good rather than evil; and his ethical teaching was such that it could be recognised as showing, more fully than the common morality of the time, the demands of Reality for the living of human life. Second, he saw and offered a vision of Reality as ultimately good and such that a new and better existence is possible within or in relationship to it. And third, as people have taken the step of living in terms of this vision, they have in fact been transformed (whether suddenly or gradually) and so have received a first-hand assurance that Reality has indeed been mediated to them.

But after the initial impact of the original revelatory event the new vision, and its transformation of human life, became in each case diffused throughout a culture or family of cultures; whilst in the Hindu instance, with no individual founder, the developing tradition was always culturally incarnated. Thus, whether the basic vision originated suddenly or gradually, aspects of it have been major ingredients in the development of cultures, whilst other and more ultimately demanding aspects have effectively moulded the lives of only a relatively few individuals and small communities, though still haunting the majority as an unattained ideal.

Cultures exist in the lives of peoples and nations, sharing their fortunes amid the contingencies of history. Each religious culture has enjoyed its high periods of flourishing and creativity and has endured periods of stagnation and depression. But through all these ups and downs their distinctive visions have continued and lives have been in varying degrees transformed through their influence. Men and women have been uplifted, and have moved towards human fulfilment, continuously or spasmodically, quietly or dramatically, amidst all the political turmoil and moral and spiritual ambiguities of the different phases of history. At the same time, whilst the religious visions have in varying degrees transformed many living within them, others have used those traditions to validate their own acquisitiveness and lust for power. Thus each tradition, viewed as an historical reality spanning many centuries, is an unique mixture of good and evil, embodied in the lives of saints and sinners, sometimes forming liberating but more often oppressive social structures, giving birth both to human nobility and to human beastliness, to justice and injustice, to beauty and ugliness. Each is a unique historical totality, a spiritual mansion within which millions live, being formed by it from birth and contributing in some small measure to shape its continuing development from generation to generation.

Now our question is whether, and if so how, we can grade these vast religio-cultural totalities.

We have, I suggest, two tools with which we can try to measure and grade aspects at least of them. One is reason applied to their beliefs; and the other is conscience, or moral judgement, applied to the historical out-working of those beliefs. Let us first deploy the rational tool. Can we apply it to the basic religious experiences, and the visions of reality which inform them? It does not appear, first, that we can speak of the rationality or irrationality of an experience. It is not experiences, but people and their beliefs and reasonings, that are rational or irrational. The distinctive experiences of Gautama, Jesus, Muhammad, and the Hindu saints, which lie at the originating basis of Buddhism, Christianity, Islam and Hinduism, were not rational constructs; they were, putatively, encounters with reality. Each of these root experiences was overwhelmingly powerful, and could only be accepted as authentic by the person whose experience it was. The test of the veridical character of such an experience must thus be the test of the larger religious totality which has been built around it. And such a test can only be pragmatic: is this complex of religious experience, belief and behaviour soteriologically effective? Does it make possible the transformation of human existence from self-centredness to Reality-centredness? This is an empirical rather than a rational test.

Nor does it appear, second, that we can speak of the rationality or irrationality of the visions of reality associated with those basic experiences. For they are linguistic pictures or maps of the universe, whose function is to enable us to find salvation/liberation, the limitlessly better quality of existence that the nature of reality is said to make possible. They accordingly test themselves by their success or failure in fulfilling this soteriological function. The final verification is thus eschatological. For a few the eschaton has already been realised in the present; but for the great majority its complete fulfilment lies in the future. In that future it may turn out that the root visions were maps of different possible universes, of which only one at most is actualised; or it may turn out that they were analogous to maps of the same world drawn in radically different projections, each method of projection distorting reality in a different fashion and yet enabling the traveller successfully to find his or her way. But it is clear that the character of the universe and our place within it will become known to us, if at all, by experience and observation, not by reasoning; and so it does not seem that the tool of reason can enable us to test and assess the different basic religious experiences and their associated visions of reality.

We have already noted however that around each basic vision subsequent generations of thinkers have built interpretative systems of thought, which are Christian or Muslim theologies and Hindu or Buddhist religious philosophies. Rational scrutiny of these systems is clearly in principle possible. We can try to assess such a system in respect of its internal consistency and its adequacy both to the particular form of experience on which it is based and to the data of human experience in general. The four major religions that we are considering have in fact produced a rich variety of theologies and philosophies, and within each tradition there is ample scope for argument as to which of these is most adequate to the basic vision or most successful in interpreting that vision to a new age. We can also compare the family of theories within a given tradition with that created within another tradition. I do not think, however, that such a comparison can lead to the conclusion that one set of theories intellectually outclasses the rest. Each family, of course, contains more impressive and less impressive members. But their best representatives seem to constitute intellectual achievements of the first rank. I doubt whether the great enduring systems of Thomas Aquinas, al-Ghazali, Shankara, and Buddhaghosha can realistically be graded in respect of their intellectual quality. They seem, broadly speaking, to be equally massive and powerful systematisations of different basic visions. Each system of course focuses its attention upon some aspects of human experience and knowledge whilst being relatively indifferent to others. Each accordingly accounts for some facts better than for others. But any grading of them in this respect has to fall back upon a grading of the basic visions which they articulate; and this, we have noted, cannot be achieved by any intellectual test. The test is whether these visions lead to the better, and ultimately the limitlessly better, quality of existence which they promise. And so I conclude, thus far, that we cannot grade the great world traditions by means of the tool of reason.

Let us then turn from the intellectual to the spiritual and moral fruits of a basic religious experience and vision. We need to look both at the ideal fruit, visible in the saints of a given tradition, and also at the ordinary life of millions of ordinary people as it takes place within the actual history of that tradition.

The transformations of human existence which the different major visions produce appear, as we see them described in their scriptures and embodied in the lives of their saints, to be equally radical in their nature and equally impressive in their outcomes. Each involves a voluntary renunciation of ego-centredness and a self-giving to, or self-losing in, the Real – a self-giving which brings acceptance, compassion, love for all humankind, or even for all life.

Thus the Christian gives himself or herself to God in Christ in a total renunciation of the self-centred ego and its concerns. The Christian can then say, with St Paul, 'it is no longer I who live, but Christ who lives in me' (Galatians 2:20). And in this new state, as part of the communal Body of Christ, the Church, the believer acts, ideally, in self-giving love toward all humankind. The two interlinked commands are to love God and to love one's neighbour – who is anyone with whom one has to do. For, 'if anyone says, "I love God", and hates his brother, he is a liar; for he who does not love his brother whom he has seen, cannot love God whom he has not seen' (1 John 4:20). This ideal of self-giving love, whilst always part of the Christian tradition, has been particularly prominent within the modern period of liberal and democratic thought. Whereas in early and medieval Christianity the person recognised as a saint was often a solitary ascetic, practising fearsome austerities, today the ideal is that of the great servant of humanity, seen in the past in St Francis and exemplified in our own century by, for example, Albert Schweitzer or Mother Teresa.

The Muslim, too, totally submits to God, renouncing the self-centred ego and its concerns, and living as a servant of Allah. The Muslim is taught by the prophet Muhammad that 'All creatures of God are His family; and he is most beloved of God who loveth His creatures.'⁵ The virtues of the good Muslim are described in the Qu'rān in characteristically concrete and earthly terms. A Muslim should be kind to all: 'Be kind to parents, and the near kinsman, and to orphans, and to the needy, and to the neighbour who is of kin, and to the neighbour who is a stranger, and to the companion at your side, and to the traveller, and to that your right hands own' (4:40). A Muslim should be humble, for 'The servants of the All-merciful are those who walk in the earth modestly and who, when the ignorant address them, say "Peace"' (25:64); and forgiving: 'But if you pardon, and overlook, and if you forgive, surely God is All-forgiving' (64:14). A Muslim should be honest and trustworthy: 'And fill up the measure when you measure, and weight with the straight balance' (17:37) (Arberry's translation). The ethical ideal of Islam is summed up in the words of the Prophet in his sermon on entering Medina; it is that of 'loving God with all their heart and loving one another in God' (Ibn Hisam, Sira II, 348).

The aim of the Buddhist, again, is finally to transcend the ego, with its desires and anxieties, and to enter the ego-free state of *nirvāṇa*. The way to this is the Noble Eightfold Path, which is both spiritual and ethical. It produces compassion (*karuna*) and loving-kindness (*metta*) for all mankind, and indeed for life in every form. The disciple of the Buddha is 'to pervade each of the four quarters of the horizon with a heart charged with love, with pity, with sympathy in joy, with equanimity'.⁶ This universal love of the selfless person is embodied in the ideal of the Bodhisattva, who voluntarily renounces the bliss of *nirvāṇa* until all mankind had been brought to the same point. The universal unity of humanity is a basic Buddhist conviction.

When we turn to Hinduism we find that its only essence is that it has no essence; for the name is an umbrella term for most of the religious life of India over a period of three millennia. In this pluralistic religious universe different ways of liberation are recognised and on each way there are stages, so that what is appropriate at one stage may not be appropriate at another. In India's most influential scripture, the *Bhagavad Gita*,* two ways are set forth, both involving the ideal of universal love and compassion which had been introduced into the religious thought of India centuries earlier by the Buddha. One way, that of meditation, leads to union with the Ultimate as the non-personal Brahman. Of those who follow this path it is said that they are 'in all things equal-minded, taking pleasure in the weal of all contingent beings' (12:4). The other way is that of action in the world, but action without concern for the fruits of action, in communion with the Ultimate Person, who speaks in the *Gita* as Krishna. And to those who follow this path of devotion and selfless action the Lord says, 'Let a man feel hatred for no contingent being, let him be friendly, compassionate; let him be done with thoughts of "I" and "mine", the same in pleasure as in pain, long-suffering, content and ever-integrated, his purpose firm, his mind and soul steeped in ME' (12:13–14).

These are, in briefest cameo, the ideal ways of life which follow from the different root experiences and visions of reality around which the four traditions have grown. If every Christian and Muslim, every Hindu and Buddhist, fully incarnated their respective ideals, they would live in a basic acceptance and love of all their fellow human beings. For they would have turned away from the self-centredness which is the source of acquisitiveness, dishonesty, injustice and exploitation. A world which practised the common ethical ideal of these traditions would have realised human brotherhood on earth. But of course in fact the ideal has only been realised in any substantial way in the lives of comparatively rare individuals and small religious communities, and spasmodically and in varying degrees in much larger ranges of individuals. The actual histories of Hindu, Buddhist, Christian and Muslim societies include, as a prominent part of the story, violence and war, oppression, exploitation and slavery, deceit and dishonesty, ruthless cruelty and a selfish grasping for wealth and power. These traditions have all nurtured not only saints and leaders in righteousness who have given themselves for the welfare of their fellows, but also evil and demonic figures, leaders in aggression and aggrandisement, who have cruelly exploited and oppressed their fellows.

Amidst history's long and depressing catalogue of 'man's inhumanity to man', can any one of the great religio-cultural streams

---

* All quotations from the *Bhagavad Gita* are based on the translation by R. C. Zaehner (Oxford: Clarendon Press, 1969).

of life claim a relatively greater virtue and establish itself as ethically superior to the others? I want to suggest that it is entirely possible that there is an ethical ranking of religious civilisations, with one rightly appearing at the top of the list. But I also want to suggest that we are not in fact able to make the comparative assessment which might lead to such a result. Thus, if we consider the case, widely accepted within Western society, for the moral superiority of Christian civilisation over the Muslim, Hindu and Buddhist civilisations, we find that for each evil that the Christian can point to in one of the other streams of religious history there is an equally evident evil within his own; and that it is impossible realistically to weight these often incommensurate evils against each other.

How are we to weigh the lethargy of many Eastern countries in relation to social and economic problems, so that they suffer from endemic poverty, against the West's ruthlessly competitive greed in the exploitation of the earth's resources – the Western capitalist rape of the planet at the expense of half the world and of all future generations? How are we to weigh the effect of Hindu and Buddhist 'otherworldliness' in retarding social, economic and technological progress against the use of the Christian Gospel to validate unjust social systems in Europe and South America, and to justify and perpetuate massive racial exploitation in South Africa? How are we to weigh the unjust caste-system of India against the unjust class-system and pervasive racism of much of the Christian West? How do we weigh the use of the sword in building great Muslim, Hindu and Buddhist empires against the use of the gun in building the great Christian empires? How do we weigh the aggressive Muslim incursion into Europe in the fourteenth century against the previous Christian incursion into the Middle East known as the Crusades? How do we weigh the hideous custom of the 'voluntary' burning of widows (*sutte*) in India against the equally hideous burning of 'witches' in Christian Europe and North America? How do we weigh the savage aspects of life in some Eastern and Middle Eastern countries – the bloody massacres at the time of the partition of India, the cutting off of a thief's hands under Islamic law – against the Christian persecution of the Jews throughout the ages and above all in our own century?

The fact is that each of these four strands of history exhibits its own distinctive mixture of virtues and vices. Each has a relatively good record in some respects but a bad record in others. Broadly speaking, for example, Christianity has done well in stimulating the creation of wealth and the goods which wealth can make possible, but is badly stained by a record of perennial violence and persecution; whilst Buddhism, in contrast, has been much more peaceful, never giving rise to wars of religion, but has often failed to combat poverty and social injustice. And comparable contrasts occur with any other pair. The resulting patterns are so different that it is, surely, impossible to sustain either the common Christian assumption, or the parallel Muslim, Hindu, or Buddhist assumption, that one's own strand of history is haloed with a discernible moral superiority.

But does not Christianity perhaps have a unique historical position as the tradition within which our modern conceptions of universal human equality and freedom have arisen, in the light of which we have been identifying the evils of the different traditions? These modern liberal ideas have indeed first emerged in the West; but they are essentially secular ideas, which have been and are as much opposed as supported within the Christian churches. Contemporary Marxist, humanist and feminist critiques of economic, racial and sexual oppression have become common currency in Western liberal thinking, and have evoked their echoes in liberation and black and feminist theologies. But it would be erroneous to conclude, from the fact that these ideas have affected Western Christianity first among the religions, that Christianity has a proprietary interest in them. Our contemporary Western liberal-democratic, politically, racially and sexually liberated form of Christianity represents a creative synthesis of the Christian tradition with secular liberalism; and analogous syntheses are beginning to emerge within the other traditions. When today we condemn slavery, the Inquisition and, say, the nineteenth-century persecutions of the Jews, we do so from the modern liberal standpoint, not from that of the Christian populations which engaged in those activities. And it is through its participation in this same modern liberal standpoint that India has officially renounced the caste-system, that polygamy is dying out and women are seeking their liberation in modern Muslim countries, and that Shinto and Buddhist Japan has become one of the world's most efficient industrial powers.

Let me now offer my conclusions.

First, religious phenomena – patterns of behaviour, experiences, beliefs, myths, theologies, cultic acts, liturgies scriptures, and so forth – can in principle be assessed and graded; and the basic criterion is the extent to which they promote or hinder the great religious aim of salvation/liberation. And by salvation or liberation I suggest that we should mean the realisation of that limitlessly better quality of human existence which comes about in the transition from self-centredness to Reality-centredness.

But, second, the ways to salvation/liberation are many and varied, and it is often not easy to recognise a religious practice or a vision of reality that is strikingly different from our own as part of another way from ego-centredness to Reality-centredness. The main kinds of way have long been known as the mystical way of contemplation and knowledge, the practical way of action in the world, and the way of loving devotion to the Real experienced as personal. It should be noted, incidentally, that these are not to be identified with different religions; for each of the great traditions includes all three ways, although often in characteristically different proportions. We should respect ways other than our own, whether or not we truly appreciate them.

And, third, whilst we can to some extent assess and grade religious phenomena, we cannot realistically assess and grade the great world religions as totalities. For each of these long traditions is so internally diverse, containing so many different kinds of both good and evil, that it is impossible for human judgement to weigh up and compare their merits as systems of salvation. It may be that one facilitates human liberation/salvation more than the others; but if so this is not evident to human vision. So far as we can tell, they are equally productive of that transition from self to Reality which we see in the saints of all traditions.

This is a broad conclusion about the great traditions as totalities, each with a life spanning many centuries and occupying large areas of the world. However, it may well be that a great tradition constitutes in some periods of its history, and in some regions of the world, and in some of its branches or sects, a better context of salvation/liberation than in others. Thus it may well be more auspicious to be born into a given religion in one period of history than in another; and, at a given period, in one country or region rather than in another; and again, within a given period or region, into one sect or branch rather than another. And, likewise, it may well be more auspicious to be born into a good period, region, or branch of religion A than into a bad period, region, or branch of religion B. And when we come down to the concrete circumstances

198 A John Hick Reader

of each human individual, the respects in which his or her unique situation may be religiously auspicious or inauspicious are virtually unlimited and of virtually endless complexity. But amidst all this untraceable detail the broad conclusion stands that, whilst we can assess religious phenomena, we cannot assess and grade religious traditions as totalities. We can, I suggest, only acknowledge, and indeed rejoice in the fact, that the Real, the Ultimate, the Divine is known and responded to within each of these vast historical complexes, so that within each of them the gradual transformation of human existence from self-centredness to Reality-centredness is taking place.

NOTES

1. J. O. Percy (ed.), *Facing the Unfinished Task: Messages Delivered at the Congress on World Mission* (Grand Rapids, Mich.: Eerdman, 1961) p. 9.
2. Ernst Troeltsch, 'The Place of Christianity among the World Religions', in J. H. Hick and B. Hebblethwaite (eds), *Christianity and Other Religions* (London: Collins; and Philadelphia: Fortress Press, 1981) p. 25.
3. Hans Küng, in J. Meuner (ed.), *Christian Revelation and World Religions* (London: Burns and Oates, 1967) p. 27.
4. Probably numbering several million in the USA alone, according to Harvey Cox, *Turning East* (New York: Simon and Schuster, 1977) p. 93.
5. Quoted by Dwight M. Donaldson in *Studies in Muslim Ethics* (London: SPCK, 1963) p. 255.
6. Maha-Govinda Sutanta 59, *Digha-Nikaya*, II. 250, in *Dialogues of the Buddha*, tr. T. W. and C. A. F. Rhys Davids, 4th edn (London: Luzac, 1959) p. 279.

Index